Mastering
Project Management with ClickUp
for Work and Home Life Balance

A step-by-step implementation and optimization guide
to unlocking the power of ClickUp and AI

Edward Unger

Mastering Project Management with ClickUp for Work and Home Life Balance

Group Product Manager: Aaron Tanna

Publishing Product Manager: Uzma Sheerin

Book Project Manager: Manisha Singh

Senior Editor: Nisha Cleetus

Technical Editor: Jubit Pincy

Copy Editor: Safis Editing

Proofreader: Nisha Cleetus

Indexer: Tejal Soni

Production Designer: Ponraj Dhandapani

DevRel Marketing Coordinator: Deepak Kumar and Mayank Singh

First published: June 2024

Production reference: 1210624

Published by Packt Publishing Ltd.

Grosvenor House

11 St Paul's Square

Birmingham

B3 1RB, UK

ISBN 978-1-83546-873-9

www.packtpub.com

This book is dedicated to Norm Stapleton, an amazing human being who is a husband, best friend, father, silly, coach, mentor, leader, entertainer, jokester, prankster, smiler, creator of laughter, kind lover of people, impact maker, legacy creator, and lover of life.

Anyone could go on forever and ever talking about all his amazing qualities, but one thing that's for sure is that anyone who knew or was influenced by Norm will carry on the amazing and funny qualities that he always left everywhere, like glitter. (You know, the kind that you keep finding days later?) Because that's the kind of guy he was. He stuck with you through thick and thin and was always there for you no matter what the cost.

Norm always had incredible words of wisdom to share with you, a trick to show you, a joke to tell, a quote to add perfectly to a moment, or... if you couldn't find him, he scared you and laughed with you about it! Needless to say, he has already been so missed by thousands of people that he impacted directly and indirectly, but his legacy will live on through all of us." - Natalie Stapleton

Norm Stapleton III (May 23, 1978 to Dec 27, 2021)

Norm, you are a friend and mentor who was in my life for such a short time in comparison to the impact of your brightly burning light, passing your flame of hope and belief from your leadership and mentorship to everyone you met, changing their life and ultimately influencing change in my life and family in ways I never knew were possible in which I am forever grateful. I miss you, I love you, and I can't wait to learn and laugh with you again one day.

– Edward Unger

Foreword

Call me Coyne. It's pronounced like money but spelled kinda funny. As the **Chief Technology Officer (CTO)** of SERHANT., I'm living the dream job every tech enthusiast fantasizes about. Each morning, I wake up knowing my work is significant—not just to those around me but also to millions worldwide, inspiring them to be their best by following our example, incorporating our teachings, and striving to match our standards of excellence that we're fortunate to be trendsetting in the various industry segments we operate within.

It's always been an exciting challenge for us when making decisions since there's no other company to compare ourselves to. SERHANT. is a media company that happens to be the most followed real estate brand in the world. We're a luxury real estate brokerage, a film and media production studio, a creative agency, a software development company, an online sales education company, and the subject of Netflix's very first NYC-based real estate reality TV show, *Owning Manhattan*. Perhaps it goes without saying, early on there was a lot to untangle and evaluate to ensure successful growth for the future.

My love affair with technology began just before the age of 3, as I sneaked behind my parents' backs to tinker with our family's Commodore 1802A. This journey, like a rollercoaster designed by Escher, has been filled with twists, turns, challenges, and opportunities. Never did I imagine I'd be steering the technology vision of an organization as accomplished and prestigious as SERHANT., a company I helped co-found in 2020. From a scrappy team of fewer than 20 people on September 15, 2020, we've ballooned to nearly 1,000, working in harmony across dozens of markets and states, supporting an education community of more than 35,000 members across 128 countries. Our growth has been fueled by collaboration, teamwork, and, candidly, a precarious hold on sanity.

At SERHANT., we were already using ClickUp but were scattered and siloed, living in scope-creep, and wasting valuable time and money figuring it out ourselves. That's when I found Edward Unger, a partner consultant who brought us together, guiding us to build out and rely on ClickUp to power our growth. Edward's approach wasn't just about implementing a tool; it was about fostering a mindset of collaboration and efficiency. It was like watching a master conductor turn a cacophony into a symphony, except the orchestra was made up of exhausted executives, directors, and managers.

Edward's brilliance isn't just in his technical know-how but in his human touch. He understands that technology is only as good as the people who use it. His empathetic leadership transformed our scattered efforts into a cohesive, well-oiled machine. Instead of imposing changes, he guided us with understanding and patience, making the complex seem simple and the daunting feel achievable.

Why my opinion matters is also because I come from a long line of innovators. My grandfather's ingenuity and inventive spirit have been passed down through generations of Coynes, a legacy I proudly carry forward. He was the first in the line, beginning his life as an orphan in East New York

Brooklyn, going on to modify and improve machines in a Novacane factory at 16 years old, then becoming decorated in World War II, naming my father Russell after his closest friend who fell in battle beside him. He went on to innovate dozens of improvements to ground and air technologies for United Airlines in Denver before passing away at 92 with his trusty Gameboy at his side, a Tetris cartridge still inside that had never once been removed. Everyone who knows me knows I'm a talker, and true to my genetics, my grandfather's AOL screenname was Rambler93.

One of my favorite experiences with Edward was a conversation we had a few months into our collaboration. Edward spoke so authoritatively about our company's various departments, their goals, and initiatives that it dawned on me that he understood SERHANT. as well as any of us—perhaps even better. As the orchestrator of interconnecting everything we were in the midst of and had still yet to achieve, his insights were invaluable.

In *Mastering Project Management with ClickUp for Work and Home Life Balance*, Edward distills his vast knowledge into a guide that is both practical and inspiring. This book tackles the universal challenges of both personal and professional realms, offering innovative solutions that are as refreshing as the first sip of a drink that took obnoxiously long to arrive at your table on a hot summer day. It's like having a trellis for your vine to grow on, providing the structure and support you need to flourish.

Edward has a knack for storytelling, and this book is no exception. He weaves in anecdotes and examples that make the content relatable and engaging. Whether you're a seasoned project manager or just starting, "ClickUp" has something for everyone. It's not just about mastering a tool; it's about transforming your approach to work and achieving a harmonious balance between your professional and personal life.

I often say, *"Humanity doesn't have a technology problem; technology has a humanity problem."* Technology, like a screwdriver, can assemble a baby's crib or be used for harm. It doesn't decide how it's used; it amplifies our flaws and our greatest aspirations. Edward's book is a testament to this philosophy. It shows how we can harness technology like ClickUp to bring more life into our lives, making us more efficient, connected, and fulfilled.

So, dear reader, I invite you to embark on this journey with an open mind and a readiness to transform your life. Edward's wisdom and guidance will undoubtedly lead you to new heights of efficiency and fulfillment. As someone who has witnessed the impact of his methods firsthand, I can confidently say that this book is a game-changer.

Dive in, explore, and let the magic of ClickUp and Edward Unger guide you to a better, more balanced, more life-filled life.

Nerdy regards,

Ryan Coyne

CTO, SERHANT.

Contributors

About the author

Edward Unger is a renowned entrepreneur, family man, educator, studio owner, DJ, music producer, productivity enthusiast, and author dedicated to helping individuals unlock their productivity potential. With over two decades of freelancing experience, Ed has mastered time management and efficiency. His quest to optimize workflows led him to discover ClickUp, a transformative project management tool. Ed shares practical strategies in this book to help readers reclaim their time and achieve their goals. Whether DJing or creating content, Ed is committed to enabling individuals to be their best and maximize every moment.

More about the author

Edward Unger is an efficiency consultant, project manager, and ClickUp expert. With over 20+ years of experience in business systems efficiency and process implementation, Edward has helped numerous organizations optimize their efficiency and productivity.

As a published author, Edward's book on ClickUp and project management will provide valuable insights and strategies for mastering project management and achieving work-life balance. He has worked with small and large teams, building business operating systems and processes from scratch.

Edward's unique approach to ClickUp sets him apart. With extensive experience in project management, CRM, and business systems, he brings a fresh perspective. His proficiency in agile project management principles and frameworks and his knack for developing streamlined processes and workflows make him a valuable asset. ClickUp contains his 'accomplishment system' to spend time with family, passion projects, and pursue purpose with his strengths.

Edward's commitment to continuous learning is evident in his diverse certifications and reports. He holds over 34 technical training certificates in project management, agile methodologies, AI, productivity, time management, leadership, and more. This extensive knowledge base allows him to apply his expertise across various industries and disciplines.

Beyond his professional achievements, Edward has a passion for DJing and music production. He enjoys spending time with his family, engaging in family activities, and playing ice hockey. He is also a fan of John Maxwell and actively pursues leadership development.

With his wealth of experience, certifications, and interests, Edward brings a unique perspective to his consulting work. He aims to help individuals and organizations achieve optimal efficiency, productivity, and work-life balance through effective project management and streamlined processes.

Acknowledgments

-Thank you to my fantastic family and friends during the times away from you while writing this book.

-I am so proud to know and love you, Frany. You are a precious flower of love and support. Thank you.

-Thank you, Aden and Victoria, for being the most amazing son and daughter a father could ask for. I'm so proud of the young men and women you are.

-My Father, for his example of silent leadership and living the lessons of no matter how tough it gets, keep learning, keep working hard, and keep taking the high road. Hard work always pays off, and wisdom is worth more than gold.

-My Mother for her love and laughter and learning to smile and laugh with as many faces as you can find (and pinch all their grandchildren's cheeks for hours lol)

-My Sister for her big heart, sunshine smile, profound wisdom, and simplicity. Seeing you and Eric and AJ and Liam thrive in love and to see all of you with those sunshine smiles of yours is a sight to behold :)

-My Brother Phil: I am so thankful to call you brother and excited to see the return on all that you have invested. Now is your time and I am excited to see the amazing things you will do and be.

-Thank you to Rose DeLeon, Puneet Kaur, Nisha Cleetus, Uzma Sheerin, Manisha Singh, Prajakta Naik, Marcus Sousa, Gabriel Hoffman, Aaron Tanna, and all the rest of the Packt Team for your help and collaboration from preparation to publishing.

-Coyne: A light of encouragement, technology, and comedy wrapped in a heart of love and fierceness to serve and bring thousands of people together as if it just miraculously happens by chance... I learned it all happens from who you are and the excellent example of leadership with humility, empathy, and compassion you embody with everyone you work with and in everything you do.

The Stapletons: Your example of love, leadership, and grace towards others nursed me back to health in some of the toughest seasons of my life. You equipped me to overcome challenges and pay it forward as a lifestyle in ways I did not know existed. Weathering the storms of life and the beautiful treasures in life together with all of you is an experience beyond words and a storybook all on its own that I cherish daily.

-Mariam Hency Varghese - working under your leadership, with One Hope's love and compassionate culture, was one of the first times I saw down the rabbit hole of an organization that matches the service they provide with the same level of excellence within the organization, watching your compassion to help your team and those in need. Thank you for your leadership and example, for helping uncover my strengths and getting comfortable with being uncomfortable.

-Perry and Kim Santoloci, working with and learning from you changed my life trajectory. I wish all the blessings and love your grace gives to everyone who comes to you, your family, and all those who know you.

Daniel Guelzo, you were one of my first mentors before I knew what that meant. You Miyagi'd me. :) Our time together in Atlanta was short, but your impact on my life remains.

-Thank you to everyone who I have worked with and connected with.

-Thank you to all fathers, mothers, mentors, and leaders who stand in the gap and pay it forward to love and mentor those who could never repay.

..It's okay if the beginning of your journey didn't turn out how you thought, as long as it doesn't stay that way. -Norm Stapleton

About the reviewers

Marcus Sousa is founder of MS Gestão Empresarial and a project manager offering solutions for implementing operations, processes, and workflows with ClickUp. He is also a global ambassador and ClickUp consultant leading implementations in the Americas, Europe, and Asia. Marcus is also number 1 in the ClickUp Verified VIP ranking!

Gabriel Hoffman, has been a ClickUp user since 2017 and a ClickUp Global Consultant since 2019 He currently works as a ClickUp Innovation Lead at a Diamond partner. Gabriel has worked with more than 500 companies worldwide across a wide array of niches and use cases and has been a Product Consultant and Alpha Tester for many ClickUp features. He is also a Lead Trainer of ClickUp Experts in Latin America, working alongside ClickUp's internal Professional Services team to deliver the best designs for enterprise customers. Gabriel is a VIP guest at the latest ClickUp Level Up event (at the time of reviewing this book) and a Brand Ambassador of ClickUp in Brazil.

Table of Contents

2

Discovering Your Benefits of Using ClickUp   31

3

Setup and Preparation Steps for Unlocking ClickUp   45

Part 2: Understanding ClickUp

4

Collaborating with Team Members in ClickUp   67

5

Defining and Managing Project Scope   79

6

Organizing Projects, Tasks, and Clearing Your To-Do Lists by the End of the Day   91

7

Tracking Goals, Project Progress, and Productivity with KPIs, Dashboards, and Reporting   107

8

Integrating ClickUp with Your Other Tools and Apps   121

Part 3: Understanding ClickUp

9

Personal Task Management with ClickUp   129

10

Project Management and Collaborating on Personal Events with Friends and Family   147

11

Managing Household Chores and Home-Life Responsibilities   173

12

Personal Habits, Goal Achievement, and Routines for Success   193

Part 4: Understanding ClickUp

13

14

15

Recommendations, Troubleshooting, FAQs, and AI-Powered Productivity   241

16

Next Steps – Personal and Professional Growth with ClickUp   255

Preface

Welcome to an innovative journey into the world of ClickUp, a dynamic project management and productivity platform that transforms how we structure, coordinate, and enhance our work. This book serves as your guide to understanding the capabilities of ClickUp, empowering you to leverage its potential for personal and professional growth.

What is ClickUp?

ClickUp is a versatile project management solution that integrates tasks, documents, objectives, and time management within an interface. Its adaptability enables users to tailor workflows, streamline operations, and foster collaboration among team members. Whether you're an entrepreneur, a team leader overseeing projects, or an individual seeking to boost productivity, ClickUp provides customized solutions for all.

Why choose ClickUp?

Juggling projects, assignments, and deadlines can feel overwhelming in today's fast-paced environment. Simply put, ClickUp has features and functionalities that help create time by consolidating task management software services and providing a central knowledge base integrated with AI and ClickUp Brain. This allows the everyday person, from small businesses to enterprise businesses, to streamline efficiencies that were not available before.

This book is designed to guide you through the fundamentals of ClickUp and techniques that will enhance your mastery of the platform. Here's what you can anticipate:

- **Building a strong foundation**: We'll kick off with the basics covering how to set up and navigate ClickUp. You'll grasp the principles and features that make ClickUp a valuable tool.

- **Enhancing Efficiency**: Going beyond the basics, we'll delve into ways to tailor ClickUp to suit your workflow requirements. This involves utilizing task views, creating templates, and establishing processes.

- **Exploring advanced functions**: We'll delve into the capabilities of ClickUp, including its AI features, automation tools, and integrations. You'll learn how to utilize these functions to save time and increase productivity.

- **Real-life scenarios**: We'll illustrate how ClickUp is effectively utilized in various industries through real-world examples and case studies. You'll gain insights into applications and proven strategies.

- **Success Strategies**: Lastly, whether leading a team or working independently, you'll learn strategies for implementing and maintaining a ClickUp environment.

A Message

With over twenty years of experience tackling the complexities of project management and efficiency, I recognize the significance of utilizing the tools. My introduction to ClickUp revolutionized how I organize my time, projects, and collaborations. This book aims to be a guide that empowers you to leverage ClickUp's capabilities to reach your objectives and boost your productivity.

I was overjoyed when I learned ClickUp is big enough to manage everything I wanted to accomplish according to my purpose. I have hundreds of thousands of strategies, workflows, processes, and documents from years of Word docs, Google Notes, Trello, Evernote, Apple Notes, Notion, and countless other software.

For over twenty years, I have built systems, life hacks, and how-to articles on owning and running a business, websites, digital marketing agencies, music businesses, and more.

The information from this content library of principles and methodologies included in this book can be used with any software. However, ClickUp's experience provides many time-saving features that increased productivity gains from 40% to 60% in my work and family time, allowing me to accomplish my yearly goals before the target date. It also increased profits by 30% in the first year of ClickUp adoption.

ClickUp Brain and AI integration are the keys to getting a work-home life balance and increased productivity gains to the 65%–90% range.

It is recommended that you read one chapter after another, or you can skip around to find the content you need immediately. Practice the steps, dive deeper into ClickUp, and download your free workbook at bluecreative.com/clickup.

I look forward to joining you on your journey and am a few steps away.

Who this book is for

This book provides tips for individuals seeking to enhance their time management skills, lower stress levels, and balance work and personal life. Whether you're a working professional, a student, or just someone needing organization, this book caters to your needs.

The target audience of this book includes four groups:

- **ClickUp users**: For those using ClickUp, whether you're just starting out or a user aiming to maximize its features, this book will guide you in unleashing its capabilities.

- **ClickUp professionals**: ClickUp experts, implementers, and optimization specialists will find valuable insights in this book on handling ClickUp for themselves and others effectively.

- **Business professionals**: Business professionals like owners, operations managers, and project managers can discover how ClickUp can streamline workflows and enhance efficiency.

- **Anyone seeking organization**: Individuals seeking organization will benefit from this book regardless of whether they use ClickUp;

- **Students**: Students can learn effective ways to manage their studies and personal commitments.
- **Freelancers**: Freelancers can improve efficiency and increase productivity.
- **Busy professionals**: Busy professionals can find strategies for handling projects while maintaining a work-life balance.

What this book covers

Chapter 1, What is ClickUp, and Why Should I Care? (Getting Started: Simplified), dives into how ClickUp empowers individuals and businesses of all sizes. It explores how ClickUp can be tailored to your specific workflow, boost efficiency and productivity, and facilitate seamless collaboration.

Chapter 2, Discovering Your Benefits of Using ClickUp, explores how ClickUp can benefit users of all levels, from solopreneurs to enterprise executives, by helping them customize workflows, boost efficiency, collaborate seamlessly, and track progress towards goals.

Chapter 3, Setup and Preparation Steps for Unlocking ClickUp, equips new ClickUp users with the essential steps to set up their workspace, including structure design, custom fields, templates, and integrations for efficient project management.

Chapter 4, Collaborating with Team Members in ClickUp, describes how to collaborate with team members in ClickUp. It covers assigning tasks, tracking progress, promoting accountability, simplifying communication, and sharing files and documents.

Chapter 5, Defining and Managing Project Scope, is a guide to managing projects effectively within ClickUp. It covers defining project scope, setting realistic deadlines and milestones, and prioritizing tasks and resources. The chapter offers valuable insights for various users, from individual business owners to enterprise executives.

Chapter 6, Organizing Projects, Tasks, and Clearing Your To-Do Lists by the End of the Day, is a guide to using ClickUp to improve your project and task management skills. It covers structuring projects and tasks, prioritizing your to-do list, and maximizing productivity using ClickUp's features.

Chapter 7, Tracking Goals, Project Progress, and Productivity with KPIs, Dashboards, and Reporting, dives into using ClickUp to track goals, project progress, and productivity. It emphasizes the importance of Key Performance Indicators (KPIs) and ClickUp's features such as dashboards and reports to achieve this.

Chapter 8, Integrating ClickUp with Your Other Tools and Apps, focuses on maximizing ClickUp's efficiency by integrating it with other apps such as Slack and Google Drive. It showcases how these connections streamline workflows and boost productivity across teams.

Chapter 9, Personal Task Management with ClickUp, dives into using ClickUp to manage your personal tasks. It covers organization, time management, and goal setting with features such as priority levels and the SMART goal framework.

Chapter 10, Project Management and Collaborating on Personal Events with Friends and Family, dives into ClickUp's functionalities to streamline personal event planning. It covers essential project management aspects, task delegation for collaboration, and budget management with ClickUp's features and integrations.

Chapter 11, Managing Household Chores and Home-Life Responsibilities guides you through using ClickUp to streamline household tasks and responsibilities, regardless of your household structure. It offers valuable insights for individuals, busy professionals, and even project managers at large organizations.

Chapter 12, Personal Habits, Goal Achievement, and Routines for Success, guides you through using ClickUp to develop habits that lead to achieving personal goals. It applies to individuals at various professional levels, from solopreneurs to enterprise executives.

Chapter 13, Processes, KPIs, and Automation: Simplified, dives into using ClickUp to streamline your work by creating efficient processes, workflows, and automation.

Chapter 14, Workflows: Designing User Experience in ClickUp, dives into using ClickUp to manage all aspects of your life, not just work. It covers creating a home workspace, integrating personal and work tasks, and achieving work-life balance with ClickUp's features.

Chapter 15, Recommendations, Troubleshooting, FAQs, and AI-Powered Productivity, equips ClickUp users with advanced knowledge to maximize the platform's potential and troubleshoot common issues. It also dives into ClickUp's AI features designed to boost productivity.

Chapter 16, Next Steps: Personal and Professional Growth with ClickUp, emphasizes the importance of having a growth mindset and using ClickUp's features (custom fields, automation, dashboards) to foster innovation. You'll also learn how ClickUp can be a hub for innovation projects, streamline workflows, and facilitate collaboration.

To get the most out of this book

While reading this book, continue researching terminologies and project management ideas and be familiar with productivity tools. It is essential to build consistent research, learning, and "doing it" habits. While you don't need experience with ClickUp, additional research and testing of tools and apps will enhance your understanding of this guide. This book presumes that you aim to enhance your efficiency and effectiveness, whether for work-related reasons or not, and you're willing to embrace new tactics for streamlining your tasks and projects.

Topic	Description	ClickUp Feature	Example
Growth Mindset	Importance of embracing challenges, learning from mistakes, and fostering a culture of continuous improvement.	N/A	- Research fostering experimentation and risk-taking

Topic	Description	ClickUp Feature	Example
Custom Fields	Adding specific data points to tasks, projects, and other ClickUp elements.	Custom Fields	- Software company tracking bug statuses and feature requests. - Monitoring progress on a sustainability project (e.g., energy usage, water consumption).
Automation	Setting up rules to automate repetitive tasks.	Automation	- Generating tasks upon lead creation. - Assigning tasks based on type or priority.
Dashboards	Visualizing data and tracking progress with customizable dashboards.	Dashboards	- Marketing team monitoring campaign effectiveness. - Project manager identifying at-risk projects.
Advanced Functionalities	ClickUp offers additional features for complex workflows.	- Gantt charts (project timelines) - Dependencies (linking tasks) - Portals (sharing with external users) - Webhooks (integrations with other apps)	- The product development team is integrating ClickUp with CRM using webhooks.
Fostering Innovation	Creating a culture that encourages creativity, provides resources, and celebrates achievements.	N/A	- Encouraging brainstorming and out-of-the-box thinking.
Managing Change	Effectively communicating changes, gaining stakeholder buy-in, and providing support and training.	N/A	

Topic	Description	ClickUp Feature	Example
Sustainable Innovation	Developing solutions that meet current needs without compromising the future.	N/A	- The company is using ClickUp to reduce its carbon footprint (track progress and identify areas for improvement).
ClickUp as Innovation Hub	Using ClickUp to manage all aspects of innovation projects.	- Custom fields, Automation, Dashboards	- Collaborating on sustainable agriculture initiatives (tracking progress, working with stakeholders).

Download the color images

You can download the color images in this book from our free graphic bundle: `https://packt.link/gbp/9781835468739`.

Conventions used

There are a number of text conventions used throughout this book.

Bold: Indicates a new term, an important word, or words that you see onscreen. For instance, words in menus or dialog boxes appear in bold. Here is an example: "Simply click the **Generate** button on the **AI Summary** field when viewing an item in your list."

> **Tips or important notes**
> Appear like this.

Get in touch

Feedback from our readers is always welcome.

General feedback: If you have questions about any aspect of this book, email us at `customercare@packtpub.com` and mention the book title in the subject of your message.

Errata: Although we have taken every care to ensure the accuracy of our content, mistakes do happen. If you have found a mistake in this book, we would be grateful if you would report this to us. Please visit `www.packtpub.com/support/errata` and fill in the form.

Piracy: If you come across any illegal copies of our works in any form on the internet, we would be grateful if you would provide us with the location address or website name. Please contact us at `copyright@packt.com` with a link to the material.

If you are interested in becoming an author: If there is a topic that you have expertise in and you are interested in either writing or contributing to a book, please visit `authors.packtpub.com`.

Share Your Thoughts

Once you've read *Mastering Project Management with ClickUp for Work and Home Life Balance*, we'd love to hear your thoughts! Scan the QR code below to go straight to the Amazon review page for this book and share your feedback.

`https://packt.link/r/183546873X`

Your review is important to us and the tech community and will help us make sure we're delivering excellent quality content.

Download a free PDF copy of this book

Thanks for purchasing this book!

Do you like to read on the go but are unable to carry your print books everywhere?

Is your eBook purchase not compatible with the device of your choice?

Don't worry, now with every Packt book you get a DRM-free PDF version of that book at no cost.

Read anywhere, any place, on any device. Search, copy, and paste code from your favorite technical books directly into your application.

The perks don't stop there, you can get exclusive access to discounts, newsletters, and great free content in your inbox daily

Follow these simple steps to get the benefits:

1. Scan the QR code or visit the link below

https://packt.link/free-ebook/9781835468739

2. Submit your proof of purchase

3. That's it! We'll send your free PDF and other benefits to your email directly

Part 1: Understanding ClickUp

In this part, you'll dive into the basics of ClickUp, understanding what it's all about, its benefits, and what it can do. You'll get the hang of navigating the workspace, adjusting settings to suit your needs, and using features with ClickApps. Whether you're new to ClickUp or a user looking to broaden your knowledge, this information will be helpful. By mastering the concepts and capabilities of ClickUp, you can set up your workspace for maximum workflow efficiency, boost productivity, and effectively handle projects and tasks using the platform. Moreover, with ClickUp AI, you can automate tasks, improve teamwork, and make informed decisions to drive your projects forward.

This part has the following chapters:

- *Chapter 1: What is ClickUp, and Why Should I Care? (Getting Started: Simplified)*
- *Chapter 2: Discovering your Benefits of Using ClickUp*
- *Chapter 3: Setup and Preparation Steps for Unlocking ClickUp*

1

What Is ClickUp, and Why Should I Care? (Getting Started – Simplified)

Welcome to *Chapter 1*, where we will explore the robust project management tool ClickUp, highlighting its significance for everyday people, solo owners, small businesses, and enterprise-level executives. ClickUp has an exhaustive list of features, literally. However, after taking a moment to learn and finish your training, ClickUp becomes like a second language. Whether you're a business owner or a project manager, this chapter offers valuable insights into the advantages of utilizing ClickUp.

In this chapter, we will cover the following topics:

- Understanding ClickUp's features
- Enhancing productivity with ClickUp
- Efficient communication and collaboration play a vital role in streamlining project management
- ClickUp for the everyday person, solo owners, and hobbyists
- ClickUp for small businesses
- ClickUp for enterprise-level executives

By the end of this chapter, you will have a comprehensive understanding of ClickUp's multifaceted utility in project management. This chapter will guide business owners and project managers through a journey of exploration, elucidating the distinctive features of ClickUp and how they can be harnessed to bolster productivity. You will grasp the integral role efficient communication and collaboration play in project streamlining, gaining insights into how ClickUp facilitates seamless interaction. Tailored discussions on ClickUp's applicability to solo owners, small businesses, and enterprise-level executives will provide you with nuanced perspectives, offering you a roadmap for leveraging ClickUp's advantages across diverse organizational scales. Whether you're seeking individual task optimization, orchestrating mid-sized project launches, or managing complex enterprise-level operations, you will conclude this chapter equipped with the knowledge to unlock ClickUp's potential and make informed decisions on how to integrate it into unique project management contexts.

Understanding ClickUp's features

ClickUp stands out as an effective project management solution that provides various features to facilitate streamlined workflows and goal achievement for teams of varying sizes. In this section, we will explore some of the critical elements of ClickUp and discuss how they can benefit different roles within your organization.

Task management

ClickUp's task management features make creating, assigning, and tracking tasks easy. You can complete tasks from anywhere in ClickUp and add due dates, descriptions, and subtasks to each task. ClickUp also allows you to prioritize tasks and set dependencies so that you can ensure that your team is working on the most critical studies first.

Goal setting

ClickUp's features help you set and track your team's goals. You can create plans at the project, task, or individual level and track your progress toward each goal. ClickUp also offers a variety of goal templates to help you get started.

Time tracking

ClickUp's time-tracking features make tracking the time you and your team members spend on tasks easy. Your team can start and stop timers with a single click and view detailed reports about your time-tracking data. Using this relevant information can enhance productivity and efficiency.

Team collaboration

ClickUp's team collaboration features make communicating and collaborating with your team members on tasks and projects easy. You can leave comments on assignments, mention team members, and share files. ClickUp also offers a variety of chat and collaboration tools, such as video chat and screen sharing.

Other features

In addition to the features mentioned previously, ClickUp also offers a variety of other features, including the following:

- **Custom fields**: You and your team can create custom fields to track any information that's critical to your team. You can create phases for process workflows and automation steps and use custom fields for automation triggers and integrations into other software systems.

- **Custom views**: You and your team can create custom views to see the best data for you, including a list view, a Kanboard Board style view, a Team Workload, a Gantt chart, a Timeline, Chat, and Dashboard KPIs.

- **Documents**: ClickUp's documents provide a unique "Wiki"-style experience that's perfect for writing and maintaining processes, meeting notes, and important documents. They are all in one area that can be searched by user permissions.

- **Custom workflows and automation**: You can create workflows to automate your work processes. Workflows are a series of steps you do in your work and home life. Make maintaining your workflows simple by writing your steps down in a document and maintaining your processes. From adding assignees, priorities, due dates, and comments, you have the tools to get creative with your workflow.

- **Integrations**: ClickUp imports and integrates with thousands of the top business tools. It's easy to migrate many disparate software applications and easily import them into ClickUp.

- **Templates**: ClickUp templates are a good starting point for testing different phases and process steps and finding the perfect standardized action statuses and custom fields.

Examples and case studies

Here are a few examples of how businesses are using ClickUp to improve their project management processes:

- **Fender**: ClickUp enabled Fender to streamline project management across departments, enhance team collaboration, and drive innovation. By leveraging ClickUp's flexibility and features, Fender can continue to create legendary instruments and exceptional customer experiences, keeping the music world rocking.

- **HubSpot**: HubSpot leverages the ClickUp integration within its platform to empower its teams and offer a more comprehensive project management experience for its clients. This integration bridges the gap between HubSpot's CRM functionalities and ClickUp's robust project management features.

- **Appsumo**: AppSumo relies on ClickUp to centralize deal management, streamline workflows, enhance team collaboration, and improve task management. Since integrating ClickUp into its processes, AppSumo has seen enhancements in its e-commerce operations. ClickUp is a tool for AppSumo as it helps them streamline e-commerce tasks, foster team collaboration, and boost efficiency in managing software deals. This enables them to consistently provide top-notch experiences for their customers.

ClickUp is a robust project management tool that's equipped with a diverse set of features that are designed to assist teams in optimizing their workflows and attaining their objectives. By comprehending the characteristics of ClickUp and leveraging them, you can select the appropriate features for your team and begin experiencing the benefits of ClickUp firsthand.

While this section delved into ClickUp's robust feature set, from efficient task management to goal-setting tools, we'll shift our focus to the practical application of these features. In the upcoming section, we'll explore how ClickUp's intuitive interface, customizable workflows, and powerful automation capabilities can be leveraged to streamline work processes, optimize your team's time, and ultimately unlock significant productivity gains within your organization.

Enhancing productivity with ClickUp

ClickUp stands out as a robust project management solution that's capable of enhancing the productivity of businesses across various scales. This section will discuss how ClickUp's intuitive interface, customizable workflows, and automation capabilities can help optimize your work processes, saving time and resources. It gives an everyday person to an enterprise-level team the ability to manage tasks, manage knowledge, optimize communication, and ultimately, time management.

Intuitive interface

ClickUp has designed its interface to be user-friendly and easy to navigate and makes continuous improvements to the user experience. Even new users can quickly learn to use ClickUp to create tasks, manage projects, and collaborate with their team members.

ClickUp also offers a variety of customization options so that you can tailor the interface to your specific needs. For example, you can create custom fields, views, and dashboards. You can also change the look and feel of the interface to match your branding.

Customizable workflows and whiteboard templates

Creating workflows with ClickUp allows you to streamline and automate your work processes. You can map out custom workflows for any process steps, such as new customer onboarding, product development, personal task management, or marketing campaign management:

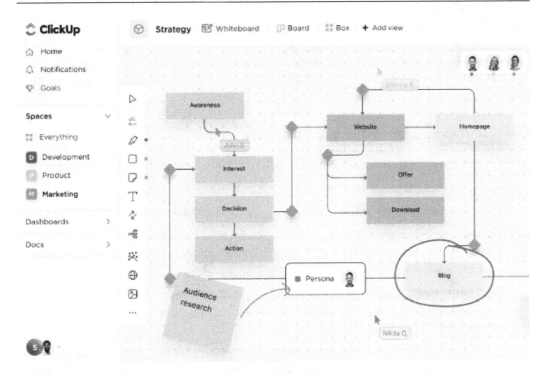

Figure 1.1 – Sample workflow (https://clickup.com/blog/workflow-templates/)

Automation capabilities

ClickUp's automation capabilities allow you to automate repetitive tasks, saving time and energy. You can create automation rules for various tasks, such as assigning tasks, sending notifications, and moving jobs between lists:

Figure 1.2 – The New Automation button (https://help.clickup.com/hc/
en-us/articles/6312102752791-Intro-to-Automations)

To generate an automation rule, click the **New Automation** button and choose the desired rule type. You can then set the trigger for the rule, such as when a new task is created or updated, and the action, such as assigning the task to a specific user or sending a notification. A good starting point to discovering automation that saves you time is to experiment with the AI feature and type in what you want to automate.

How ClickUp can improve productivity

ClickUp can improve productivity for businesses of all sizes in various ways. Here are a few examples:

- **Everyday people**: Organize your life with one app. Design how you want to live your life with family, friends, work, hobbies, and ambitious pursuits as a professional without even trying.

- **Solo owners**: They can use ClickUp to manage their entire business, from tasks and projects to contacts and invoices. ClickUp can help solo owners stay organized, track their progress, and avoid feeling overwhelmed.

- **Small businesses**: ClickUp is a valuable solution for small businesses, aiding them in managing their teams and projects more effectively. It can help them streamline their workflows, improve collaboration, and increase productivity.

- **Enterprise-level executives**: Enterprise-level executives can use ClickUp to track the progress of their teams and identify areas for improvement. This can help them make better decisions and improve the performance of their businesses.

Here are a few specific examples of how ClickUp can be used to improve productivity:

- **Use ClickUp to create a central hub for all your work**: ClickUp can manage all aspects of your business, from tasks and projects to contacts and invoices. This can help you save time and avoid switching between different tools.

- **Use ClickUp to automate repetitive tasks**: ClickUp's automation capabilities help you automate repetitive tasks, such as assigning tasks, sending notifications, and moving tasks between lists. For example, when creating tasks in a project list, you can use automation to assign yourself a priority and a due date and save time.

- **Use ClickUp to improve collaboration**: ClickUp's collaboration features make communicating with your team members and sharing files easy. You can @ comment team members with updates on a project. When added as a watcher, you'll receive instant notifications of the task's progress, making sure nothing slips through the cracks. This can help you get work done more quickly and efficiently.

- **Use ClickUp to track your progress**: ClickUp's reporting features can help you track the progress of your projects and identify areas for improvement. Create real-time reports on a list to gather custom metrics and goals within the same project view. Each task item can add an auto-progress option to give a visual reference to the percentage of work remaining. This can help you make better decisions and improve your daily life and business performance.

In general, ClickUp stands out as a potent project management tool that's capable of enhancing productivity for businesses of various sizes. Its unique flexibility makes it a key component of any home or business operating system. Its intuitive interface, customizable workflows, and automation capabilities allow you to optimize your work processes, saving time and resources.

While this section explored how ClickUp's user-friendly interface, workflows, and automation features optimize individual productivity, let's shift gears and delve into the crucial role of communication and collaboration in successful project management. ClickUp, equipped with features such as real-time chat, file sharing, and task comments, empowers teams to work together seamlessly, ensuring everyone stays aligned and contributes effectively toward shared goals. This collaborative aspect of ClickUp further amplifies the productivity gains we explored earlier, ultimately leading to project success.

Efficient communication and collaboration play a vital role in streamlining project management

Effective communication and collaboration play vital roles in achieving success in project management. ClickUp facilitates seamless communication among team members, clients, and stakeholders through various features, including real-time chat, file sharing, and task comments. This ensures that everyone is aligned and striving toward common objectives. Let's take a closer look.

Real-time chat

The real-time chat feature in ClickUp enables team members to communicate instantly within the platform, eliminating the need to navigate away. When using real-time chat and chatting in comments, some organizations have eliminated the need for software such as Slack, Discord, and other messaging software. This functionality is particularly beneficial for remote teams or those with members in different time zones:

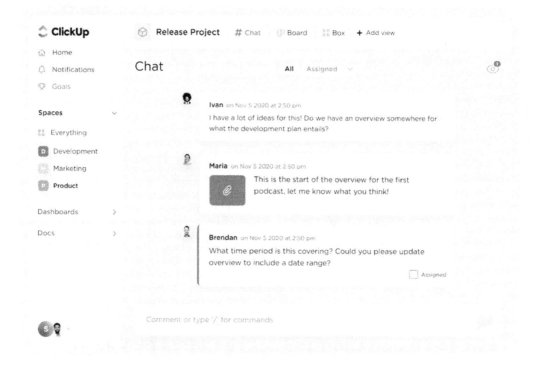

Figure 1.3 – ClickUp's real-time chat feature (https://clickup.com/blog/slack-vs-google-chat/)

To use ClickUp's real-time chat feature, click the chat icon in the top-right corner of the screen. You can then select the person or people you want to chat with. The chat window will open up on the right-hand side of the screen. At this point, you can type your message and press *Enter* to send it. The other person(s) will receive your message immediately.

File sharing

ClickUp also makes it easy to share files with team members and stakeholders. To share a file, click the **Attach** button in the task or comment editor. You can select the file you want to share from your computer or ClickUp's cloud storage:

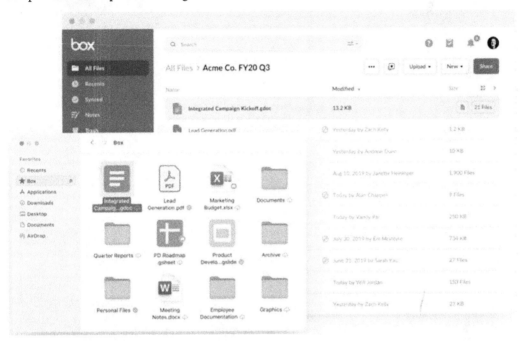

Figure 1.4 – ClickUp's file-sharing feature (https://clickup.com/blog/file-sharing-software/)

ClickUp will upload and share the file with the person or people you selected. They can then download the file and view it in their browser.

Task comments

ClickUp's task comments feature allows team members to leave comments on tasks. Similar to messaging software, by using @ comments, teams help prevent communication from being lost and replaced by the newest messages that can be unrelated. Without comments being connected to tasks, other messaging software becomes like the "water cooler of remote teams," where everyone hangs out to pass the time in the office. ClickUp task comments can be used for posting meeting notes, asking questions, providing feedback, or sharing updates, centralized on the task's focus:

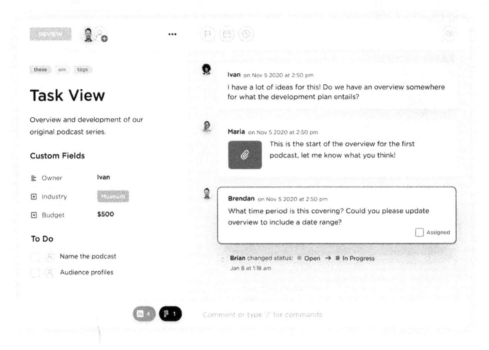

Figure 1.5 – ClickUp's task comments feature (https://clickup.com/features)

To comment on a task, click the **Comment** button in the task editor. You can then type your comment and press *Enter* to post it.

Other communication and collaboration features

In addition to the features mentioned previously, ClickUp also offers several other communication and collaboration features, including the following:

- **Mentions**: You can @ mention other team members in task comments, chat messages, and documents. This will notify them that they have been mentioned and that they may need to take action.

- **Inbox notifications**: ClickUp will send you notifications when you are mentioned in a task comment, chat message, or document when a task is assigned to you, or when the due date is approaching.

- **Task boards**: ClickUp's task boards provide a visual way to track the progress of tasks. Team members can leave comments and attachments on tasks directly on the task board.

- **Wiki**: ClickUp's docs feature a Wiki-type experience that allows teams to create and share knowledge bases. This can centralize leadership knowledgebase, team processes, procedures, and best practices.

Benefits of efficient communication and collaboration

Efficient communication and collaboration can lead to several benefits, including the following:

- **Increased productivity**: Effective communication and collaboration among team members contribute to increased efficiency in reducing the amount of time and communication "touchpoints" when completing tasks

- **Improved quality of work**: When team members can share ideas and feedback and know that responses are guaranteed within 24 to 72 hours, the quality of work improves

- **Reduced errors**: When team members can communicate, and it feels natural to collaborate effectively, errors are less likely to occur

- **Increased team morale**: Team morale increases when members feel like they are part of a team and their voices are heard

Examples and case studies

Here are a few examples of how businesses are using ClickUp's communication and collaboration features to improve their project management:

- **Webflow**: Webflow utilizes ClickUp to optimize workflows, improve communication and collaboration, and enhance project management. ClickUp plays a role in Webflow's operations by empowering its design and development teams to work together, resulting in outstanding web design experiences for its clients.

- **Mailigen**: Mailigen considers ClickUp an essential tool that helps them streamline email marketing workflows, foster team collaboration, and deliver campaign experiences for their clients. By utilizing ClickUp's features, Mailigen empowers businesses to achieve success in email marketing endeavors.

- **Airbyte**: Airbyte values ClickUp's contribution to streamlining data integration project management tasks, enhancing team collaboration efforts, and advancing its mission of democratizing data accessibility for all companies. ClickUp's flexibility and scalability enable Airbyte to innovate and offer top-tier data integration solutions.

Successful project management relies heavily on efficient communication and collaboration. ClickUp offers features such as real-time chat, file sharing, task comments, and more to facilitate seamless communication and collaboration, enabling teams to stay connected and work together efficiently.

In essence, ClickUp is a robust project management tool that enhances team communication and collaboration. Using ClickUp's communication and collaboration features, teams can streamline workflows, foster real-time interaction, and enhance overall project coordination. This, in turn, leads to increased efficiency, better task management, and a more cohesive team environment, ultimately contributing to improved project outcomes. In the next section, you will learn that while ClickUp empowers teams to collaborate seamlessly, it is also an effective project management tool for solo owners.

ClickUp for everyday people, solo owners, and hobbyists

The everyday person and solo business owners face unique challenges when managing projects. They often have to wear multiple hats and juggle a variety of tasks. This can make it challenging to stay organized and on top of everything.

ClickUp proves to be an effective project management tool, aiding individual owners in overcoming these challenges. It offers many features and tools to help solo owners stay organized, track progress, and manage tasks effectively.

Specific features for the everyday person

ClickUp offers several features that are specifically designed for solo owners, including the following:

- **To Do**: ClickUp's **To Do** feature allows you to create a centralized list of tasks. Solo owners can then prioritize their tasks and track their progress:

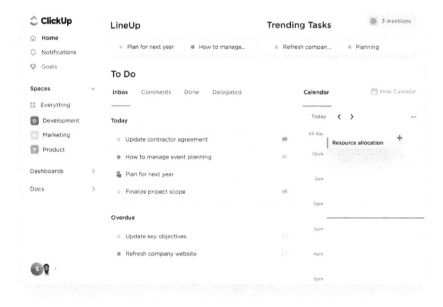

Figure 1.6 – ClickUp's To Do feature (https://clickup.com/online-to-do-list)

- **Task Management**: ClickUp's **Task Management** feature allows solo owners to create, assign, and track tasks. Solo owners can also set due dates, priorities, and task dependencies:

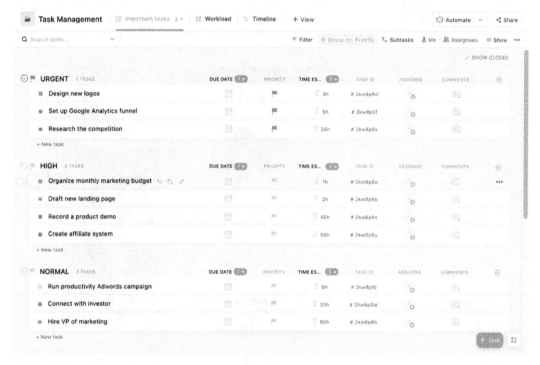

Figure 1.7 – ClickUp's Task Management feature (https://clickup.com/blog/task-management-templates/)

- **Time Tracking**: ClickUp's **Time Tracking** feature allows solo owners to track their time on tasks. This information can then identify areas where time is wasted and improve productivity:

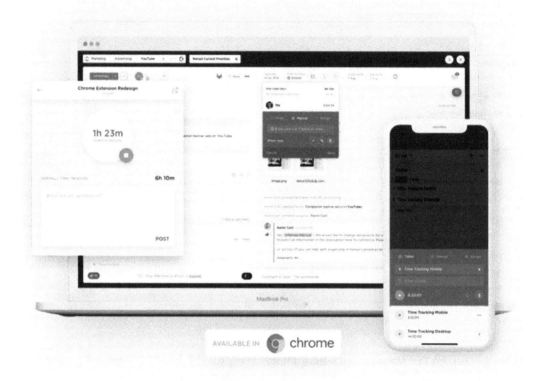

Figure 1.8 – ClickUp's Time Tracking feature (https://clickup.com/blog/time-tracking-software-developers/)

- **Reporting**: ClickUp's **Reporting** feature allows solo owners to track progress and identify improvement areas. Solo owners can generate reports on task completion rates, time spent on tasks, and other vital metrics:

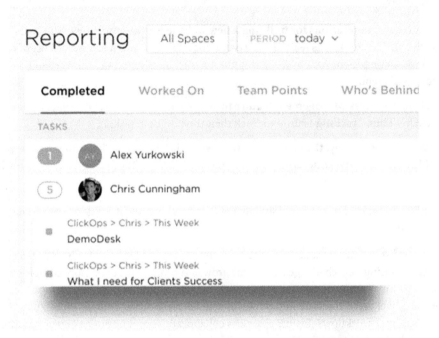

Figure 1.9 – ClickUp's Reporting feature (https://clickup.com/features/reporting)

Strategies for maximizing productivity

Solo owners can leverage the following ClickUp features and strategies to maximize their productivity:

- **Use the To Do list feature to create a centralized list of your tasks.** This will help you to stay organized and on top of everything.

- **Use the Task Management feature to create, assign, and track tasks.** This will help you keep your projects on track and meet deadlines.

- **Use the Time Tracking feature to track your time on tasks.** This information can then identify areas where time is wasted and improve productivity.

- **Utilize the Reporting feature to monitor your progress and pinpoint areas for improvement.** This functionality aids in making well-informed decisions regarding allocating time and resources.

Real-life scenarios and case studies

Let's look at an example of how an everyday person and solo owner can use ClickUp to manage their projects effectively:

- **Organize all preparations for building a new website for their business.** They use ClickUp's **To Do** and **Custom Fields** features to create website phases with a centralized list of tasks that need to be completed, such as designing the website, developing the website, and writing the website's content.

- **Use ClickUp's Task Management feature to assign each task and set due dates.** They also use ClickUp's **Time Tracking** feature to track their time on each task.

- **At the end of each day, the solo owner reviews their ClickUp task list to see their progress and identify any overdue tasks.** They also use ClickUp's **Reporting** feature to track their overall progress on the project.

Using ClickUp's features and strategies, solo owners can stay organized, track progress, and manage their projects effectively.

Having equipped solo entrepreneurs with the tools to thrive, ClickUp seamlessly scales to empower small businesses facing new challenges. As teams grow and projects become more complex, the need for robust project management solutions intensifies. Let's dive into how ClickUp's adaptable features, honed for individual users, translate into powerful benefits for growing companies. We'll explore how ClickUp streamlines workflows, fosters seamless collaboration, and optimizes resource allocation, allowing small businesses to navigate expansion while maintaining control and efficiency.

ClickUp for small to medium-sized businesses

Small businesses require robust project management solutions to handle their growing operations. ClickUp is a flexible and scalable project management tool that can accommodate the needs of medium-sized teams. It offers many features to help small businesses streamline their project management processes, improve team collaboration, and allocate resources effectively.

Scaling your business

ClickUp is designed to scale your business. As your business grows, you can add more users and features to ClickUp to meet your changing needs. ClickUp also offers a variety of pricing plans to fit the budget of any small to medium-sized business.

Features for small businesses

ClickUp offers a variety of features that are specifically designed for small businesses, including the following:

- **Team collaboration**: ClickUp's functionalities simplify project communication and collaboration among team members. These features include real-time chat, file sharing, and task comments:

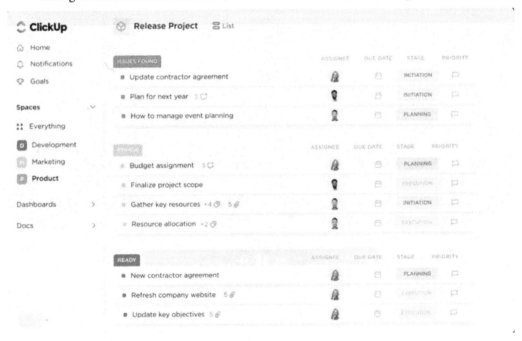

Figure 1.10 – ClickUp – team collaboration (https://clickup.com/
blog/project-management-collaboration-tools/)

- **Resource allocation**: ClickUp's resource allocation features help small to medium-sized businesses allocate resources effectively. These features include workloads, views, resource calendars, and task dependencies:

Figure 1.11 – ClickUp – resource allocation (https://clickup.com/blog/capacity-planning-in-excel/)

- **Customizable workflows**: ClickUp's workflows allow small businesses to automate their work processes. This helps save time and improve efficiency:

Figure 1.12– ClickUp – customizable workflows (https://clickup.com/custom-project-management)

- **Reporting and analytics:** ClickUp's reporting and analytics features help small businesses track their progress and identify areas where improvement is needed. These features include project status reports, task completion reports, and time tracking reports:

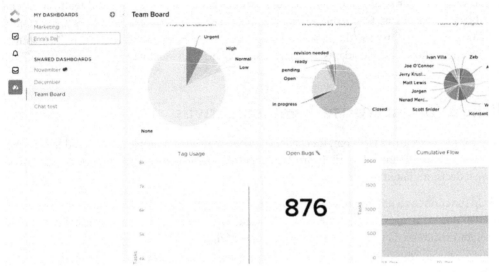

Figure 1.13 – ClickUp – reporting and analytics (https://clickup.com/blog/crm-reporting/)

Real-life scenarios and case studies

Let's look at an example of how a small business can use ClickUp to manage its projects effectively:

- **A small to medium-sized marketing agency uses ClickUp to manage its client projects.** The agency uses ClickUp's team collaboration features to communicate and collaborate with its team members on each project. The agency also uses ClickUp's resource allocation features to allocate resources effectively across all its projects. By adding clients as guests to the list, they were able to follow along with the project in their own time.

- **The agency has created custom workflows in ClickUp to automate its work processes.** For example, the agency has created a custom workflow for onboarding new clients. Using custom fields and forms, this workflow automates the process of creating new projects, assigning tasks, and setting deadlines.

- **The agency also uses ClickUp's Reporting features to track its progress and identify improvement areas.** For instance, the agency utilizes ClickUp to monitor time allocations for individual projects and pinpoint the most lucrative ones while identifying key indicators of team members being over or under-utilized.

Using ClickUp's features, the marketing agency can streamline its project management processes, improve team collaboration, and allocate resources effectively.

Having empowered small businesses to navigate growth and complexity, ClickUp now ascends to a new challenge: catering to the unique needs of enterprise-level executives. While executives at the helm of large organizations appreciate streamlined processes and team collaboration, their focus shifts toward broader strategic concerns. Let's explore how ClickUp's powerful features extend beyond task management, transforming into a comprehensive tool for executives seeking visibility, risk identification, and informed decision-making across their vast projects and teams. This shift in focus highlights how ClickUp adapts to different user needs while maintaining its core strengths in organization and efficiency.

ClickUp for enterprise-level executives

Enterprise-level executives face complex challenges when managing multiple projects and teams. They need to have visibility into all of their projects, identify potential risks and bottlenecks, and make informed decisions about resource allocation.

ClickUp functions as a potent project management tool that assists executives at the enterprise level in overcoming challenges. It offers several features and tools crafted to enhance project visibility and control for executives. Let's take a closer look at some of them.

Task types

ClickUp offers more than task management – it lets you customize it to fit your specific workflows. By using custom task types, you can convert tasks into categories such as **Projects**, **Initiatives**, **Contacts**, or even **Inventory Items**. It also allows you to add icons and descriptions to further define your workload. This flexible feature allows you to organize and handle your tasks in a manner that suits your requirements perfectly:

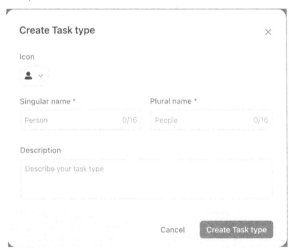

Figure 1.14 – Task types (https://help.clickup.com/hc/en-us/articles/17564381376919-Custom-task-types)

You can simplify your work process by setting up default task categories for your ClickUp lists. This convenient feature automatically assigns a category (such as "Milestone" or "Person") to every task you create within that list. This helps maintain uniformity and saves time – no category assignments – for each new task. Just keep in mind that this change only affects tasks. You can always use the bulk action toolbar to update existing tasks if necessary. What's more convenient is that the **Add task** button shows the default category, making it easy for you to add items to your list with just one click:

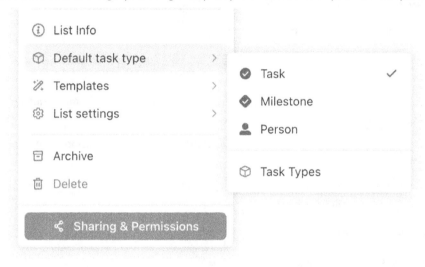

Figure 1.15 – Custom task types (https://help.clickup.com/hc/en-us/articles/17564381376919-Custom-task-types)

Don't worry about limiting your options. Setting a default task type won't prevent you from adding more custom types to your ClickUp list. Here's how to set a default type:

1. In the list view, click the three dots (**...**) next to the list's name.

2. Choose **Default task type** and select your desired type. Now, all new tasks in this list will automatically inherit that type, saving you time and keeping things organized.

As an administrator or owner, you have the authority to establish and oversee task categories. The procedure is straightforward: simply designate a title, symbol, and description for your category.

You can allocate custom task categories to existing tasks, define defaults for lists, and even update task categories in bulk for enhanced productivity. Keep in mind that only administrators and owners can create and modify task categories. However, individuals with edit or full permissions can alter the category that's been assigned to a task.

Milestone Gantt view

What are milestones? Imagine reaching a major accomplishment in your project, such as launching a new product or completing a critical development phase. ClickUp's milestones feature helps you celebrate those victories and stay on track toward your goals.

Why use milestones?

Here are some reasons why you should use them:

- **Visualize progress**: Milestones act like checkpoints on your project timeline, giving you a clear picture of your overall progress
- **Stay motivated**: Reaching milestones provides a sense of accomplishment and keeps your team motivated
- **Organize complex projects**: Break down large projects into smaller, more manageable steps with milestones
- **Track epics progress**: Use milestones to organize and keep tabs on the progress of your epics (large, long-term projects)

How to use milestones

Using milestones is straightforward. Here's how:

- **Upgrading is optional**: Milestones are available on the Free Forever plan, with a limit of 20. Paid plans offer unlimited milestones.
- **Who can create them?**: Anyone on your team with edit or full permissions can create milestones (guests included).

Turning tasks into milestones

Follow these steps:

1. Open a task you want to mark as a milestone.
2. Click the three dots icon (…) in the top-right corner (or to the right of the task name in the List, Board, or Calendar view).

3. Select **Task Type** and choose **Milestone**:

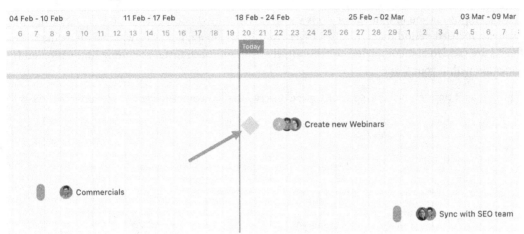

Figure 1.16 – Milestone Gantt view (https://help.clickup.com/
hc/en-us/articles/6304458574615-Milestones)

Spotting milestones in the Gantt view

The Gantt view offers a visual representation of your project timeline. Here's how to identify milestones in this view:

- Look for the diamond icon next to the task name
- Milestone tasks might also appear in different colors, depending on your chosen color scheme settings

Viewing milestones easily

Need to take a quick look at your milestones? ClickUp lets you filter tasks to show only milestones:

1. Open the **Filter** option located in the corner (the icon with three lines).
2. Select **Filters** at the top of the screen.
3. Choose **Task type** from the list.
4. Opt for **Milestone** from the task types.

By integrating milestones into your workflow on ClickUp, you can efficiently oversee projects and commemorate accomplishments. Ensure your team remains focused on reaching their goals.

Sprint management

ClickUp empowers you to manage projects using the Agile methodology's core concept: Sprints. A Sprint is a focused period that typically ranges from 1 week to a few weeks, where a predefined set of tasks are tackled and completed collaboratively. This approach fosters ongoing innovation and adaptation within your team:

A Sprint is a set time interval during which specific work has to be completed and made ready for review.

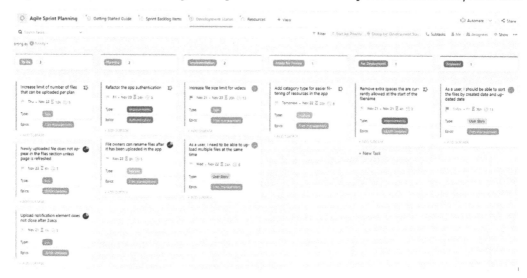

Figure 1.17 – Sprints (https://clickup.com/features/sprints)

ClickUp equips your team to thrive in a Sprint environment. You can easily assign tasks, track progress, and foster communication – all within a centralized platform. This fosters a collaborative atmosphere where team members can hold each other accountable and celebrate achievements together, leading to successful Sprint completion and ongoing project improvement.

Custom reporting

ClickUp empowers executives with the ability to delve deep into their projects through custom reporting. Unlike pre-built reports with limited data points, ClickUp allows them to pull information from any field within the platform:

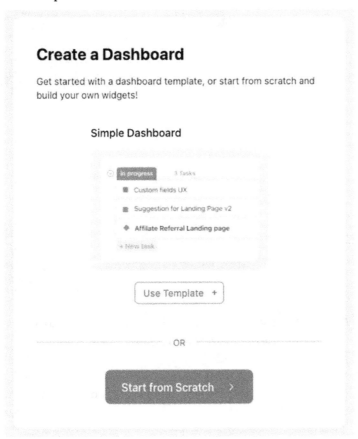

Figure 1.18 – ClickUp – custom reporting (https://clickup.com/blog/excel-kpi-dashboard/)

Custom reporting provides unmatched flexibility – imagine generating reports that showcase not just deadlines and completion rates but also custom fields tracking resource allocation, budget spending, or even client satisfaction scores. With this level of granularity, executives gain a holistic view of project health, enabling them to make data-driven decisions that optimize workflows and drive success.

Dashboards hub

You can utilize the **Dashboards** hub to arrange, search for, and craft dashboards all in one spot. The hub categorizes dashboards into three cards and a table, each equipped with filters and functions to help you effectively handle your dashboards:

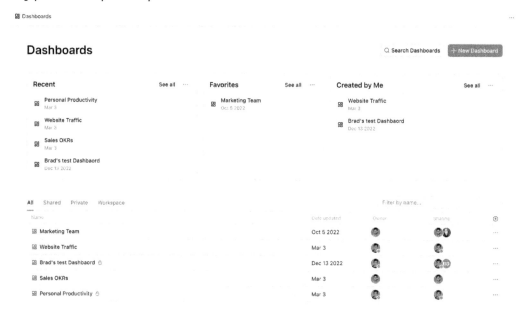

Figure 1.19 – ClickUp's Dashboards hub (https://help.clickup.com/
hc/en-us/articles/14236332445335-Dashboards-Hub)

Anyone with a ClickUp account can access the **Dashboards** hub, regardless of their plan. However, creating and modifying dashboards is limited to paying plans (Unlimited and above). The good news is that even guests can view dashboards shared with them within the hub, allowing them to stay in the loop on project progress.

Integration

ClickUp integrates with other business tools, such as CRM systems, HR systems, and marketing automation platforms. Additionally, further workflows are available with the Zapier and Make.com software, which connects thousands of apps for advanced workflows and automation. This helps executives keep all of their data in one place and to streamline their workflows:

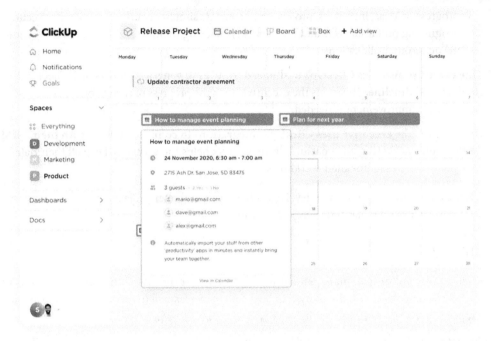

Figure 1.20 – ClickUp's integrations (https://clickup.com/blog/best-clickup-integrations/)

Benefits for enterprise-level executives

ClickUp provides enterprise-level executives with several benefits, including the following:

- **Improved visibility**: ClickUp's custom admin roles, Sprints, and task types give enterprise-level executives a comprehensive view of their projects. This helps executives identify potential risks and bottlenecks and make informed decisions about resource allocation.

- **Increased productivity**: ClickUp's custom reporting and integration features help enterprise-level executives streamline workflows and save time. This frees up executives to focus on more strategic tasks.

- **Improved decision-making**: ClickUp's robust analytics capabilities provide enterprise-level executives with the insights they need to make informed project decisions.

Real-life scenarios and case studies

Let's look at an example of how an enterprise-level executive can use ClickUp to manage their projects effectively:

- **An enterprise-level executive is responsible for managing a portfolio of software development projects.** The executive uses different spaces, folders, Sprints, and task-type features to separate the progress of ideas, initiatives, projects, and contacts simultaneously. This aids the executive in recognizing potential risks and bottlenecks, enabling them to make informed decisions regarding resource allocation.

- **The executive also uses ClickUp's dashboard features to generate reports on project status, budget, and timeline.** This helps the executive track the progress of their projects and identify areas where improvement is needed.

- **In addition, the executive uses ClickUp's integrations to connect ClickUp with their CRM system and marketing automation platform.** This helps the executive keep all their data in one place and streamline their workflows.

Using ClickUp's features, an enterprise-level executive can gain better project visibility and control, improve productivity, and make better project decisions.

Summary

ClickUp is a powerful project management tool. This chapter discussed the various features of ClickUp, how it can enhance productivity, and how solo owners, small to medium-sized businesses, and enterprise-level executives can use it.

The information in this chapter was helpful because it provided a comprehensive overview of ClickUp and how it can be used to improve project management processes. This chapter also discussed specific examples of how businesses can use ClickUp to enhance productivity and efficiency.

Now that you understand Clickup, it's time to move on to the next chapter. There, you will learn about the specific features of ClickUp that are most beneficial for solo owners, small businesses, and enterprise-level executives, as well as real-world examples of how enterprises use ClickUp to improve project management processes.

Sign up to download your free workbook and productivity resources for each chapter

ClickUp is constantly evolving. Get help and explore each chapter in depth, receive the latest productivity updates and ClickUp tips, and download your free workbook at `http://bluecreative.com/clickup`. Specializing in ClickUp implementation, configurations, systems development, process implementation, and more.

Unger, E. (2024). Clickup. BLUECREATIVE.

`https://bluecreative.com/clickup`

2

Discovering Your Benefits of Using ClickUp

Welcome to *Chapter 2*, where we will explore the personal benefits that everyday users, solo owners, moderate-sized company owners, and enterprise-level executives can gain from using ClickUp. This chapter will explore how ClickUp can cater to your needs and help you achieve your goals.

In this chapter, we will cover the following topics:

- Tailoring ClickUp to your workflow
- Increasing efficiency and productivity
- Fostering seamless collaboration and communication
- Tracking progress and achieving goals

By the end of this chapter, you will have gained a comprehensive understanding of the various benefits ClickUp offers to solo owners, small businesses, mid-sized companies, and enterprise-level executives. Through detailed exploration, you will learn the art of tailoring ClickUp to seamlessly align with your unique workflows, unlocking a personalized project management experience. Moreover, you will discover strategies for enhancing efficiency and productivity, leveraging ClickUp's features to streamline tasks and operations effectively. This chapter will help provide the necessary knowledge for you to get started and maximize its benefits.

Tailoring ClickUp to your workflow

ClickUp is an adaptable project management tool that can be effortlessly tailored so that it aligns with the unique workflow needs of any team or organization. With ClickUp, you can customize everything from the task statuses and views to the custom fields and automation. This flexibility and adaptability make ClickUp a powerful tool for streamlining work processes and boosting productivity. In the upcoming subsections, we will delve into specific features and customization options offered by ClickUp, exploring how these capabilities can be leveraged strategically to optimize workflow efficiency and enhance collaborative productivity.

Creating task statuses and views

ClickUp allows you to create task statuses and views that align with your workflow. For example, you could create a standard set of statuses for "Open," "In Progress," "In Review," and "Closed." You can also create custom views to group tasks by project, priority, or due date. *It is a best practice to commit to one set of custom statuses that is used throughout the workspace.* This is important when you're creating your dashboard KPI metrics and keeping all data in sync across projects, teams, and reporting:

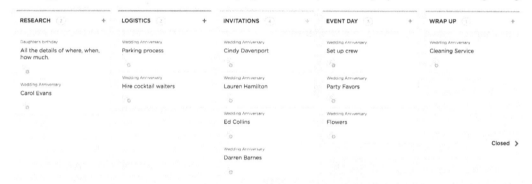

Figure 2.1 – Custom task statuses (https://clickup.com/features/custom-task-statuses)

Creating custom fields

ClickUp also allows you to create custom fields to track any essential data for your team. For example, you could complete custom fields to track project budgets, resource allocation, or customer satisfaction. A great feature when using custom fields is to use them for process steps, automation, categories, and any other custom field name that will enhance your workflow:

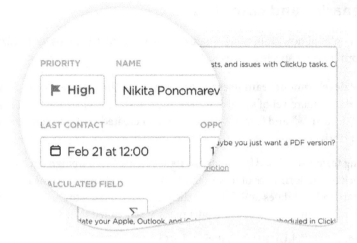

Figure 2.2– Custom fields (https://clickup.com/blog/feature-custom-fields/)

Automating tasks

ClickUp's automation features allow you to automate repetitive tasks, such as assigning tasks, sending emails, notifications, custom fields, and changing task statuses. Once you've defined your workflow, it's recommended that you write down the steps to continually optimize it. Then, you can implement the workflow with automation and free up time so that you can focus on other important things in your life:

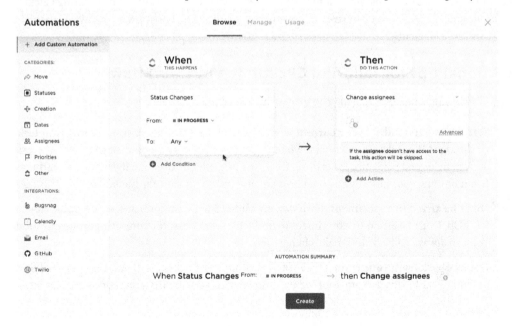

Figure 2.3 – Automations (https://clickup.com/features/automations)

Real-life scenarios and case studies

Here are a few examples of how teams and organizations are using ClickUp's customization features to tailor the platform to their specific needs:

- **A software development team uses ClickUp to track the progress of their sprints.** They have created a standard set of statuses for each action stage of the sprint, such as "To Do," "In Progress," "In Review," and "Done." They have also created custom views to group tasks by sprint and priority.

- **A marketing team uses ClickUp to manage its social media campaigns.** It has created custom fields to track the performance of its social media posts, such as reach, engagement, and clicks. By using start and due dates and defining their process into custom fields, the team has also automated the posting of new social media posts at scheduled times.

- **A sales team uses ClickUp to track their sales pipeline.** They have created custom fields with each stage of the sales pipeline, such as "Prospect," "Qualified Lead," "Demo Scheduled," and "Closed Won." They have also created automation to send notifications to team members when a lead moves to a new pipeline stage. Additional automation was added to move a lead through the sales process to trigger the fulfillment team with automated assignee, start and due dates, a custom field stage, and a standard set of action statuses.

ClickUp's customization features make it a powerful tool for teams and organizations of all sizes to use open source software. Teams can customize it according to how business operations work, while users and departments can customize it to their individual views and workflows. By tailoring ClickUp to your unique workflow, you can streamline your work processes, boost productivity, and achieve your goals more efficiently.

Additional tips for tailoring ClickUp to your workflow

Here are a few other tips for tailoring ClickUp to your workflow:

- **Start by understanding your current workflow**: What are the different stages that your tasks go through? What data is essential to you to track? Once you know your stages, you can create custom fields and prioritize tasks using ClickUp's priorities of Urgent, High, Normal, and Low. Begin filtering your tasks by custom views and use the board view for Kanban to sort priorities.

- **Don't be afraid to experiment**: Each day, set aside 15 to 30 minutes and select a new view of ClickUp. Don't be afraid to experiment to find what works best for your team or organization. You can always go back and make changes later on.

- **Get feedback from your team**: Once you've customized ClickUp so that it fits your workflow, be sure to get feedback from your team. This will help you identify areas for improvement.

Following these tips, you can tailor ClickUp to your unique workflow and create a project management system that works for you and your team.

Having explored ClickUp's customizable features for tailoring to specific workflow needs, we'll transition to the next section, which focuses on increasing efficiency and productivity within the platform. While customization allows users to adapt ClickUp to their unique requirements, the upcoming section delves into specific features and strategies to enhance overall workflow efficiency and productivity.

Increasing efficiency and productivity

ClickUp is a comprehensive project management tool that's tailored to elevate the efficiency and productivity of individuals, businesses of all scales, and enterprise-level organizations.

In this section, we'll cover a few specific features and strategies that you can use to streamline your work processes and accomplish more in less time with ClickUp.

Task management

ClickUp's task management features make creating, assigning, and tracking tasks easy. You can also establish due dates, prioritize tasks, and define function dependencies. This helps you to stay organized and on top of your workload:

Figure 2.4 – Task management (https://clickup.com/templates/task-management-t-4404185)

Time tracking

ClickUp's time-tracking features allow you to track the time you spend on tasks. This information can then identify areas where time is wasted and improve productivity:

Figure 2.5 – Time tracking (https://help.clickup.com/hc/en-us/
articles/6304291811479-Intro-to-Time-Tracking)

Reporting

ClickUp's reporting features allow you to track progress and identify improvement areas. This information can then be used to make informed decisions about allocating your time and resources:

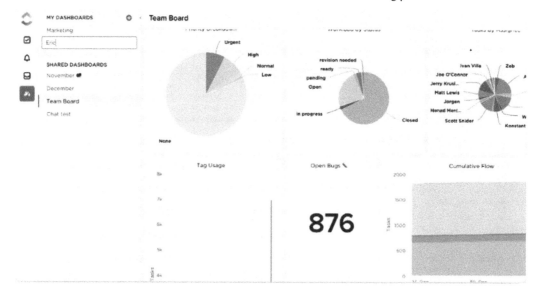

Figure 2.6 – Reporting (https://clickup.com/blog/kpi-reporting/)

Here are a few additional tips for using ClickUp to increase your efficiency and productivity:

- **Use templates to save time**: ClickUp provides many pre-built templates for diverse project and task types, catering to various needs. These templates serve as a solid foundation, enabling you to get started on your projects and streamline your workflow quickly. You can use these templates to create rapidly and avoid repeatedly recreating the same schemes.

- **Set realistic deadlines**: When setting task deadlines, be realistic about your available time. It is better to set a deadline that you can achieve than to set a deadline that you are likely to miss.

- **Take breaks**: Remember to take breaks throughout the day to avoid burnout. ClickUp's timer can help you stay focused and take breaks at regular intervals.

- **Delegate tasks**: If you can delegate tasks, do so. This will free up your time to focus on more critical studies.

Real-life scenarios and case studies

Let's look at an example of how a solo business owner can use ClickUp to increase their efficiency and productivity:

- **A solo owner is working on a new website for their business.** They use ClickUp's task management features to create a list of tasks that need to be completed, such as designing the website, developing the website, and writing the website content.

- **The solo owner then uses ClickUp's customizable workflows to automate repetitive tasks, such as emailing clients and updating the website's status.** By automating and delegating routine tasks, solo owners can reclaim their time and focus on high-impact activities that drive business growth, such as content creation and strategic marketing initiatives.

- **The solo owner also uses ClickUp's time tracking features to track their time on tasks.** This information is then used to identify areas where time is being wasted and to make improvements.

Solo owners can effectively streamline their work processes by leveraging ClickUp's comprehensive features and strategic functionalities, enhancing efficiency and productivity gains.

Here's an example of how small to mid-sized businesses can use ClickUp to increase their efficiency and productivity:

- A mid-sized enterprise is launching a new product. It uses ClickUp's task management features to create a list of tasks to be completed, such as developing the product, marketing it, and selling it.

- Harnessing ClickUp's customizable workflows, small businesses can automate repetitive tasks, such as report generation and customer email communication, streamlining operations and enhancing efficiency. This frees up time to focus on more critical tasks, such as developing products and building customer relationships.

- By leveraging ClickUp's robust reporting features, mid-sized enterprises can effectively track their progress, gain valuable insights into their operations, and identify areas ripe for improvement. This information is then used to make informed decisions about allocating their time and resources.

Using ClickUp's features and strategies, small businesses can streamline their work processes and increase efficiency and productivity.

ClickUp emerges as a versatile project management solution that's been meticulously crafted to elevate the efficiency and productivity of individuals, small and mid-sized businesses, and enterprise-level organizations.

Using ClickUp's features and strategies, you can streamline your work processes, automate repetitive tasks, and track your progress. By streamlining your workflow and eliminating distractions, ClickUp can free up your time, allowing you to focus on the most critical tasks and achieve your goals more efficiently.

Having delved into the various features and strategies for increasing efficiency and productivity within ClickUp, we'll focus on fostering seamless collaboration and communication in the upcoming section. While this section emphasized individual productivity through task management, time tracking, customizable workflows, and reporting, the forthcoming section will explore how ClickUp facilitates effective collaboration and communication among team members. This transition highlights the interconnected nature of productivity and collaboration, underscoring how optimizing both aspects leads to overall project success within ClickUp's framework.

Fostering seamless collaboration and communication

Effective collaboration and communication are the cornerstones of successful project management. ClickUp emerges as a versatile project management solution that's been meticulously crafted to elevate the efficiency and productivity of individuals, small and mid-sized businesses, and enterprise-level organizations. At the core of its success lies a comprehensive suite of features and tools that have been crafted to streamline collaboration communication and ensure everyone is aligned and working toward shared objectives.

Features for collaboration and communication

ClickUp offers a variety of features that are specifically designed for collaboration and communication, including the following:

- **Real-time chat**: ClickUp's real-time chat functionality facilitates seamless communication among team members. This can help answer questions, resolve issues, and brainstorm ideas.

- **File sharing**: ClickUp's file-sharing feature allows team members to share files easily. This can help you collaborate on documents, images, and other types of files.

- **Task comments**: ClickUp's task comments feature allows team members to leave comments on tasks. This can help you discuss charges, provide feedback, and ask questions.

- **Whiteboards**: ClickUp's whiteboards feature allows team members to brainstorm ideas and visually collaborate on projects.

- **Integrations**: ClickUp integrates with other business tools, such as Slack, Microsoft Teams, Google Drive, Box, and more. This can help teams keep all their communication and collaboration in one place.

Strategies for improving collaboration and communication

Here are a few plans for using ClickUp to enhance the cooperation and communication:

- **Boost collaboration and reduce meetings**: ClickUp's real-time chat keeps everyone on the same page, minimizing email clutter and unnecessary meetings and fostering clear communication and shared goals.

- **Goodbye, outdated files**: ClickUp's file-sharing ensures everyone always works with the latest documents, eliminating confusion caused by outdated information and streamlining project flow.

- **Unified communication and feedback**: ClickUp's task comments keep everyone informed about the task itself, reducing miscommunication and fostering clear discussions and feedback loops.

- **Supercharge brainstorming**: ClickUp's whiteboard unleashes team creativity! It allows you to brainstorm ideas visually, share concepts, and gather feedback collaboratively, accelerating problem-solving and innovation.

- **All-in-one hub**: Connect ClickUp with your favorite business tools to centralize communication and collaboration across your entire workflow, keeping everything organized and accessible for the team.

Examples and case studies

Here's an example of how a solo owner can use ClickUp to improve collaboration and communication with their clients:

- **A solo owner is working on a project for a client.** The solo owner uses ClickUp's real-time chat feature to communicate with the client. This allows the solo owner to quickly answer the client's questions and resolve any issues.

- The solo owner also uses ClickUp's file-sharing feature to quickly share files with the client. This ensures that the client can access the latest documents and other files.

- In addition, the solo owner uses ClickUp's task comments feature to discuss tasks with the client and to provide feedback. This helps keep the client on the same page and avoid misunderstandings.

Using ClickUp's features and strategies, the solo owner can improve collaboration and communication with their client.

Here's an example of how a mid-sized business can use ClickUp to improve collaboration and communication between team members:

- **A mid-sized enterprise uses ClickUp to manage its projects.** By leveraging ClickUp's real-time chat feature, the company has effectively streamlined communication among team members, reducing the reliance on emails and meetings.

- **The business also uses ClickUp's file-sharing feature to allow team members to share files easily and use ClickUp as storage.** This allows for easy access through ClickUp's universal search and ensures everyone works with the most accurate and up-to-date information, promoting efficiency and consistency.

- In addition, the business uses ClickUp's task comments and chat view feature to allow team members to discuss tasks, provide feedback, and ask questions. This helps to keep everyone on the same page to avoid misunderstandings.

Effective collaboration and communication are cornerstones of success in the dynamic realm of small to medium-sized businesses. ClickUp emerges as a powerful project management tool that's been meticulously crafted to elevate teams to new heights of productivity and synergy. By leveraging ClickUp's comprehensive suite of features and strategies, small businesses can transform their collaboration landscape, fostering seamless communication and achieving remarkable results.

Having explored the significance of effective collaboration and communication within project management, we'll transition to tracking progress and achieving goals in the upcoming section. While collaboration and communication are fundamental for aligning teams and driving synergy, monitoring progress and goal attainment are equally crucial for project success. In the next section, we will delve into ClickUp's diverse array of features and tools that are designed to track progress and facilitate goal achievement, highlighting how these aspects seamlessly integrate with the collaborative framework we established earlier.

Tracking progress and achieving goals

Tracking progress and achieving goals is essential for success in any business or organization. ClickUp offers a variety of features and tools that can help you track progress and achieve your goals, regardless of whether you are a solo owner, medium-sized business owner, or enterprise-level executive.

Goal-setting features

ClickUp's goal-setting features make setting goals easy. Have you ever found yourself staring at a daunting goal, feeling overwhelmed and unsure where to start? This feeling is common, especially when faced with large, complex objectives. However, by breaking down your goals into smaller, more manageable tasks and milestones, you can transform these once-intimidating aspirations into achievable steps.

Progress-tracking features

ClickUp's progress-tracking features allow you to track your progress toward your goals in real time. You can see your progress, identify where you fall behind, and adjust as needed:

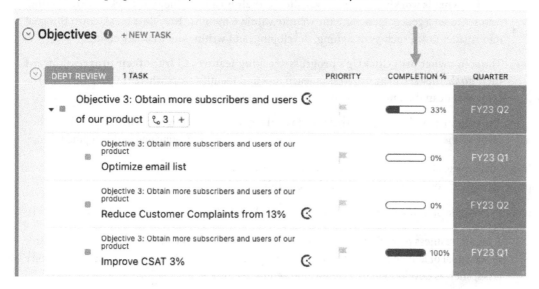

Figure 2.7 – Clickup's progress-tracking features (https://help.clickup.com/hc/en-us/articles/6327987972119-Use-ClickUp-to-track-goals-and-OKRs)

Strategies for Success

Here are a few strategies for using ClickUp to track progress and achieve your goals:

- Set specific, measurable, achievable, related, and time-bound goals to enhance your chances of success and maintain motivation. This will help you stay on track and motivated.

- Transform overwhelming goals into manageable steps. This will make your goals more manageable and achievable.

- Track your progress in real-time. This will help you identify areas where you must catch up and adjust as needed.

- Regularly review your goals. Consistent evaluation ensures you stay on track and consistently progress toward your objectives.

- Acknowledge and celebrate your triumphs. When you accomplish a goal, take a moment to savor your success. This will revitalize your motivation and fuel your pursuit of future achievements.

Real-life scenarios and case studies

Here's an example of how a solo owner can use ClickUp to track progress and achieve their goals:

- **A solo owner is working on a new website for their business.** They use ClickUp's goal-setting features to set a goal of launching the website within 6 months. They then break down this goal into smaller tasks, such as designing, developing, and writing the website's content.

- **The solo owner uses ClickUp's progress-tracking features to track their progress toward their goal.** They see their progress on each task and identify areas where they fall behind. The solo owner can then make adjustments as needed to stay on track.

- **The solo owner also reviews their goal regularly to ensure they are still progressing.** They celebrate their successes, such as completing the website's design or launching its development phase.

Using ClickUp's goal-setting and progress-tracking features, the solo owner can track their progress and achieve their goal of launching the website within 6 months.

Here's an example of how a small business can use ClickUp to track progress and achieve their goals:

- **A small business is working on a new product launch.** It uses ClickUp's goal-setting features to set a goal of launching the product within 1 year. It then breaks down this goal into smaller tasks, such as developing, marketing, and selling the product.

- **Mid-sized enterprises leverage ClickUp's progress-tracking features to monitor their progress toward their objectives.** They assess the progress of individual tasks and pinpoint any areas where they lag. Subsequently, adjustments can be made to ensure they remain on track. Moreover, ClickUp seamlessly integrates with time management and mapping software.

- **Small to medium-sized businesses also regularly review their goals to ensure they are still progressing.** They celebrate their successes along the way, such as completing the development of the product or generating a certain number of leads for the product.

Using ClickUp's goal-setting and progress-tracking features, small businesses can track their progress and achieve their goal of launching the product within 1 year.

ClickUp is a unified project management platform that empowers businesses of all scales to streamline task management, track progress, and achieve their objectives effectively. Whether you're a solo entrepreneur or an enterprise-level executive, ClickUp can streamline your workflows and boost productivity.

ClickUp boasts the following features:

- "ClickUpBrain" is a feature that remarkably enhances team productivity by seamlessly integrating management software with advanced AI capabilities.

- Powerful task management allows you to create, assign, and track tasks with ease.

- Customizable workflows enable you to tailor ClickUp to fit your unique needs.

- Real-time collaboration facilitates seamless teamwork with your colleagues.

- Comprehensive reporting provides valuable insights into your project progress.

- The accessible mobile app allows you to seamlessly manage tasks and stay connected, regardless of location.

When seeking a robust project management tool to empower your goal attainment, ClickUp emerges as a compelling choice. With its user-friendly interface and powerful features, ClickUp can help you take your business to the next level.

ClickUp empowers you to establish goals, dissect them into manageable tasks and milestones, monitor your progress in real time, conduct regular goal assessments, and commemorate your achievements.

Summary

This chapter explored the personal benefits that solo owners, small business owners, and enterprise-level executives can derive from using ClickUp, a versatile project management tool. This chapter delved into tailoring ClickUp to individual workflows, increasing efficiency and productivity, fostering seamless collaboration and communication, and tracking progress to achieve goals.

The first part of this chapter discussed tailoring ClickUp to specific workflows by customizing task statuses, views, and fields and automating tasks. It emphasized ClickUp's adaptability to align with the unique needs of any team or organization, showcasing examples and case studies of software development, marketing, and sales teams effectively using ClickUp's customization features.

The second part highlighted ClickUp's role in increasing efficiency and productivity while presenting features such as task management, time tracking, customizable workflows, and reporting. It provides additional tips, including using templates, setting realistic deadlines, taking breaks, and delegating tasks. Case studies were provided to illustrate how solo owners and small to medium-sized businesses can leverage ClickUp for enhanced efficiency and productivity.

The third section focused on fostering seamless collaboration and communication while emphasizing features such as real-time chat, file sharing, task comments, whiteboards, and integrations with other business tools. Strategies for improvement were outlined, and examples demonstrated how ClickUp can facilitate collaboration for solo owners and small businesses.

The final part of this chapter discussed tracking progress and achieving goals using ClickUp's goal-setting and progress-tracking features. It encouraged setting SMART goals, breaking them down into manageable steps, tracking progress in real time, regularly reviewing plans, and celebrating successes. Case studies were provided to illustrate how solo owners and small businesses can effectively use ClickUp for goal achievement.

In conclusion, this chapter provided a comprehensive understanding of ClickUp's diverse benefits, empowering you to tailor the tool to your workflows, increase efficiency and productivity, foster collaboration and communication, and track progress toward your goals effectively. Through practical examples and strategic insights, you've gained valuable knowledge that you can use to maximize ClickUp's potential for your specific needs and objectives.

In the next chapter, you will learn about the setup and preparation steps that are required to unlock ClickUp's full potential. This chapter will guide you through the process of getting started with ClickUp, including account creation, platform customization, and initial configuration. By following the setup and preparation steps outlined in the upcoming chapter, you will be equipped to seamlessly integrate ClickUp into your workflow and harness its capabilities to achieve your goals more efficiently.

Sign up to download your free workbook and productivity resources for each chapter

ClickUp is constantly evolving. Get help and explore each chapter in depth, receive the latest productivity updates and ClickUp tips, and download your free workbook at `http://bluecreative.com/clickup`. Specializing in ClickUp implementation, configurations, systems development, process implementation, and more.

Unger, E. (2024). Clickup. BLUECREATIVE.

`https://bluecreative.com/clickup`

Setup and Preparation Steps for Unlocking ClickUp

Welcome to *Chapter 3*, where we will guide you through the essential setup and preparation steps for unlocking the full potential of ClickUp. Whether you are a solo owner, a medium-sized business owner, or an enterprise-level executive taking on the project manager role, this chapter will provide simple instructions to figure out your ClickUp structure and hierarchy and overcome any obstacles.

In this chapter, we're going to cover the following main topics:

- Assessing your project management needs
- Designing your ClickUp structure and hierarchy
- Setting up custom fields and templates
- Integrating ClickUp with other tools

By the end of this chapter, you will have gained a comprehensive understanding of the crucial setup and preparation steps necessary to harness the full capabilities of ClickUp. This chapter guides solo owners, medium-sized business owners, and enterprise-level executives assuming project management roles through a step-by-step process. You will learn to assess their project management needs, design a ClickUp structure and hierarchy tailored to your desired workflows, and effectively set up custom fields and templates. Additionally, the chapter illuminates the seamless integration of ClickUp with other tools, providing the knowledge and skills needed to optimize their project management experience. As a result, you will be well-equipped to overcome obstacles, enhance organizational efficiency, and unlock the full potential of ClickUp for their specific needs and goals.

Assessing your project management needs

Assessing your project management needs is the first step in defining the scope of your ClickUp implementation. By taking the time to understand your current challenges and goals, you can create a plan to tailor ClickUp to your specific requirements.

Step 1: Identify your main obstacles

What are the biggest challenges you face when managing projects? Once you understand your pain points well, you can start thinking about how ClickUp can help you overcome them.

Some common project management obstacles include:

- Lack of visibility
- Communication challenges
- Collaboration difficulties
- Inefficiency
- Lack of standardization of processes

Lack of visibility

It can be challenging to track the progress of tasks and projects, especially when working with a distributed team. This can lead to missed deadlines, overruns, and confusion.

Communication challenges

Communication can lead to better understanding, missed deadlines, and other problems. Teams may be using different tools and platforms to communicate, making it challenging to keep everyone on the same page.

Collaboration difficulties

It can be challenging to collaborate effectively on projects, especially when working with multiple teams or departments. This can lead to duplicated work, missed deadlines, and frustration.

Inefficiency

Manual tasks and repetitive processes can save time and resources. If teams spend less time on these tasks, they have less time to focus on more important work.

Lack of standardization of processes

Inconsistent processes can lead to errors and inefficiencies. Teams may use different methods to complete tasks, making it difficult to track progress and identify areas for improvement.

Step 2: Define your goals

What do you want to achieve with your project management tool? Once you know your goal, you can identify the ClickUp features and functionality to help you reach your goals.

Some common project management goals include:

- Improve visibility
- Enhance communication
- Streamline workflows
- Standardize processes
- Increase productivity

Improve visibility

Gain real-time visibility into the progress of tasks and projects. This will help you identify potential problems early on and make necessary adjustments to keep projects on track.

A Gantt chart is a powerful tool that helps you plan projects and track their progress.

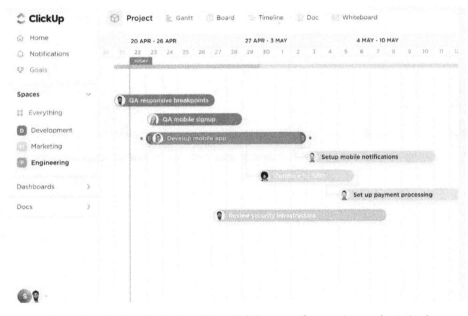

Figure 3.1 – ClickUp Gantt chart (https://clickup.com/features/gantt-chart-view)

ClickUp's Gantt chart brings your projects to life, visualizing your roadmap with interactive timelines and effortless collaboration.

Enhance communication

Improve communication and collaboration between team members. This will help reduce misunderstandings and missed deadlines and create a more efficient team.

ClickUp comments are one of the most powerful tools for collaboration.

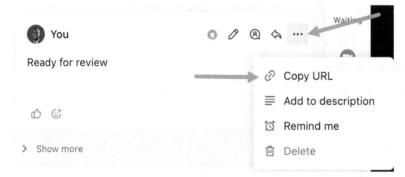

Figure 3.2 – ClickUp comments section (https://help.clickup.com/hc/
en-us/articles/6309646134295-Intro-to-comments)

ClickUp's comments become your project brain-trust, sparking discussion, assigning action, and keeping everyone in sync, line by line.

Streamline workflows

Automate tasks and repetitive processes to streamline workflows and save time. This will free your team to focus on more critical work, such as creative tasks and problem-solving.

ClickUp automations are location-based and affect all tasks beneath them in the Hierarchy.

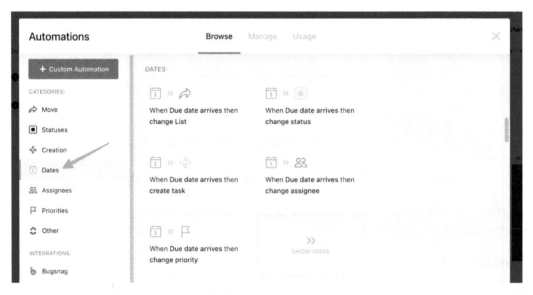

Figure 3.3 – ClickUp automations (https://clickup.com/blog/automation-examples/)

ClickUp's automation becomes your tireless teammates, handling repetitive tasks and streamlining workflows like magic.

Standardize processes

Create and enforce standardized processes to improve efficiency and consistency. This will help reduce errors and ensure all tasks are completed to a high standard.

ClickUp task templates can break down projects of any size into customized tasks.

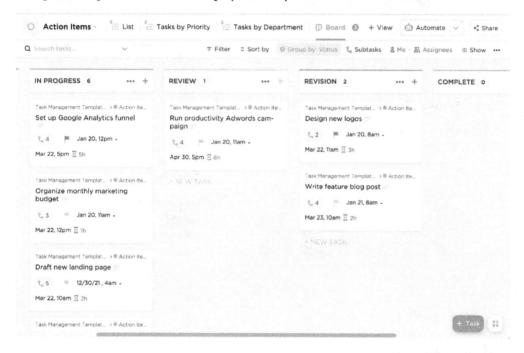

Figure 3.4 – ClickUp task templates (https://clickup.com/templates/task-management-t-4404185)

ClickUp task templates save time, boost consistency, and scale flawlessly with ready-made task blueprints.

Increase productivity

Use project management tools to increase productivity and achieve goals more efficiently. ClickUp's comprehensive features can help you manage all aspects of your projects, from task management to time tracking to reporting.

ClickUp reports gather every critical metric and are ready for instant analysis.

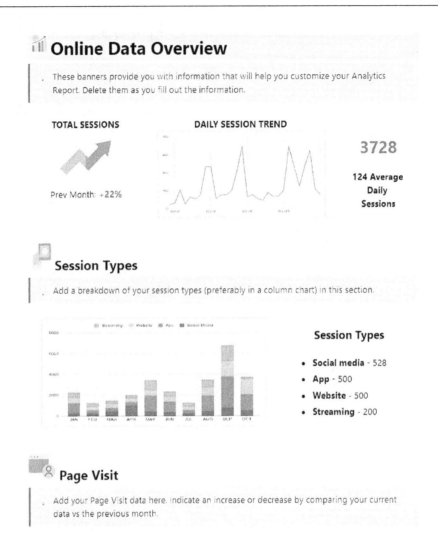

Figure 3.5 – ClickUp reports (https://clickup.com/templates/analytics-report-kkmvq-6104008)

ClickUp's reports transform project data into actionable insights, guiding your decisions and lighting the path to success.

Step 3: Create a solutions plan

Once you have identified your main obstacles and defined your goals, you can create a solution plan. This plan should outline the specific ClickUp features and functionality that you will use to address your challenges and achieve your goals.

The following is an example solution plan:

Obstacle/Goal	ClickUp Solution
Lack of visibility	Use Gantt charts and Kanban boards to track the progress of tasks and projects in real-time.
Enhance communication	Use comments, mentions, and real-time chat to improve communication and collaboration between team members.
Streamline workflows	Use automation to automate repetitive tasks and workflows.
Standardize processes	Create doc instructions and SOPs, custom task and project phase templates, and checklists to standardize processes across the team.
Increase productivity	Use ClickUp's comprehensive set of features to manage all aspects of your projects, from custom views, filters, and time tracking to reporting.

Table 3.1 – Example solutions plan

In a real-world example, a software development company grappled with keeping multiple projects on track and fostering seamless team collaboration. Feeling the strain of disorganization, they sought a solution. ClickUp, with its potent project management capabilities, stepped in as the answer. By implementing ClickUp, the company effectively tracked progress across diverse projects, dismantling departmental silos and paving the way for enhanced communication.

Here is another real-life example: feeling swamped by managing social media campaigns and email marketing blasts for various clients, a fast-growing marketing agency needed help maintaining a cohesive workflow. Chasing deadlines and scattered communication across different platforms caused confusion and missed opportunities. ClickUp's centralized platform proved to be the solution. With ClickUp, the agency streamlined campaign creation, assigned tasks efficiently between copywriters and designers, and ensured real-time collaboration, leading to a significant boost in both client satisfaction and overall project delivery.

Having laid the groundwork by assessing your project management needs and goals, let's delve into the next crucial step: crafting your ClickUp structure and hierarchy. This vital framework is the foundation for organizing your projects, teams, and data within ClickUp. By aligning your chosen structure with your specific requirements, you unlock the platform's full potential to streamline workflows, foster collaboration, and achieve your project goals. Remember, the success of your ClickUp implementation hinges on establishing a well-organized and efficient structure that reflects your unique needs. This section will guide you through essential considerations and best practices for building a robust ClickUp structure that empowers your team to thrive.

Designing your ClickUp structure and hierarchy

Once you have assessed your project management needs and defined the scope of your ClickUp implementation, you can start to design your ClickUp structure and hierarchy.

Why is a well-designed ClickUp structure important?

A well-designed ClickUp structure can help you to:

- **Improve organization and efficiency**: A logical structure makes finding what you need easy and managing your work effectively.

- **Enhance collaboration**: A clear and shared structure helps team members understand their roles and responsibilities and collaborate more efficiently.

- **Increase productivity**: A well-designed structure can help you to streamline your workflows and to focus on the most critical tasks.

The following steps can help you to design a well-structured ClickUp hierarchy:

1. **Identify your main project areas**: What are the different projects you work on? Group these projects into broad categories.

2. **Create a ClickUp Workspace for each primary project area**: This will help you to keep your projects organized and separate.

3. **Within each Workspace, create Folders to group related projects together**. For example, if you are a software development company, you might have Folders for different projects, such as web development, mobile development, and desktop development.

4. **Within each Folder, create Lists to further organize your projects**: For example, you might have a List for each stage of the software development process, such as requirements gathering, design, development, testing, and deployment.

5. **Within each List, create Tasks to represent the tasks that must be completed**. You can also create subtasks to break down large tasks into smaller, more manageable pieces.

ClickUp's Workspace organizes your world; Folders categorize, Lists prioritize, and Tasks fuel action.

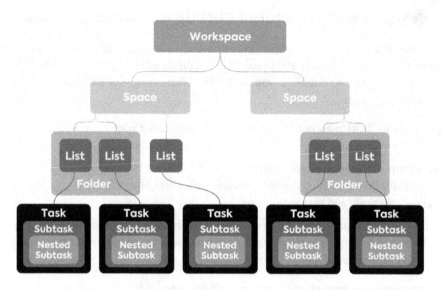

Figure 3.6 – ClickUp hierarchy (https://clickup.com/hierarchy-guide https://help.clickup.com/hc/en-us/articles/6311450560407-Intro-to-Folders https://help.clickup.com/hc/en-us/articles/7255448709655-Make-Spaces-Folders-Lists-and-tasks-private)

Lists are in the middle of ClickUp's Hierarchy and hold every task in your Workspace. Tasks cannot exist outside of Lists. Folders are optional and can hold multiple Lists, creating a more granular organizational structure.

Tips for designing an effective ClickUp structure

Here are a few tips for designing an effective ClickUp structure:

- **Use a consistent naming convention**: This will make it easier to find the information you need and to collaborate with team members.

- **Use custom fields to organize your work**: Custom fields allow you to add additional information to your tasks, such as priority, due date, and status.

- **Use views to customize how you see your work**: ClickUp offers a variety of views, such as Gantt charts, Kanban boards, and lists. Choose the views that work best for you and your team.

How to design a well-structured ClickUp hierarchy workflow

To create a workflow for your ClickUp structure, assess the work to be done and document the steps to accomplish all your tasks. To save additional time, simply journal while you achieve the task and continue to document your workflows as you work. Here is an example of a workflow to create your ClickUp workspace structure.

1. **Sign up for a ClickUp account and create a Workspace for your team or project.** This will serve as the overarching container for your Spaces, Folders, and Lists.

2. **Create your ClickUp workspace structure** using Spaces, Folders, and Lists. Spaces act as containers for Folders, which contain Lists and Tasks. This hierarchy helps you structure your workflow effectively and manage your workload.

3. **Within your workspace, structure your data differently according to your objectives**: You can structure your workspace into one company or your custom workspace for a personalized day-to-day experience of how you would like to live your life.

    A. **The space structure of one company will include** all departments, such as Marketing, Operations, Development, Finance, Technology, Support, etc. All supporting processes, workflows, documents, and system content will reside in folders and tasks within the lists.

    B. **The space structure of your personalized approach to life** creates Spaces representing the crucial areas of your life. For instance, if you build a company or hobby and are very active in your personal life, you can track everything separated by spaces according to your categories of life. Examples of structures for spaces for everyday people: the spaces can be categories of life, including Health, Work, Home, Relationships, Hobbies, and more.

    C. If your ClickUp workspace is an enterprise agency, spaces can be different companies with which the agency is in contract. Each company can be built out as a space with each company's requirements included in the space by folder, list, and task.

4. **Within each Folder, create Lists to further categorize your tasks.** Lists can represent specific projects, features, or any other relevant divisions within your workflow.

5. **Finally, create tasks within the appropriate Lists to represent the individual work items in your workflow**. Add task details, assignees, due dates, and more to each task.

By following this hierarchy and organizing your tasks in Spaces, Folders, and Lists, you can create a structured workflow in ClickUp. Explore additional features like custom statuses, board view, and proofing to enhance your workflow further.

Examples and case studies

Here is an example of a ClickUp structure for a software development company:

Workspace: Software Development

Folders:

- Web Development
- Mobile Development
- Desktop Development

Lists:

- Requirements Gathering
- Design
- Development
- Testing
- Deployment

Tasks:

- Write the requirements document for the new website feature
- Create a mockup of the new website feature
- Develop the new website feature
- Test the new website feature
- Deploy the new website feature

Docs:

- Knowledgebase documents for the ClickUp structure, business operations, and all SOPs that run the business or are important things in your life.

This structure is just an example; you can customize it to fit your specific needs. For example, you might need to add additional Folders or Lists if you work on different types of projects or have a larger team.

Real-life scenarios and case studies

In a real-life example, a disorganized marketing team juggling numerous projects and campaigns across a scattered toolset yearned for a centralized solution. Enter ClickUp. ClickUp transformed its workflow by creating a dedicated workspace for marketing efforts. Folders and lists within this workspace provided a clear structure, meticulously organizing projects and campaigns for effortless access and progress tracking. The team implemented custom fields to gain deeper insights, with custom fields, capturing crucial details like priority, deadlines, and project status. This enabled them to easily filter and sort tasks, pinpointing potential roadblocks before they escalated. ClickUp's unified platform streamlined project management and empowered seamless collaboration, propelling the marketing team toward peak efficiency.

Another example is a busy veterinary clinic struggling to juggle appointment scheduling, medical records, and pet care reminders across different platforms, craved a more organized approach. ClickUp came to the rescue! By implementing ClickUp, the clinic created a central hub for all animal care needs. Pet profiles housed sub-lists for appointments, medications, and vaccination records, ensuring every furry friend received the best possible care. Custom fields allowed them to track vital details like allergies, upcoming procedures, and owner contact information, facilitating efficient prioritization and communication. ClickUp's centralized platform streamlined daily operations, boosting overall clinic efficiency and ensuring no pet's well-being ever slipped through the cracks.

By using a well-organized structure in ClickUp, the marketing team improved their efficiency and productivity. They could also collaborate more effectively and achieve their goals more quickly.

Having established a transparent and efficient ClickUp structure as your project management foundation, let's delve into two powerful tools that further amplify its capabilities: custom fields and templates. These customizable features help you tailor ClickUp to your specific needs, capturing and tracking vital information unique to your projects. By leveraging custom fields and templates, you can streamline workflows, automate repetitive tasks, and ensure consistent project execution across your team. This transition highlights the connection between a well-designed structure and the added power of custom fields and templates, showcasing how they work together to optimize your ClickUp experience.

Setting Up Custom Fields and Templates

Custom fields and templates are two powerful features in ClickUp that can help you streamline your project management processes and capture and track essential information specific to your projects.

Custom fields

Custom fields allow you to add information to your tasks, such as priority, due date, status, and budget. You can create custom fields for any data type and customize them to fit your specific needs.

ClickUp custom fields categorize and analyze your data, revealing hidden patterns and fueling better decisions.

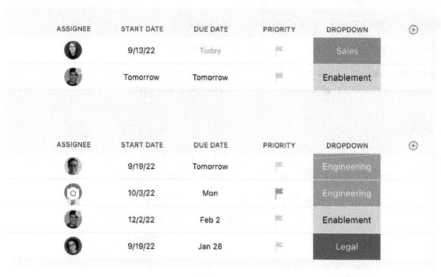

Figure 3.7– ClickUp custom fields (https://help.clickup.com/hc/en-us/articles/6303536766231-Intro-to-Custom-Fields)

Use Custom Fields to customize your Workspace. Different Custom Fields contain various types of data. Custom Fields can be added to Lists, Folders, Spaces, or your entire Workspace. You can use the same Custom Field in multiple locations.

How to create a custom field

To create a custom field, follow these steps:

1. Go to **Settings** > **Custom Fields**.
2. Click **Create Custom Field**.
3. Enter a name and description for your custom field.
4. Select the data type you want to store in the custom field.
5. Click **Create**.

Once you have created a custom field, you can add it to your tasks by clicking the **Custom Fields** tab on the task page.

Using custom fields

Custom fields can be used to track any type of information that is relevant to your projects. For example, you might use custom fields to track the following:

*   **Priority**: Track the priority of each task so that you can focus on the most critical tasks first.
*   **Due date**: Track the due date of each task to ensure that all tasks are completed on time.

- **Status**: Track each task's status so you can see how each task is progressing.
- **Budget**: Track the budget for each task to stay within budget.
- **Other information**: Track any other information relevant to your projects, such as the client name, project manager, or estimated time to complete the task.

Templates

Templates allow you to create pre-populated tasks and projects to use as a starting point for your new work. This can save you time and effort and help you ensure that your new projects are set up correctly.

The Template Center is a library of both pre-made templates and templates you've saved. You can also find templates created by members of your Workspace or the ClickUp community.

Figure 3.8 – ClickUp templates (https://clickup.com/templates/
sales-and-crm, https://clickup.com/templates)

Save tasks, Docs, and views as templates to apply an established format to new Workspace items efficiently.

How to create a template

To create a template, follow these steps:

1. Go to **Settings** > **Templates**.
2. Click **Create Template**.
3. Enter a name and description for your template.
4. Select the type of template that you want to create (task or project).

5.   Add the tasks or subtasks that you wish to include in your template.

6.   Click **Create**.

Once you have created a template, you can create new tasks or projects by clicking the Create from Template button.

Using templates

Templates can be used to create a variety of different types of projects, such as:

- Software development projects

- Marketing campaigns

- Content creation projects

- Customer support projects

- Event planning projects

You can also use templates to create recurring tasks, such as weekly status meetings or monthly reports.

Real-life scenarios and case studies:

Here is an example of how a software development team uses custom fields and templates to manage their projects:

The team uses custom fields to track the following information for each task:

- Priority

- Due date

- Status

- Assigned to

- Estimated time to complete

The team also uses templates to create new projects for each type of software development project they work on. For example, they have templates for web, mobile, and desktop development projects.

Using custom fields and templates, the software development team streamlines their project management processes and tracks essential information specific to their projects.

In another real-world example, in a bid to conquer their ever-growing workload, a marketing team drowning in multiple projects and campaigns across various tools sought a unified solution. ClickUp became their answer. By implementing ClickUp, the team created a dedicated workspace for their marketing efforts. Folders and lists within this space provided a clear structure, organizing projects and campaigns for easy access and progress tracking. Custom fields were then implemented to capture vital details like priority, deadlines, status, and budget. This enabled effortless filtering, sorting, and identification of any potential roadblocks across projects. Additionally, pre-built templates for various campaign types (social media, email marketing, paid advertising) streamlined project initiation, saving valuable time and ensuring consistency. ClickUp's centralized platform empowered the marketing team to manage their workload effectively, fostering a collaborative and efficient environment.

Here's another real-world example: Feeling overwhelmed by managing complex cases, overflowing inboxes, and scattered documents, a mid-sized law firm sought to streamline its workflow. ClickUp offered the perfect solution. By implementing ClickUp, the firm created a central hub for all its cases. Client folders housed sub-lists for tasks, deadlines, and documents, ensuring nothing fell through the cracks. Custom fields allowed them to track critical details like case type, opposing counsel, and key dates, facilitating efficient filtering and prioritizing. Additionally, ClickUp's document-sharing capabilities fostered seamless collaboration among lawyers and paralegals, leading to a significant boost in both client satisfaction and overall case management.

By using ClickUp's custom fields and templates, the marketing team improved its efficiency and productivity. It also collaborated more effectively and achieved its goals more quickly.

Having harnessed the power of custom fields and templates to tailor ClickUp to your specific needs, let's now explore how you can expand its functionality even further through integrations. ClickUp seamlessly connects with a wide range of other tools, enabling you to centralize data, automate tasks, and streamline workflows across your entire ecosystem. This integrated approach fosters an interconnected workspace, eliminating the need to juggle multiple platforms and offering a holistic view of your projects and processes. Remember, a streamlined workflow empowers your team to work smarter, not harder, ultimately driving greater efficiency and achieving your project goals with ease.

Integrating ClickUp with other tools

ClickUp can be integrated with a variety of other tools to enhance your project management capabilities and streamline your workflows. This allows you to keep all of your data in one place and to automate tasks between different tools.

Popular Clickup integrations

Some of the most popular ClickUp integrations include:

- **Slack**: ClickUp can be integrated with Slack to receive notifications about task updates, deadlines, and other important events. You can also create and manage ClickUp tasks directly from Slack.

- **Google Drive**: ClickUp can be integrated with Google Drive to attach files to tasks and to collaborate on documents with your team.

- **GitHub**: ClickUp can be integrated with GitHub to track code changes, create issues, and manage pull requests.

- **Asana**: ClickUp can be integrated with Asana to import and export tasks and projects between the two tools.

- **Trello**: ClickUp can be integrated with Trello to import and export boards, cards, and lists between the two tools.

- **Figma**: ClickUp can be integrated with Figma to streamline design workflow.

Benefits of integrating Clickup with other tools

There are many benefits to integrating ClickUp with other tools, including:

- **Improved efficiency**: Integrations can help you to streamline your workflows and to save time by automating tasks between different tools.

- **Increased visibility**: Integrations can give you a complete overview of all of your work, even if it is spread across multiple tools.

- **Improved collaboration**: Integrations can make it easier to collaborate with your team members, even if they are using different tools.

- **Reduced errors**: Integrations can help to reduce errors by eliminating the need to manually enter data into multiple tools.

How to integrate Clickup with other tools

To integrate ClickUp with other tools, you can use the following methods:

- **Native integrations**: ClickUp offers native integrations with a variety of popular business tools. To set up a native integration, simply go to **Settings** > **Integrations** and click on the tool that you want to integrate with.

- **Third-party integrations**: ClickUp also supports third-party integrations through Zapier. Zapier is a platform that allows you to connect different tools and automate tasks between them. To set up a third-party integration, you will need to create a Zapier account and connect ClickUp and the other tool that you want to integrate with.

Examples and case studies

Here is an example of how a marketing team uses ClickUp integrations to streamline their workflows:

- **The team uses ClickUp to manage all of their marketing campaigns**. They have integrated ClickUp with Slack to receive notifications about task updates and deadlines. They have also integrated ClickUp with Google Drive to attach files to tasks and to collaborate on documents with their team.

- **The team also uses Zapier to automate tasks between ClickUp and other tools**. For example, they have created a Zap that automatically creates a new ClickUp task when a new lead is generated in their CRM system.

By using ClickUp integrations, the marketing team is able to streamline their workflows and to save time on manual tasks. This has helped them to improve their efficiency and productivity.

Case study

- **A software development team needed help managing their multiple projects and tasks**. They were using a variety of tools to track their work, which made it difficult to get a complete overview of their progress.
- **The team decided to implement ClickUp to manage all of their projects and tasks in one place**. They also integrated ClickUp with Slack, GitHub, and Google Drive.

By integrating ClickUp with other tools, the software development team was able to streamline their workflows and improve their collaboration. They were also able to get a complete overview of their progress and to identify any areas where they were falling behind.

Summary

This chapter empowered you to unlock ClickUp's full potential, regardless of your role - solo owner or enterprise executive. Throughout this chapter, you've undertaken a comprehensive journey in honing your ClickUp skills. Beginning with a meticulous assessment of project management needs, you adeptly tackled challenges ranging from visibility issues to communication breakdowns and workflow inefficiencies. Subsequently, you delved into the art of designing a well-structured ClickUp hierarchy, recognizing its pivotal role in enhancing organization, collaboration, and overall productivity. Through hands-on practice, you skillfully created workspaces, folders, lists, and tasks, drawing on valuable tips and real-world case studies for optimal structuring. Moving forward, you explored the dynamic realm of configuring custom fields and templates, gaining insights into their flexibility through practical examples. Witnessing the efficiency of templates in pre-populating tasks and projects, you gleaned knowledge from case studies showcasing their real-world applications. Finally, you embarked on a journey into the realm of integration, discovering how to seamlessly integrate ClickUp with popular tools such as Slack, Google Drive, and Asana. Unveiling both native and third-party integration methods, including Zapier, you grasped the transformative benefits of improved efficiency and visibility. The ensuing examples and case studies illuminated how teams strategically streamline their workflows through integration.

This chapter equipped you with the knowledge and tools to transform your project management experience. By implementing the strategies you learned, you can overcome common challenges, optimize workflows, and boost collaboration within your team, whether you're a solo owner or part of a large enterprise.

The next chapter delves deeper into ClickUp's advanced features, empowering you to further customize and optimize your project management environment. You'll explore automation tools, reporting and analytics capabilities, and resource management strategies to take your ClickUp mastery to the next level.

Sign up to download your free workbook and productivity resources for each chapter

ClickUp is constantly evolving. Get help and explore each chapter in depth, receive the latest productivity updates and ClickUp tips, and download your free workbook at `http://bluecreative.com/clickup`. Specializing in ClickUp implementation, configurations, systems development, process implementation, and more.

Unger, E. (2024). Clickup. BLUECREATIVE.

`https://bluecreative.com/clickup`

Part 2: Understanding ClickUp

This part provides valuable insights on optimizing your projects for work or your business, streamlining workflow, and collaborating effectively with different team members using ClickUp. It covers task management, time tracking, integrations, reporting, and how to custom-tailor the system to your requirements. Regardless of your role – project manager, team leader, or individual contributor – this information will enable you to unlock ClickUp's complete potential, leading minimally to improving your workflow efficiency. This part will provide the maximum potential to scale your hobby ideas or business to be sold or will pave the path for you to grow your passion to exponential growth – you decide.

This part has the following chapters:

- *Chapter 4: Collaborating with Team Members in ClickUp*
- *Chapter 5: Defining and Managing Project Scope*
- *Chapter 6: Organizing Projects, Tasks, and Clearing Your To-do Lists by the End of the Day*
- *Chapter 7: Tracking Goals, Project Progress, and Productivity with KPIs, Dashboards, and Reporting*
- *Chapter 8: Integrating ClickUp with Your Other Tools & Apps*

4

Collaborating with Team Members in ClickUp

Welcome to *Chapter 4*, where we will explore how to collaborate with team members in ClickUp. Regardless of whether you're an owner, a medium-sized business owner, or an executive taking on the role of a project manager at an enterprise level, this chapter will provide valuable insights into how you can utilize ClickUp's collaboration features to enhance teamwork and achieve project success. In this chapter, we will cover the following topics:

- Boosting team productivity with ClickUp's task management

- Simplifying communication with comments and mentions

- Collaborating in real time with ClickUp's chat feature

- Sharing files and documents in ClickUp

By the end of this chapter, you will gain a set of skills and knowledge that will empower you to implement effective collaboration strategies within ClickUp. This will enable you to boost teamwork, streamline project workflows, and contribute toward the success of your projects.

Boosting team productivity with ClickUp's task management

By utilizing ClickUp's task assignment and tracking features, teams can efficiently collaborate and ensure tasks are assigned accurately, progress is tracked, and accountability is promoted. Additionally, these features facilitate clearer productivity mapping by tracking individual task completion times and overall productivity.

Assigning tasks in ClickUp

You can assign tasks effortlessly in ClickUp by clicking the **Assign** button and selecting team members or teams while also leveraging the / shortcut for various mentions:

Figure 4.1: ClickUp task assignment (https://help.clickup.com/hc/
en-us/articles/6309783246103-View-all-your-tasks)

Figure 4.1. showcases how task assignment works in ClickUp.

Tracking task progress in ClickUp

To track task progress in ClickUp, you can use various features:

- **Status**: Each task can be assigned a status based on its current progress. ClickUp offers default statuses such as **New**, **In Progress**, **On Hold**, and **Completed**. Additionally, you can create custom statuses that align with your needs.

- **Dates**: It's important to set deadlines for tasks so that you can keep track of when they're due and ensure completion.

- **Estimated time**: Estimating the time required for each task helps you prioritize effectively and monitor your team's progress over time.

- **Time tracking**: You can keep tabs on how much time you and your team members spend on each task:

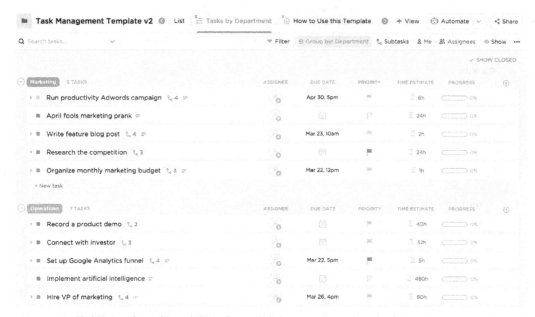

Figure 4.2: ClickUp's task-tracking abilities (https://clickup.com/templates/task-management-t-4404185)

By utilizing the assignment and tracking features available in ClickUp, teams can streamline their workflow, improve productivity, and successfully collaborate toward achieving their goals. This information has the potential to be valuable in improving estimations and identifying areas where efficiency can be optimized.

Promoting accountability in ClickUp

ClickUp offers a variety of features that can help you promote accountability within your team. Let's look at some of the available features:

- **Mentions/'@'**: You can mention team members in tasks and comments to bring information to their attention directly, making sure communication doesn't slip through the cracks
- **Start and due dates**: With start and due dates, you can hold each team member directly accountable to you and across your organization
- **Notifications**: Stay updated on task progress, deadlines, and other significant events through notifications.
- **Reports**: Generate reports to track your team's progress and pinpoint areas that need improvement

- **Goals**: Monitor the achievement of set objectives and track progress toward them with ClickUp's **Goals** feature

A project schedule is a simplified roadmap of activities, resources, and due dates that help your team meet a final goal. It breaks down the who, what, when, and how of your project:

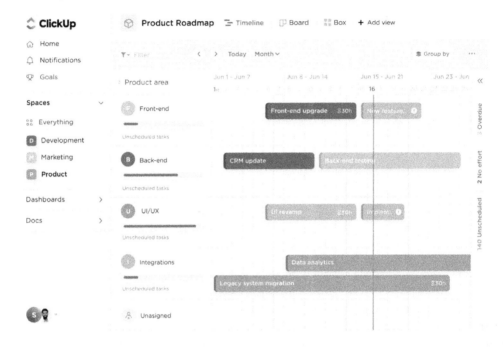

Figure 4.3: ClickUp's project schedule (https://clickup.com/blog/project-schedule/)

The process involves gathering background information, including which team members will be responsible for what tasks, and establishing deadlines that should be met.

Real-life scenarios and case studies

Let's consider how a marketing team leverages ClickUp task assignment and tracking capabilities to manage their social media campaigns:

- *The team utilizes ClickUp to create and monitor all their social media posts.* Each post is assigned to a team member with a designated date. They also keep track of the status of each post while estimating the time required for completion.

- *By utilizing ClickUp's notifications feature, the team receives alerts whenever tasks are updated or approaching deadlines.* Additionally, they use the **Reports** feature provided by ClickUp to monitor their progress and identify any areas that need improvement.

- The marketing team utilizes ClickUp's features to assign and monitor tasks so that they can manage their social media campaigns.

- They also use PostFlow, which is integrated with ClickUp, to handle social media posting directly from ClickUp, saving time by keeping the entire workflow within ClickUp.

Another case study

A software development team faced challenges in keeping track of projects and tasks. They were using disparate tools, making it difficult for them to gain an overview of their progress. To overcome this, the team implemented ClickUp as a centralized solution for managing all their projects and tasks. They also integrated ClickUp with Slack to receive notifications about task updates and deadlines with an external team.

With the help of ClickUp's task assignment and tracking features, the software development team significantly improved collaboration among its members and external teams. They successfully ensured the completion of all tasks while identifying areas where they could enhance their processes.

Moving on from optimizing team efficiency with ClickUp's task management tools, let's explore how ClickUp streamlines communication with its comments and mentions features.

Simplifying communication with comments and mentions

Effective collaboration heavily relies on communication. ClickUp offers comments and mentions features that facilitate communication within teams, ensuring clarity among members.

Utilizing comments in ClickUp

Comments serve as a means to ask questions, provide feedback, and share information related to tasks. To leave a comment on a task, simply click on the **Comments** tab and type your comment. You can also mention team members in your comments to draw their attention to the information.

Using mentions/'@' in ClickUp

Mentions can be utilized to notify team members about tasks, comments, and other significant events:

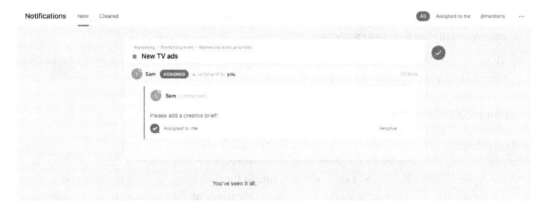

Figure 4.4: ClickUp's mentions feature (https://help.clickup.com/hc/
en-us/articles/6326004036887-Intro-to-notifications)

To mention a team member, just type the @ symbol, followed by their name.

Benefits of utilizing comments and mentions in ClickUp

There are advantages to using comments and mentions in ClickUp, including the following:

- **Enhanced communication**: Comments and mentions facilitate communication with your team members and allow you and others to share information regarding tasks

- **Improved collaboration**: Comments and mentions promote collaboration by enabling team members to ask questions, provide feedback, and share ideas efficiently

- **Error reduction**: Comments and mentions help minimize errors by ensuring everyone is on the same page, and all information is communicated effectively

- **Increased productivity**: Comments and mentions contribute to higher productivity levels as they reduce the need for unnecessary meetings and excessive emails

Collaborating in real time with ClickUp's chat feature

ClickUp's chat feature is a tool that enables seamless collaboration among team members. It allows for communication and information sharing without the need to switch between tools.

Benefits of using ClickUp's chat feature

There are several advantages to utilizing ClickUp's chat functionality:

- **Instantaneous communication**: With ClickUp's chat feature, you can instantly communicate with your team members, bypassing the delays associated with emails or meetings. This proves beneficial when quick problem resolution or real-time task collaboration is required.

- **Collaboration**: By leveraging ClickUp's chat feature, collaborating on tasks and projects becomes effortless. You can exchange ideas, discuss challenges, and provide feedback, ultimately fostering improved work quality and reducing task completion time.

- **Enhanced productivity**: ClickUp's chat feature increases productivity by minimizing reliance on meetings and emails. By scheduling a meeting or drafting an email, you can send a chat message to communicate with your team members.

Effective practices for leveraging ClickUp's chat functionality

To make the most of ClickUp's chat feature, here are some tips:

- **Organize your conversations using channels.** You can create channels in ClickUp for teams, projects, or topics. This helps keep discussions organized and easily accessible.

- **Utilize mentions via @ to grab someone's attention.** This ensures effective communication in ClickUp, as well as that they receive notifications. Centralize all communication by commenting within the Clickup chat.

- **Provide feedback using reactions.** You can add reactions using emojis to provide feedback or show appreciation for a colleague's message.

- **Emojis can make your chat messages more engaging and readable.** They can add personality and convey emotions.

- **When communicating on time, it is essential to be mindful of your tone.** The tone of your messages significantly impacts communication.

By following these practices, you can save time, stay focused on your work, and effectively utilize ClickUp's chat feature.

For example, in a software development team using ClickUp's chat tool for collaboration on a feature, members discuss the design, share ideas, provide feedback to one another, and ensure alignment.

The software development team benefits from collaboration and quick feature development for their product by utilizing ClickUp's chat feature.

Illustrative example

A company's media team faced challenges in their efforts. They used communication tools that made it difficult to track conversations and maintain alignment among team members. However, they witnessed improved collaboration and communication dynamics after implementing ClickUp for project and task management and utilizing its chat feature. By leveraging ClickUp's chat feature for both the media production team and the marketing team, they were able to enhance their efforts. This feature proved beneficial in reducing errors and ensuring the execution of media and marketing campaigns.

By employing ClickUp's chat feature, the media and marketing team experienced communication, enabling them to collaborate effectively. This reduced errors and allowed for the timely launch of media campaigns within budget.

The collaboration benefits of ClickUp's chat feature, including instantaneous communication, improved collaboration, and enhanced productivity, make it an essential tool for teams. By following effective practices, such as organizing conversations, utilizing mentions, providing feedback with reactions, and being mindful of tone, teams can maximize the efficiency of their communication within ClickUp. In the next section, we'll explore how ClickUp facilitates file and document sharing, further enhancing team collaboration and workflow efficiency.

Sharing files and documents in ClickUp

When it comes to sharing files and documents in ClickUp, the process is straightforward. You can share these assets with team members, entire teams, or anyone accessing the shared link.

If you want to share a file or document in ClickUp, here are the steps you need to follow:

1. Open the file or document that you want to share.
2. Click the **Share** button.
3. Enter the names and email addresses of the people you wish to share the file or document with.
4. Lastly, click **Share**.

Figure 4.5 shows how file sharing works:

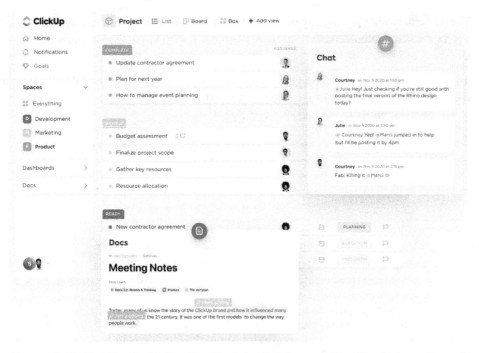

Figure 4.5: ClickUp's file-sharing functionality (https://clickup.com/blog/file-sharing-software/)

File-sharing software makes it easier for a hybrid workforce to collaborate with teams, stakeholders, and clients. From small businesses to global corporations, everyone benefits from a central location to access important work documents.

Now, let's take a look at some practices for file sharing and document management in ClickUp:

- Establish a naming convention for your files. This will make it easier for team members to find what they need.

- Organize your files into folders and subfolders for structure and accessibility.

- Use version control mechanisms to keep track of any changes that are made to files or documents, allowing you to revert if needed.

- Utilize permissions to manage access and editing rights, preventing modifications or deletions.

- Take advantage of ClickUp's search feature, which allows you to locate files and documents efficiently by name, content, or other criteria.

Let's imagine a scenario where a marketing team uses ClickUp for sharing files and documents:

- **The marketing team is currently working on a campaign**. They use ClickUp as their platform to share all campaign-related materials, such as the campaign brief, creative assets, and analytics reports.

- **To keep things organized, the team stores all their campaign files and documents in a folder on ClickUp**. They also use version control to track changes to these files while managing permissions to control access and editing rights.

By utilizing ClickUp for file and document sharing, the marketing team ensures everyone can access the necessary information while collaborating on file versions.

In another case study...

There was an instance where a software development team faced file and document management challenges. They used tools to store and exchange files, making it difficult to keep track of versions and ensure everyone had access to the required information. To streamline their project management and task handling, the team implemented ClickUp as a centralized platform for storing and sharing all their files and documents.

By utilizing ClickUp as a tool for organizing and collaborating on files and documents, the software developers experienced efficiency and improved teamwork. They also saw reduced errors and an ability to complete projects within their designated timeframes and budgets.

Summary

In this chapter, you learned about the various collaboration features of ClickUp, regardless of your role as a solopreneur-sized business owner or corporate project manager. You explored four areas.

In terms of mastering tasks, you delved into ClickUp's array of features tailored for task assignment and tracking. These include status updates, due dates, and timeframes, ensuring clear ownership, accurate progress monitoring, and shared accountability. Real-world examples from marketing and software development teams illustrated how these features streamline task management while boosting efficiency.

Moving on to boosting communication, you explored ClickUp's tools for comments and mentions, @, which serve to enhance team communication by reducing errors and fostering productivity. Case studies, such as the management of social media campaigns by marketing teams, underscored the effectiveness of these tools in streamlining collaboration.

Furthermore, you delved into real-time connection through ClickUp's chat feature and its advantages for communication and collaboration. Helpful tips were shared on optimizing its use, with real-world examples illustrating its role in enhancing productivity.

Finally, you learned about strategies for facilitating the sharing and management of documents within ClickUp. Practical examples demonstrated how teams effectively utilize these tools for collaboration. This chapter equipped you with the tools and insights necessary to enhance your team's efforts, establish responsibilities, minimize communication errors, boost productivity, and ultimately achieve project outcomes.

The upcoming chapter delves deep into ClickUp's features for managing project scope, deadlines, and priorities, empowering users to fine-tune their teamwork environment. This guide provides insights and practical strategies for navigating project management within ClickUp, from refining project scopes to meeting deadlines and prioritizing tasks. Additionally, it explores views that can be added to map due and priority tasks for enhanced organization and efficiency.

Sign up to download your free workbook and productivity resources for each chapter

ClickUp is constantly evolving. Get help and explore each chapter in depth, receive the latest productivity updates and ClickUp tips, and download your free workbook at `http://bluecreative.com/clickup`. Specializing in ClickUp implementation, configurations, systems development, process implementation, and more.

Unger, E. (2024). Clickup. BLUECREATIVE.

`https://bluecreative.com/clickup`

5

Defining and Managing Project Scope

Welcome to *Chapter 5*, where we guide you through managing project scope, deadlines, and priorities. Whether you're an owner, a sized business owner, or an executive taking on the project manager role in a large enterprise, this chapter offers valuable insights to ensure successful project execution. Within this chapter, we will delve into topics such as the following:

- Defining and managing project scope
- Setting realistic deadlines and milestones
- Prioritizing tasks and resources

By the end of the chapter, we will equip you with the knowledge and skills to navigate the elements of managing project scope, deadlines, and priorities within ClickUp. By applying these insights, you can carry out projects while maintaining focus and optimizing resource utilization for improved outcomes.

Defining and managing project scope

The following figure illustrates the components of project scope:

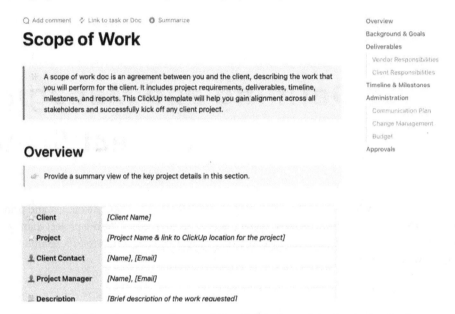

Figure 5.1 – A project scope diagram (https://clickup.com/blog/project-scope/)

Project scope refers to the entirety of work required for a project's completion. It encompasses all tasks, deliverables, and requirements essential to achieve project goals and objectives. The process of defining and managing project scope is vital to ensure success.

Establishing clear project boundaries

To ensure a project, it's crucial to establish a project scope. This involves defining what is included in the project and what is not, setting goals and objectives, identifying deliverables, determining requirements, and considering constraints such as time, budget, and resources. By doing so, you can manage stakeholder expectations effectively. Avoid scope creep. It's essential to communicate the project scope to all stakeholders to set expectations for everyone involved. Understanding the project's timeline, budget, and available resources is crucial.

Here are some tips to establish clear project boundaries:

- **Identify a project's goals and objectives**: What is the project trying to achieve?

- **Define a project's deliverables**: What products or services will be delivered as part of the project?

- **Identify a project's requirements**: What technical and non-technical requirements must be met to complete the project?

- **Identify a project's constraints**: What are the time, budget, and resource constraints that apply to the project?

Setting realistic expectations

Once you have defined the project scope, you must set realistic stakeholder expectations. This means communicating the project scope clearly and concisely to all stakeholders. It is also essential to be realistic about the project's timeline, budget, and resources.

Here are some tips for setting realistic expectations:

- Concisely communicate the project scope with all interested parties
- Be honest about the estimated project's timeline, budget, and resources
- Identify and handle risks
- Keep stakeholders updated on the project's progress and any modifications to its scope

Effectively managing changes in scope

Projects tend to experience changes in scope. However, it is vital to manage these changes to prevent delays and excessive costs.

Consider these recommendations to manage changes in scope:

- Document all changes that occur within the scope of a project.
- Evaluate how these changes impact the timeline, budget, and available resources.
- Obtain approval from stakeholders before implementing any modifications to the project's scope.
- Communicate any adjustments made to the scope with all stakeholders.

Examples

Here's an instance that demonstrates how a software development team utilizes a project scope statement to manage the extent of a software development project.

The team project scope statement encompasses the following details:

- **Objectives and goals of the project**: The aim is to design and develop a brand mobile app that caters to our company's customers.
- **Project deliverables**: This involves delivering the app, a user manual, and a test plan.
- **Project requirements**: Technical requirements utilize a programming language and development framework. Non-technical requirements involve ensuring compatibility with a mobile operating system and incorporating features.

- **Project limitations**: The team has set a completion deadline of six months and allocated a budget of $100,000.

The team relies on this project scope statement as their guiding document to help them streamline their work processes and make decisions throughout the project's lifespan. For example, if a stakeholder proposes a feature for the app, the team will evaluate its impact on timelines, budgetary constraints, and available resources. If approved, they will incorporate this feature into the revised version of the project scope statement.

In the real world, even the best-laid plans can encounter unexpected deviations. Consider a construction company building a 10-story office building. Everything was progressing smoothly until the client requested changes mid-construction. These modifications involved adding an extra floor and switching building materials, impacting the project's timeline and budget.

However, the construction company rose to the challenge. They maintained open communication with the client, meticulously documented all alterations, and negotiated a change order to cover the additional costs. This proactive approach ensured transparency, minimized confusion, and ultimately led to a successful project completion despite the scope changes.

Here are some valuable pointers to define and manage project scope:

- **Engage all stakeholders throughout the process of defining and managing project scope**: This ensures everyone is on board and fully aware of a project's objectives, goals, and requirements.

- **Utilize a crafted project scope statement to document all aspects of your project scope in a concise yet manner.**

- **Regularly review your project scope**: Make adjustments when required. It's crucial to maintain flexibility and adapt the project scope according to changes in the business environment.

With a solid foundation in defining and managing project scope, it's now crucial to establish timelines and milestones to ensure smooth progress and successful completion. The next topic delves into setting realistic deadlines and milestones, exploring how they act as crucial roadmaps to guide your project toward achieving its goals within the defined scope. Remember, well-defined milestones mark progress and serve as checkpoints for adjustments and course corrections if needed.

Setting realistic deadlines and milestones

The following figure shows a task timeline, illustrating how tasks with deadlines and milestones are interconnected and emphasizing their importance.

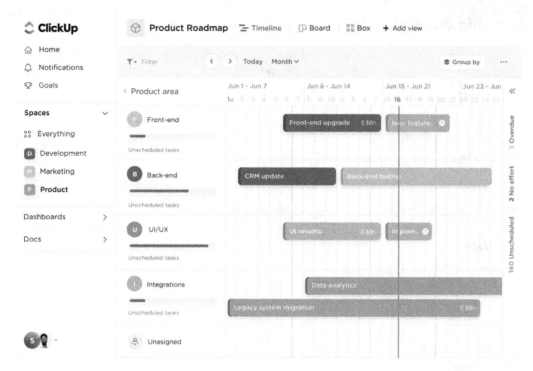

Figure 5.2 – A ClickUp task timeline (https://clickup.com/blog/project-schedule/)

Establishing deadlines and milestones is vital for the success of any project. By estimating project timelines, managing dependencies, and ensuring task completion, you can increase your chances of completing your projects on time and within budget.

Accurately estimating project timelines

Estimating project timelines involves setting realistic deadlines and milestones. This can be challenging due to factors affecting a project's duration, such as scope, task complexity, and resource availability.

Here are some tips to estimate project timelines:

- Break down a project into tasks to facilitate estimating each task's duration
- Consider the varying complexity levels of tasks; some may require more time than others
- Estimate the necessary time for each task while being realistic about potential risks or challenges involved
- To ensure that your estimates are accurate, it's essential to include a buffer to account for any delays

Managing dependencies

Managing dependencies is crucial for the completion of a project. Dependencies refer to the relationships between tasks, indicating which tasks must be finished before others can begin. Here are some helpful tips to manage dependencies:

- Start by identifying all the project dependencies. You can create a dependency map to visualize these relationships.

- Prioritize the tasks based on their dependencies.

- Schedule the tasks to minimize the impact of these dependencies on the timeline.

- Monitor each task's progress and adjust the schedule as needed.

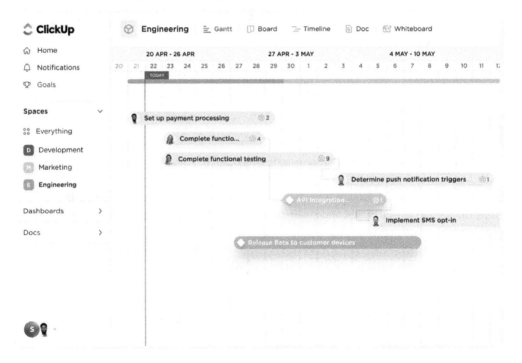

Figure 5.3 – A dependency map (https://clickup.com/blog/dependency-mapping/)

The preceding diagram illustrates how different tasks depend on each other and highlights their influence on project timelines.

Ensuring the timely completion of tasks

Ensuring the completion of tasks relies on several factors. Once you have set deadlines and milestones, consider implementing these strategies:

- Assign tasks to team members who possess the required skills and experience

- Provide team members with all the resources they need to complete their assigned tasks

- It is vital to monitor task advancement and offer assistance when needed to ensure progress and support struggling team members

- Additionally, it is crucial to identify and address risks and challenges before they become problematic

Real-life scenarios and case studies

Real-life scenarios can demonstrate the utilization of deadlines and milestones in managing software development projects. For instance, a software development team divides a project into tasks, estimating the duration of each task. They also identify project dependencies. Create a dependency map for them, and then, based on these dependencies, they can prioritize the tasks. Schedule them strategically to minimize any impact caused by dependencies. Throughout the process, the team can closely monitor task progress. Make adjustments to keep everything on track. Ultimately, they are proactive in identifying and resolving any risks or challenges that may arise.

By adhering to deadlines and milestones, teams can complete projects within specified time frames while staying within constraints.

In another case study example from the construction industry, a company was tasked to build an office building within 12 months with a budget of $10 million. Like the scenario, they divided the project into tasks while estimating their durations. They also identified all project dependencies. They created a dependency map for understanding. The company then organized the functions by their dependencies and arranged them in a manner that minimized the impact of those dependencies. The company closely monitored the progress of the tasks. They made adjustments to the schedule. They also proactively addressed any risks or challenges.

The company completed the project within the designated timeframe and budget by setting deadlines and milestones.

Now that we've discussed the significance of establishing deadlines and milestones, let's turn our attention to the crucial element of prioritizing tasks and managing resources efficiently.

Prioritizing tasks and resources

Prioritizing tasks and allocating resources are crucial to achieve success in any project. Determining tasks, managing workloads, and optimizing resource allocation can enhance productivity and accomplish your objectives.

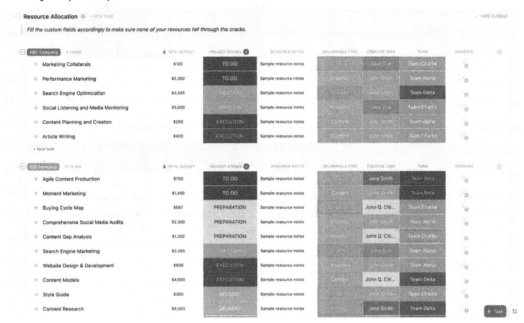

Figure 5.4 – A resource allocation chart (https://clickup.com/blog/resource-allocation/)

The preceding chart illustrates how resources, including personnel and time, are distributed among tasks.

Identifying critical tasks

Identifying tasks involves task prioritization. These tasks are indispensable for project completion and must be finished on time.

Here are some tips to help you identify tasks:

- **Consider the goals and objectives of a project**: Which tasks are necessary to achieve these goals?
- **Identify tasks with dependencies**: Tasks with dependencies need to be completed before other tasks can commence.

- **Consider the significance of each task to the project**: Some tasks will be more critical than others, and their impact on the project's success will be more significant.

Managing workloads

After identifying the tasks, it is essential to manage workloads. This entails ensuring that each team member has a workload and is focused on the crucial tasks at any given time.

The workload view visualizes the amount of work each team member is assigned during the time period selected. You can choose one or two weeks or one month. Each person's workload is compared with the capacity set for them.

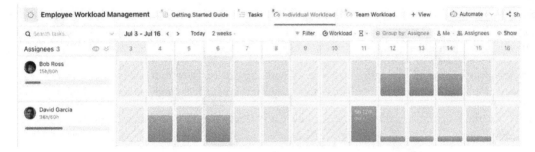

Figure 5.5 – A workload view (https://help.clickup.com/hc/en-us/
articles/6310449699735-Use-Workload-view)

Note that the one-month view is available only for spaces, folders, and lists.

Here are some helpful suggestions to manage workloads:

- Assign tasks to team members based on their skills and experience.
- Estimate the time required to complete each task and create a schedule.
- Monitor task progress and make adjustments to the schedule when needed.
- Regularly communicate with your team. Provide support to those who face challenges.

Optimizing resource allocation

Resource allocation involves assigning resources such as people, time, money, and equipment to maximize productivity. Here are some tips to optimize resource allocation:

- Take into account the importance of each task along with its resource requirements
- Prioritize allocating resources to the tasks
- Be flexible and prepared to make adjustments in resource allocation as necessary

It is crucial to maintain communication with your team and stakeholders regarding resource allocation. This ensures everyone is on the same page and can effectively manage tasks.

Examples and case studies

For instance, let's consider a marketing team handling a campaign. They have identified tasks for the campaign, such as creating a campaign brief, designing creative elements, developing a landing page, setting up an email list for the campaign, and ultimately launching it.

The team has estimated the time needed for each task to ensure progress and created a realistic schedule. They prioritize tasks at any given time while regularly monitoring their progress.

Specific roles have been assigned to team members in terms of resource allocation. These include a campaign manager who oversees the campaign and ensures timely completion within budget constraints. Other roles include a designer, web developer, content writer, and email marketer.

The team emphasizes allocating resources based on task priority. They understand that specific tasks require more attention than others. Thus, they assign resources accordingly to achieve results.

Moreover, the team remains adaptable and ready to adjust resource allocation as necessary throughout the campaign.

For instance, if the team faces an issue with the campaign landing page, they might have to assign resources to the web developer. The team regularly communicates regarding resource allocation, ensuring everyone is on the same page and working toward shared objectives.

Here's a case study:

- A software development team was engaged in a project with a 12-month deadline and a budget of $10 million.

- The team identified project tasks and devised a practical schedule. Resources were allocated to each task based on their significance.

- The team consistently monitored task progress. They made adjustments to both the schedule and resource allocation.

Thanks to the prioritization of tasks and resource allocation, the team completed the project within budget and on time.

Summary

This chapter delved into managing project scope, deadlines, and priorities within ClickUp. It provided insights that can be applied by solo owners, medium-sized business proprietors, and enterprise-level executives with project management responsibilities.

First, we focused on defining and managing project scope, which highlights the importance of establishing project boundaries, goals, deliverables, requirements, and constraints. The chapter offered tips for setting expectations and managing changes in scope. Real-world examples, such as how a software development team uses a project scope statement to make decisions, were provided.

Then, we focused on setting realistic deadlines and milestones, where strategies for estimating project timelines were shared. Additionally, it guides managing dependencies and ensuring timely task completion. Examples illustrated how a software development team successfully navigates these challenges while emphasizing risk management.

Lastly, we explored prioritizing tasks and resources by emphasizing the identification of tasks, effective workload management techniques, and optimizing resource allocation for productivity. Examples were included to showcase how a marketing team prioritizes tasks and allocates resources for a campaign, and how a software development team efficiently manages tasks and resources for a project.

In the next chapter, we will explore tips on effectively organizing your projects, prioritizing and managing your to-do lists, and fully utilizing ClickUp's productivity features.

Sign up to download your free workbook and productivity resources for each chapter

ClickUp is constantly evolving. Get help and explore each chapter in depth, receive the latest productivity updates and ClickUp tips, and download your free workbook at `http://bluecreative.com/clickup`. Specializing in ClickUp implementation, configurations, systems development, process implementation, and more.

Unger, E. (2024). Clickup. BLUECREATIVE.

`https://bluecreative.com/clickup`

Organizing Projects, Tasks, and Clearing Your To-Do Lists by the End of the Day

Welcome to *Chapter 6*, where you will delve into strategies for organizing projects and tasks and ensuring the completion of your to-do lists by the end of the day. Whether you are an everyday person, entrepreneur, business owner running a small company, or executive taking on the role of project manager in a large enterprise, this chapter will provide valuable insights on optimizing your organization and task management skills using ClickUp. Within this chapter, you will cover the following topics:

- How to structure projects and tasks in ClickUp

- Techniques for organizing and managing your to-do lists

- Maximizing productivity by utilizing ClickUp's efficiency-enhancing features

In summary, *Chapter 6* offers a guide to refine your organizational skills and enhance your task management proficiency with ClickUp. By providing tools and techniques, you will gain resources that can aid in clearing to-do lists while improving overall project management capabilities.

How to structure projects and tasks in ClickUp

ClickUp is an effective project management tool equipped with a wide array of features designed for organizing and managing projects and tasks. By structuring your projects and tasks within ClickUp's framework, you can ensure organization and clarity and streamline workflow processes while boosting productivity levels.

Developing a well-defined structure

The first step in effectively structuring your projects and tasks in ClickUp is to create a hierarchy. This involves organizing your projects and tasks in a way that makes sense for you and your team.

You can establish this hierarchy by utilizing **Spaces**, **Folders**, and **Lists** within ClickUp. Spaces represent the hierarchy level and serve as containers for your projects. Folders act as sub-levels of Spaces, enabling you to categorize your tasks. Lists, on the other hand, form the hierarchy level where individual tasks reside.

Establishing task Relationships

Once you have established a hierarchy, it's time to develop task Relationships. These relationships indicate dependencies between tasks – determining which tasks must be completed before others can start or finish.

ClickUp provides task Relationship options:

- **Precedes**: This relationship signifies that one task must be finished before another can begin
- **Follows**: This relationship indicates that one task must be finished before another task can reach completion
- **Finishes**: In this relationship, one task must be completed before another can start
- **Starts**: This relationship suggests that one task must commence before another can be executed

Utilizing these features in ClickUp allows you to effectively structure your projects and easily manage dependencies between tasks.

Establishing relationships between tasks can create an organized and efficient workflow for your team.

Figure 6.1 – ClickUp task Relationships (https://help.clickup.com/
hc/de/articles/6309965212567-Task-Relationships)

Task Relationships in ClickUp allow you to easily connect tasks throughout your Workspace. You can link tasks for reference or use them to emphasize important items for you and your team. When one task must be completed before another can begin, it's recommended to use **Dependency Relationships**.

Utilizing ClickUp's features to streamline project and task management with templates

ClickUp offers a range of features that can help streamline your project and task management process. These features include the following:

- **Custom fields**: Add information such as dates, priorities, and labels to your tasks.
- **Subtasks**: Break down large tasks into smaller, more manageable ones.
- **Checklists**: Track the progress of your tasks and ensure all necessary steps are completed.
- **Dependencies**: Indicate which tasks must be finished before others can start or finish.

- **Views**: ClickUp offers various views, such as List, Board, or Calendar views. These features will enhance the efficiency of your project and task management. You can select the view that best suits you and your team.

Utilizing the features in ClickUp will simplify your project and task management process while enhancing productivity.

Real-world examples

Let's discuss real-world examples for better understanding:

A marketing team streamlines their campaign workflow with ClickUp

Imagine a marketing agency juggling multiple social media campaigns for various clients. Staying organized can be challenging with deadlines looming and tasks piling up. Here's how ClickUp helps them keep everything under control and launch successful campaigns on time:

- **Structure for scalability**:

  - **Workspaces for agencies**: ClickUp offers Workspaces, which act as the overarching container for all projects and teams within the agency. The marketing team utilizes a dedicated Workspace to house all their client campaigns.

  - **Campaign Folders**: Within the Workspace, they create Folders for each individual marketing campaign, such as "Summer Sale Promotion for ABC Company" or "New Product Launch for XYZ Brand." This provides a clear separation between projects and keeps things organized.

  - **List hierarchy**: Inside each campaign Folder, they create Lists to categorize specific tasks. Examples include "Develop social media content," "Design email marketing materials," or "Track campaign performance." This nested structure allows for detailed organization within each campaign.

- **Prioritization and clarity**:

  - **Task dependencies**: They establish task dependencies to ensure a logical workflow. For example, the "Create Instagram posts" task must be completed before the "Launch campaign" task to avoid launching before the visuals are ready.

  - **Custom fields**: They leverage custom fields to track deadlines, assign priorities (high, medium, low), and add relevant tags (e.g., "#summer-sale," "#new-product") to each task. This allows for easy filtering, searching, and prioritization.

  - **Subtasks for efficiency**: They break down large tasks such as "Develop social media content" into smaller, more manageable subtasks such as "Research target audience," "Craft engaging copy," and "Design eye-catching visuals." This keeps the team focused and ensures each campaign element receives proper attention.

- **Benefits achieved**: By implementing ClickUp's project and task structuring features, the marketing agency's marketing team enjoys several advantages:

  - **Streamlined workflow**: A clear hierarchy ensures everyone understands their responsibilities and tasks flow logically through the campaign life cycle.

  - **On-time launches**: Dependencies prevent premature campaign launches, guaranteeing everything is ready before going live.

  - **Scalability and visibility**: The workspace structure allows for easy expansion as the agency takes on more clients while maintaining clear visibility in individual campaigns.

This example demonstrates how ClickUp empowers marketing teams within an agency to collaborate effectively, manage multiple projects efficiently, and, ultimately, launch successful campaigns for their clients.

Another real-world example – software development team tackles chaos with ClickUp

Many software development teams need help with efficient project management tools, leading to communication breakdowns and missed deadlines. Here's how ClickUp helped one team overcome these challenges and achieve project success:

- **Structure for efficiency**:

  - **Workspaces for focus**: The development team utilized a dedicated Workspace within ClickUp, creating a central hub for all their projects.

  - **Project Folders**: Within the Workspace, they created Folders for each individual software development project. This provided a clear separation between projects and fostered team focus.

  - **Organized Lists**: Inside each project Folder, they created Lists to categorize specific development tasks. Examples include "Develop core functionality," "Design user interface," or "Conduct quality assurance testing." This structure ensured all aspects of the project were meticulously tracked.

- **Collaboration and clarity**:

  - **Task Relationships**: They established task Relationships to define dependencies between tasks. This ensured tasks were completed in the correct order, preventing roadblocks and delays. Examples include "Fix bugs identified in testing" needing to be finished before "Release software update."

  - **ClickUp features**: They leveraged ClickUp's features to streamline their workflow. Features such as subtasks helped break down large tasks into manageable steps, while custom fields tracked deadlines, priorities, and assigned team members. This fostered clear communication and accountability.

- **Benefits achieved**: By implementing ClickUp's project and task structuring features, the software development team experienced significant improvements:

  - **Smoother collaboration**: Clear task dependencies and communication channels ensured everyone was on the same page, minimizing confusion and delays.

  - **Enhanced productivity**: Organized tasks and efficient workflows allowed the team to focus on their work and maximize their output.

  - **Reduced errors**: Task dependencies prevented developers from moving forward before critical tasks were completed, leading to fewer errors and a more polished final product.

  - **On-time delivery**: Streamlined workflows and clear deadlines ensured projects were completed within budget and timeframe expectations.

This example showcases ClickUp's ability to empower software development teams to collaborate effectively, manage projects efficiently, and ultimately deliver successful software solutions.

Having laid the groundwork for practical project and task structuring, we'll now focus on the crucial prioritization skill. In the next section, we'll dive into proven techniques for managing your to-do lists within ClickUp, ensuring you stay focused and conquer your daily workload. Remember, effectively prioritizing tasks leads to enhanced productivity and achievement of your project goals. Now, let's explore how ClickUp empowers you to master your to-do list and confidently tackle each day.

Techniques for prioritizing and managing your to-do lists

When managing your to-do lists, prioritization plays a role in staying organized and focused. By prioritizing tasks and utilizing ClickUp's features, you can ensure that you clear your daily to-do list by the end of each day.

Identifying priorities

To effectively identify priorities for your to-do list, consider the importance and urgency of each task. Specific tasks will hold more significance than others in terms of impacting your goals.

Some tasks may require attention and should be completed sooner. It is helpful to break down tasks into more manageable ones. This allows for prioritization and tracking of progress. Consider delegating tasks to others whenever possible to free up your time and focus on the responsibilities.

Task prioritization involves assigning an order to tasks based on their urgency and importance. The objective is to enhance time management and productivity by organizing and focusing on the tasks that need completion.

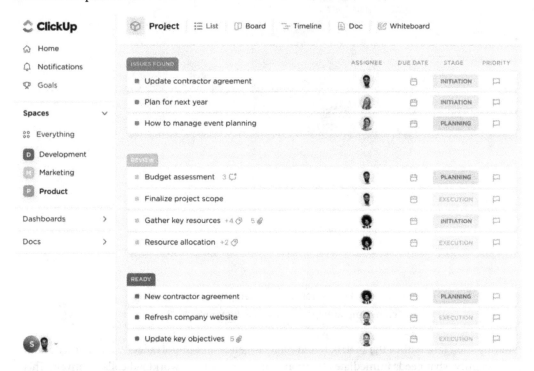

Figure 6.2 – ClickUp task prioritization (https://clickup.com/features/task-priorities)

ClickUp's priority matrix template offers a visual and collaborative way to streamline your workflow. This powerful tool utilizes a four-quadrant grid, each section color-coded to represent the urgency and importance of tasks. Imagine a matrix where the vertical axis reflects urgency (high or low) and the horizontal axis represents importance (high or low). This creates clear distinctions between critical and time-sensitive tasks (upper right quadrant) versus those that are important but not urgent (upper left quadrant).

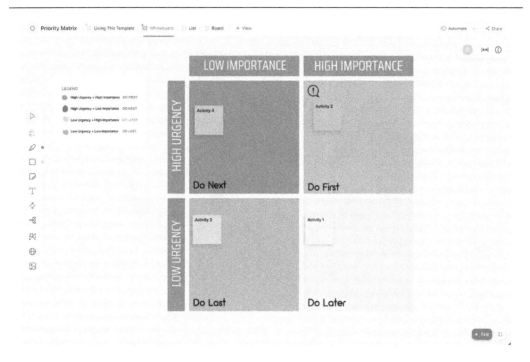

Figure 6.3 – ClickUp's priority matrix template (https://clickup.com/templates/priority-matrix-kkmvq-6322890)

By plotting each task within the matrix based on its urgency and importance level, your team can quickly identify what needs immediate attention and prioritize their workload collaboratively. This fosters clear communication and ensures everyone is aligned on which tasks deserve the most focus, propelling your projects forward efficiently.

Organizing tasks

After determining your priorities, organizing your tasks in a manner that makes sense for you is crucial. ClickUp provides features, such as Folders and Lists, which enable you to categorize your tasks.

This can assist you in staying organized and finding your tasks quickly. You can utilize dates and priorities to identify which tasks need to be completed by deadlines and determine their level of importance. Additionally, you can use tags and labels to include details about your tasks, such as the associated project or the person responsible for completing them. By using ClickUp's features, you can organize your tasks efficiently and effectively.

A vital aspect shared by all teams is task management. With ClickUp, you can focus on the tasks by accessing them through various views, such as List, Board, or Calendar.

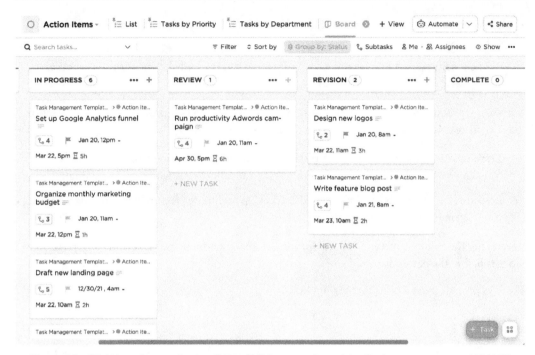

Figure 6.4 – ClickUp task organization (https://clickup.com/templates/task-management-t-4404185)

This task management template is a comprehensive toolkit for teams, streamlining organization and collaboration. You can easily sort tasks by status, priority, or department for ultimate clarity, optimize workflows based on team bandwidth and task progress, ensuring efficient resource allocation, and foster seamless collaboration across teams with features for scheduling, assigning, and completing tasks – all within a single, centralized platform. Put simply, this template empowers teams to work smarter, not harder, by providing the tools they need to achieve peak productivity.

By utilizing ClickUp's features, you can effectively organize your tasks in a manner that's both efficient and effective. Here are a few ways ClickUp can assist you in achieving this:

- **My Tasks view**: This view conveniently displays all your tasks in a list, helping you prioritize and manage them efficiently.

- **Turn emails into tasks**: ClickUp has a good feature for turning emails into tasks. You can't directly forward an email to become a new task, but you can forward it to a specific email address that ClickUp assigns to your Lists. Here's a quick rundown:

  - ClickUp allows you to create tasks by sending or forwarding emails to specific lists

  - Each List in ClickUp has a unique email address

- When you forward an email to this address, ClickUp will convert it into a new task within that List

- The email's subject line becomes the task name, and the body becomes the description

This way, you can use your email as a springboard to capture tasks and keep everything organized within ClickUp. You can find more details and instructions on using ClickUp's email-to-task feature through their resources (search Clickup to create a task from email).

- **Time tracking**: Use ClickUp's time tracking feature to monitor your time on each task. This will allow you to identify time-consuming tasks and adjust your workflow accordingly.

- **Reminders**: Never miss a task again with ClickUp's reminder feature. Set reminders to help you stay on track and avoid forgetting tasks.

By leveraging the features offered by ClickUp, you can maintain focus and efficiently complete your to-do lists before the day ends.

Task views provide perspectives for viewing tasks.

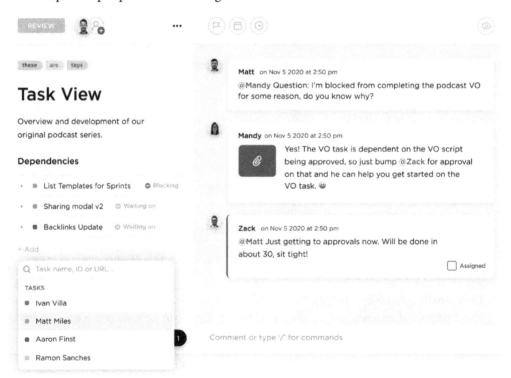

Figure 6.5 – ClickUp My Tasks view (https://clickup.com/features/tasks)

These views offer ways to visualize your tasks, allowing you to group, sort, and filter them according to your preferences. Additionally, you can save and share your customized views with others.

Examples and real-life scenarios

Let's take a look at how a software development team utilizes ClickUp to prioritize and manage their task lists:

- The team employs the My Tasks view, which lists all their tasks. They utilize the priorities feature to assign importance levels to each task. Furthermore, they use the time tracking functionality to monitor the time dedicated to each task.

- At the end of each day, they review their respective to-do lists, removing any completed tasks and rescheduling any others for the day.

By incorporating ClickUp into their workflow, the software development team has experienced productivity and decreased tasks.

Case study: A marketing team, drowning in scattered to-do lists and inefficient tools, found salvation in ClickUp. Their journey began with the My Tasks view, offering a centralized hub for all their tasks. ClickUp's priority feature became their secret weapon, allowing them to filter and focus on the most critical items. But the team didn't stop there. They harnessed the power of time tracking to identify time-consuming tasks and streamline their workflow for maximum efficiency. This case study is a testament to ClickUp's ability to transform even the most chaotic to-do lists into well-oiled productivity machines.

Adopting ClickUp for prioritizing and managing their tasks has increased productivity and reduced assignments for the marketing team.

Now that we've tackled prioritization and organization-like productivity ninjas, let's delve deeper into the next topic. Here, we'll explore ClickUp's efficiency-enhancing features, from templates to automation and integrations. Remember, maximizing productivity means conquering your to-do lists with laser focus and achieving your goals with time to spare. Let's discover how ClickUp empowers you to become a productivity powerhouse.

Maximizing productivity by utilizing ClickUp's efficiency-enhancing features

ClickUp is a project management tool that offers various features designed to enhance productivity and efficiently manage tasks. It helps streamline your workflow and ensures the completion of your to-do lists. You can optimize your productivity and accomplish your objectives by leveraging features such as task templates, automation, and integrations.

Task templates

Task templates save time and ensure task completion. With ClickUp, you can create customized task templates encompassing all details, including task names, descriptions, due dates, and priorities.

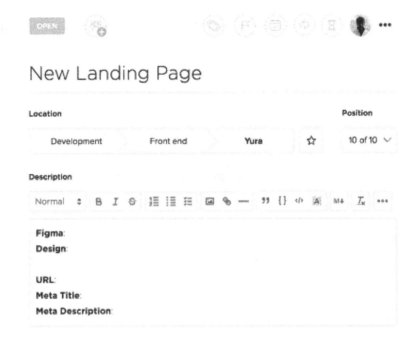

Figure 6.6 – ClickUp task templates (https://clickup.com/features/task-templates)

You can establish task templates for tasks such as recurring tasks, project-related tasks, or personal assignments. Once a task template is created, generating tasks based on the template becomes effortless with a single click.

Automation

ClickUp also offers automation. This feature allows you to automate tasks and free up time to focus on more critical responsibilities.

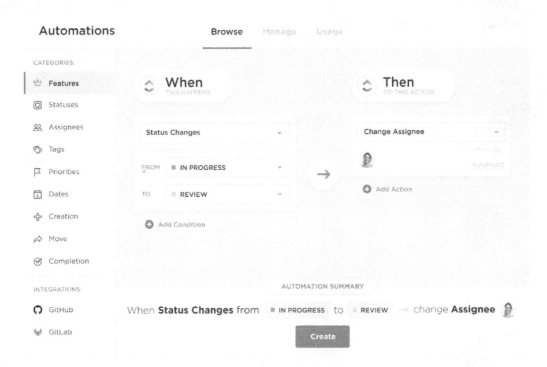

Figure 6.7 – ClickUp automation (https://clickup.com/blog/automation-examples/)

With ClickUp's automation capabilities, you can automate actions such as creating tasks, assigning them to team members, or sending notifications. Additionally, ClickUp provides built-in automations that serve as good starting points.

Integrations

ClickUp integrates with various tools, including Slack, Google Drive, and Jira. This feature allows you to centralize all your work and make your workflow more efficient.

Figure 6.8 – ClickUp integrations (https://clickup.com/blog/best-clickup-integrations/)

For instance, you can use the Slack integration to receive notifications about your tasks directly in Slack and attach Google Drive files to your tasks.

Examples and case studies

Here's an illustration of how a marketing team leverages ClickUp's productivity features for efficiency:

- The team relies on task templates for their performed tasks, such as creating blog posts and social media content. This saves them time and ensures consistency in completing their tasks.

- They also use automation to streamline tasks, such as generating tasks for each blog post or social media update. This frees their time to focus on responsibilities such as writing blog posts and crafting engaging social media content.

- Furthermore, the team capitalizes on ClickUp's integrations to consolidate all their work in one place. For instance, they use Slack integration to receive task notifications within Slack while utilizing Google Drive integration to attach files from Google Drive to their tasks.

As a result of using ClickUp's productivity features, the marketing team has seen a boost in their efficiency levels and content output.

In a real-life scenario

A software development team faced challenges in keeping up with their project demands. They were using tools to track progress, making it difficult to see the picture.

To address this issue, the team implemented ClickUp as their project management solution. They started by creating task templates for their assignments and automated repetitive tasks using its automation capabilities.

Furthermore, they integrated ClickUp with tools such as Slack and Jira. This integration allowed them to consolidate all their work in one place and streamline their workflow effectively.

Thanks to the leveraging of ClickUp's productivity features, the software development team has experienced efficiency and successful delivery of projects within designated timelines and budgets.

Bonus tips for organizing projects and tasks in ClickUp

Here are three bonus tips you can use in real-life scenarios to further enhance your ClickUp experience:

- Utilize ClickUp Docs for centralized information:

  - Don't just manage tasks in ClickUp; use ClickUp Docs to create a knowledgebase central for hubs of information

  - Store important documents, meeting notes, and reference materials within Docs linked to specific projects or tasks

  - This keeps everything organized and easily accessible to your team members, eliminating the need to search through emails or external drives

- Leverage ClickUp mind maps for brainstorming and planning:

  - ClickUp's Mind Maps are a fantastic tool for brainstorming project ideas, outlining workflows, and visually planning tasks

  - Capture free-flowing ideas, establish connections between tasks, and prioritize them visually within the Mind Map

  - This fosters collaborative planning sessions and helps visualize the project scope before diving into detailed task creation

- Master ClickUp views for tailored project insights:

  - ClickUp offers various views (List, Board, Calendar, etc.) to visualize your projects from different angles

  - Use the List view for a traditional to-do list format, the Board view for a Kanban-style workflow, and the Calendar view to track deadlines and project timelines

- Customize these views with filters and sorting options to see only the information most relevant to your needs

By incorporating these bonus tips alongside the strategies outlined in this chapter, you can unlock ClickUp's full potential and streamline your project management process.

Summary

In *Chapter 6*, you have learned essential strategies for optimizing organizational and task management skills using ClickUp, tailored explicitly for medium-sized business owners and enterprise-level executives. The chapter delves into structuring projects and tasks within ClickUp, emphasizing hierarchy and features such as task Relationships, custom fields, subtasks, checklists, and dependencies. It guides you in prioritizing and managing to-do lists effectively, demonstrating the significance of task prioritization, organization, and delegation.

Real-world examples illustrate ClickUp's practical application in marketing teams and software development projects. Additionally, the chapter explores maximizing efficiency through productivity features such as task templates and automation. The information is valuable, providing actionable insights and tools to enhance project management capabilities using ClickUp.

In the next chapter, *Chapter 7*, you will delve into tracking goals, project progress, and productivity with KPIs, Dashboards, and Reporting.

Sign up to download your free workbook and productivity resources for each chapter

ClickUp is constantly evolving. Get help and explore each chapter in depth, receive the latest productivity updates and ClickUp tips, and download your free workbook at `http://bluecreative.com/clickup`. Specializing in ClickUp implementation, configurations, systems development, process implementation, and more.

Unger, E. (2024). Clickup. BLUECREATIVE.

`https://bluecreative.com/clickup`

Tracking Goals, Project Progress, and Productivity with KPIs, Dashboards, and Reporting

Welcome to *Chapter 7*, where we'll dive into the significance of monitoring goals, project progress, and productivity by utilizing **key performance indicators** (**KPIs**), dashboards, and reporting. Regardless of whether you're an entrepreneur, a business owner running a medium-sized company, or an executive at an enterprise level taking on the role of a project manager, this chapter offers valuable insights on effectively tracking and measuring success using ClickUp's features.

In this chapter, we will cover the following topics:

- Establishing KPIs to determine success

- Creating real-time project dashboards for instant insights

- Generating reports for stakeholder communication and decision-making

This chapter will equip you with the knowledge and skills necessary to make optimal use of ClickUp's features to track goals effectively, monitor project progress efficiently, and evaluate productivity by applying KPIs, dashboards, and reporting strategically.

Establishing KPIs to determine success

KPIs are measurable values that assist businesses in tracking their progress toward specific objectives. KPIs can be employed to gauge factors such as performance, customer satisfaction levels, employee productivity metrics, and operational efficiency. By establishing and monitoring KPIs, companies can assess their strengths, as well as areas that require improvement. This data is valuable for making decisions and achieving goals effectively.

Identifying meaningful metrics

The initial step in defining KPIs involves identifying metrics that align with specific goals and objectives. When selecting metrics, it is crucial to consider the following factors:

- **Relevance**: The metric should directly relate to the goals and objectives

- **Measurability**: The metric should be quantifiable and measurable

- **Timeliness**: The metric should be available promptly for progress tracking

- **Actionability**: The metric should provide insights that enable performance improvements

ClickUp's KPI dashboard is specifically designed to facilitate tracking progress toward KPIs and objectives:

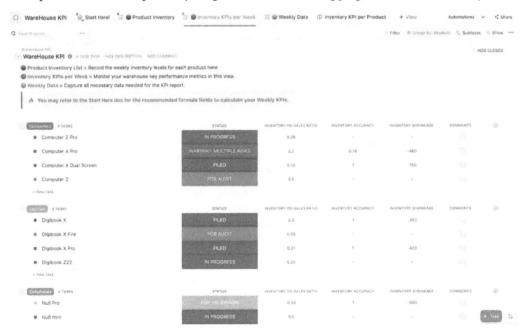

Figure 7.1 – ClickUp's KPI dashboard (https://clickup.com/blog/kpi-reporting/)

KPIs are vital for comprehending business or project success. By implementing a KPI template and monitoring performance, you can stay up to date with progress and make adjustments when required.

Setting targets

Once you've identified meaningful metrics, you need to set targets for each KPI. The targets should be specific, measurable, achievable, relevant, and time-bound:

Figure 7.2 – ClickUp's KPI target setting (https://clickup.com/blog/
how-to-use-clickup-to-set-goals-for-your-team/)

For instance, by setting a target such as "increasing sales," you can set a more precise goal, such as *"achieving a 10% increase in sales within the upcoming quarter."* This target is specific, measurable, achievable, relevant, and time-bound.

To effectively track and measure your KPIs, ClickUp provides various features you can utilize:

- **Custom fields**: You have the option to create custom fields in ClickUp to monitor your KPIs. This allows you to view your KPI data within the context of your tasks and projects.

- **Dashboards**: ClickUp's dashboards enable you to visualize your KPI data and keep track of your progress over time.

- **Reports**: ClickUp's reporting features allow you to generate reports on your KPIs. This can prove useful for sharing your progress with stakeholders or identifying areas that require improvement.

A KPI report serves as a compiled record in digital form that consolidates performance data for all the KPIs currently being tracked. It acts as a hub in the form of a KPI dashboard where you can easily understand your data and evaluate your KPIs:

Figure 7.3 – ClickUp's KPI tracking report (https://clickup.com/blog/kpi-reporting/)

KPI reports are typically designed to be appealing so that you and your team members can quickly analyze the data and identify trends or challenges related to your business objectives.

To illustrate how a marketing team utilizes ClickUp to track and measure their KPIs, let's consider a scenario.

The marketing team has established targets for themselves:

- Increase website traffic by 5% within the first quarter
- Generate 100 new leads per month
- Boost social media engagement by 10% within the first quarter

They are employing ClickUp to monitor their progress toward these goals. They have customized fields to track metrics such as website traffic, lead generation, and social media engagement. Additionally, they are utilizing ClickUp's dashboards to visualize their KPI data and monitor their progress over time.

Case study

Frustrated by missed deadlines and unclear progress, a software development team found salvation in ClickUp. Their struggle stemmed from their inability to track progress effectively, leaving them blind to potential roadblocks. Enter ClickUp's tracking prowess! They customized fields to meticulously monitor each task's start date, end date, and status. Additionally, a dedicated dashboard served as their command center, visualizing progress and highlighting any tasks at risk of derailing the schedule. This newfound transparency transformed their efficiency, allowing them to consistently meet deadlines and celebrate well-deserved project victories. ClickUp became the key to unlocking their full potential, proving that clear visibility is the fuel for success.

Now that we've discussed the significance of KPIs and how to identify measurements, let's delve into the hands-on aspect. In the next section, we'll take a look at ClickUp's dashboards, which are designed to turn your data into actionable insights in real time. By customizing your dashboards, you'll be able to track your team's progress and performance, enabling you to acknowledge achievements and tackle obstacles promptly.

Creating real-time project dashboards for instant insights

ClickUp dashboards offer a solution for visualizing project data and gaining instant insights into progress and performance. By creating custom dashboards, you can easily identify areas where your team is excelling and areas that require improvement.

Creating a dashboard

To create a dashboard in ClickUp, follow these steps:

1. Navigate to the **Dashboards** icon located in the sidebar.
2. Click on the **Create Dashboard** button.
3. Provide a name for your dashboard and select the space(s) you wish to include within it.
4. Finally, click **Create Dashboard** to complete the process.

Customizing your dashboard

After creating your dashboard, you have the option to customize it according to your requirements. To begin the customization process, simply click on the **Customize Dashboard** button located in the corner of your dashboard:

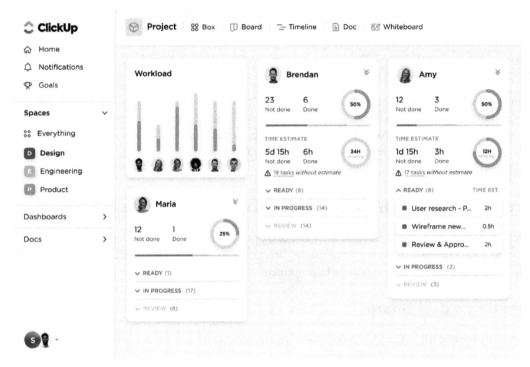

Figure 7.4 – ClickUp's dashboard customization panel (https://clickup.com/features/dashboards)

Within the **Customize Dashboard** panel, you have the flexibility to add widgets, rearrange them as needed, and apply data filters.

Adding widgets to your dashboard

ClickUp provides a range of widgets that you can incorporate into your dashboards. To add a widget, click the **Add Widget** button within the **Customize Dashboard** panel. Select the desired widget from the available options:

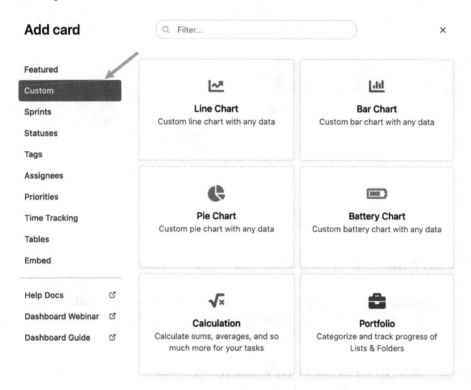

Figure 7.5 – ClickUp's dashboard cards (https://help.clickup.com/hc/
en-us/articles/6312211188759-Intro-to-Dashboard-cards)

Once a widget has been added to your dashboard, you can easily configure it to display data that is relevant to you. For example, with a **Task List** widget, you can choose whether you wish to view all tasks associated with a project or only those tasks due within the week.

Visualizing your data

ClickUp dashboards offer visualization methods for understanding and representing your data. You have various ways to represent your data, such as via bar charts, line charts, pie charts, and tables:

Figure 7.6 – ClickUp's dashboard charts (https://clickup.com/blog/project-management-chart/)

To visualize your data, go to the **Charts** tab in the **Customize Dashboard** panel and choose the type of chart you prefer. Once you've selected a chart type, you can customize it to display the data you're interested in.

Utilizing ClickUp's features to monitor projects effectively

ClickUp provides features for effectively monitoring your projects. For instance, you can utilize the following features:

- **Filters**: Use filters to narrow down your data and focus on what's most important to you
- **Timeframes**: Select a period when you wish to view your data
- **Drill-downs**: Dive deeper into your data for more information

ClickUp's dashboards act as a control center for teams. They offer a comprehensive and user-friendly project visibility system that caters to functional teams. This system promotes collaboration without complexity:

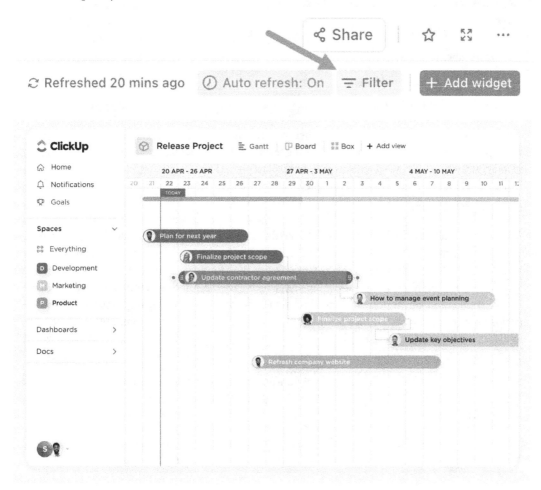

Figure 7.7 – ClickUp's dashboard filters, timeframes, and drill-downs (https://clickup.com/time-management)

For instance, imagine that you want to view tasks in a location with dates that fall on or before today, as well as tasks with start dates also falling on or before today. With ClickUp's filter capabilities, you can easily achieve this level of customization:

((**Due Date** is Today or Earlier) OR (**Start Date** is Today or Earlier)) AND **Location**…

This flexibility enables you to create tailored dashboards that precisely meet your requirements.

To illustrate its practicality, let's look at an example of how a software development team utilizes dashboards for project monitoring.

The team has set up a dashboard that tracks key metrics:

- The number of completed tasks

- The number of tasks

- The number of reported bugs

- The number of fixed bugs

This dashboard serves as a tool for tracking their progress toward project goals and identifying areas where improvement is needed. For instance, if the team notices an increase in the number of overdue tasks, they can take measures to address this issue.

Illustrative example

The marketing team was overwhelmed with data and different tools and wanted a view of their campaign progress. Their current monitoring methods made them feel like they were blindfolded, unable to track and analyze how their campaigns were performing. So, they found a solution: ClickUp's command center. They created dashboards for each campaign, which gave them access to important metrics such as website traffic, lead generation, and social media engagement – all beautifully presented through ClickUp's user-friendly widgets. This newfound transparency allowed them to monitor progress in time, identify strengths and weaknesses, and optimize their campaigns for impact. ClickUp became their weapon for transforming data into actionable insights and paving the way for marketing success.

By utilizing dashboards, the marketing team significantly improved their efficiency and gained better insights into their campaign progress. They were also able to identify areas where enhancements were required.

Now that you've mastered the art of crafting dynamic dashboards, let's shift gears. In the next section, we'll explore ClickUp's powerful reporting features, which can transform project insights into compelling narratives for stakeholders and drive data-driven decisions. We'll unveil how to generate customized reports that keep everyone informed, aligned, and empowered to achieve project success. Stay tuned as we unveil the secrets to clear communication and strategic decision-making, all fueled by the power of data.

Generating reports for stakeholder communication and decision-making

ClickUp reports play a role in communicating project progress and performance to stakeholders while facilitating informed decision-making. Through generating reports, you can share information with stakeholders effortlessly and pinpoint areas where your team needs improvement.

Best practices for report creation

When creating reports, it is essential to adhere to these recommended guidelines:

- **Identify your target audience.** Who will be reading your report? What kind of information do they require?

- **Determine your objective.** What are you aiming to accomplish with your report?

- **Arrange your data in a certain manner.** Your report should be well-structured and easy to comprehend.

- **Use succinct language.** Avoid jargon and abbreviations.

- **Utilize visual aids such as charts and graphs to emphasize findings.** These visual representations can enhance the understanding and attractiveness of your data.

- **Carefully proofread your report to ensure it's error-free.**

ClickUp's project status report is specifically designed to assist you in monitoring the progress of a project. This template includes a status feature that allows you to track the stages of your project:

Figure 7.8 – ClickUp's project status report (https://clickup.com/blog/project-status-report/)

Creating a project status report plays a pivotal role in project management. By using this report, you can keep stakeholders informed about the project's status, address any issues that arise, and ensure that your team remains on track toward achieving their goals.

Data visualization

Data visualization serves as a means of conveying information concisely and clearly. ClickUp provides a range of options for visualizing data, such as bar charts, line charts, pie charts, and tables:

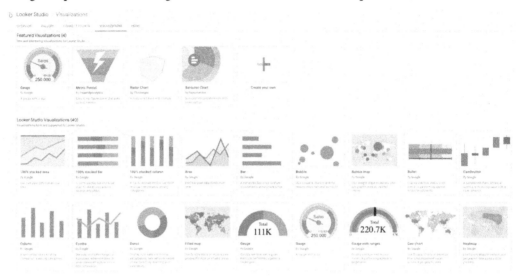

Figure 7.9 – ClickUp's report data visualization features (https://clickup.com/blog/data-visualization-tools/)

When deciding on a data visualization method, it is essential to consider the type of data being presented and the intended audience for your report. For instance, if you're presenting information to individuals who may not be technically inclined, it is advisable to opt for visualization options such as bar charts or pie charts.

Utilizing ClickUp's reporting capabilities allows you to present information accurately and clearly. Let's look at some of the available features:

- **Filters**: Utilize filters to narrow down your data and focus on the information that's been presented
- **Timeframes**: Select specific periods to examine your data within that time frame.
- **Drill-downs**: Dive deeper into your data to access more detailed insights
- **Custom branding**: Personalize your reports by adding custom branding elements
- **Exporting**: Export your reports, in PDF, CSV, or Excel format

These features contribute to creating informative reports in ClickUp. Let's look at an example of how a marketing team utilizes reports to keep stakeholders informed about project progress and performance.

The team prepares a weekly report that tracks the following key metrics:

- Website traffic
- Leads generated
- Social media engagement
- Email open rates
- Click-through rates

By sharing this report with stakeholders, the marketing team ensures everyone is up to date on their progress and identifies areas for improvement.

Real-life example

Stuck in a rut of lengthy, complex email updates that left stakeholders scratching their heads, a software development team sought a more effective communication channel. Their weekly reports were like dense novels, drowning key takeaways in a sea of text. Enter ClickUp's reporting magic! By crafting focused reports tailored to each stakeholder's specific needs, they eliminated information overload. Filters ensured relevant data took center stage, while charts and graphs transformed complex metrics into visually appealing insights. This transformation from text-heavy tomes to digestible visuals not only saved time but fostered stakeholder engagement and understanding, paving the way for smoother collaboration and project success. ClickUp's reporting features became the bridge between technical details and clear communication, ensuring everyone was on the same page and driving the project forward as a united team.

As a result of adopting reports, the software development team significantly improved their communication, with stakeholders ultimately building trust in the process.

Summary

In this chapter, you learned about the vital components of tracking goals, project progress, and productivity through the implementation of KPIs, dashboards, and reporting while utilizing the robust features of ClickUp. This information proved useful by providing insights for efficiently monitoring success, something that applies to solo entrepreneurs, medium-sized business owners, and high-level executives overseeing project management. The emphasis on KPIs as measurable values for tracking progress in various aspects, coupled with the utilization of ClickUp's features, such as custom fields, equipped you to set and track meaningful metrics aligned with your plans.

This chapter also covered how to create and customize ClickUp dashboards, offering tools for visualizing real-time project data. You gained knowledge about adding widgets, customizing dashboard layouts, and utilizing visualization options such as bar and line charts, with case studies illustrating how software development and marketing teams efficiently monitor projects using dashboards. The final section highlighted best practices for report creation while focusing on audience identification, defining purpose, logical data organization, and employing clear language and visualizations, all while focusing on ClickUp's reporting.

In the next chapter, you'll learn how to integrate ClickUp with other tools and apps, further expanding your understanding of seamless project management integration.

Sign up to download your free workbook and productivity resources for each chapter

ClickUp is constantly evolving. Get help and explore each chapter in depth, receive the latest productivity updates and ClickUp tips, and download your free workbook at `http://bluecreative.com/clickup`. Specializing in ClickUp implementation, configurations, systems development, process implementation, and more.

Unger, E. (2024). Clickup. BLUECREATIVE.

`https://bluecreative.com/clickup`

Integrating ClickUp with Your Other Tools and Apps

Welcome to *Chapter 8*, where we'll explore the potential of integrating ClickUp with your existing tools and applications. Whether you're an entrepreneur, a sized business owner, or an executive taking on the role of project manager, this chapter will provide valuable insights into how integrating ClickUp can streamline your workflows, boost productivity, and drive project success. Throughout this chapter, we'll cover the following topics:

- Understanding the advantages of integration

- Incorporating ClickUp with communication tools

- Leveraging ClickUp's integration capabilities with productivity tools

By the end of this chapter, you will have a comprehensive understanding of integration benefits and practical knowledge on effectively incorporating ClickUp into your toolsets. This unlocks possibilities for collaboration, efficiency, and successful project outcomes.

Understanding the advantages of integration

Integration involves connecting software applications to enable data sharing and enhanced functionality. ClickUp offers integration with tools and apps such as Slack, Google Drive, Jira, and Trello.

The benefits of integration

There are advantages to integrating ClickUp with tools and apps. Here are some of the benefits:

- **Enhanced data flow**: Integration can improve the flow of data between different systems, saving you time and increasing efficiency by eliminating the need for manual data entry across multiple platforms.

- **Reduced manual tasks**: Integration streamlines processes by eliminating manual tasks, such as copying and pasting data. This frees up your time to focus on responsibilities.

- **Streamlined workflow**: Integration enables a smooth workflow across various platforms, making it easier to manage your work and collaborate effectively with others.

- **Time mapping**: This functionality can visually represent how your integrations work together. This allows you to see how data flows between ClickUp and your other tools, identify bottlenecks, and optimize your workflow for even greater efficiency.

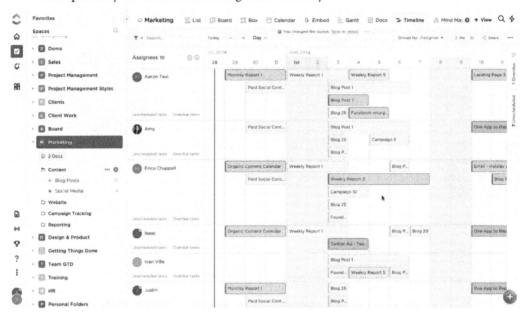

Figure 8.1 – ClickUp time mapping (https://clickup.com/blog/gantt-vs-timeline/)

ClickUp's time mapping offers a visual timeline view, where tasks are represented by colored blocks or bars reflecting their duration. You can link dependent tasks with arrows and customize colors by category. You can also zoom in and out to see specific details or the bigger picture, respectively, using filters to focus on specific projects, team members, or timelines. This functionality integrates with dependencies and time estimates, creating a comprehensive view of your project schedule.

A real-life example

Imagine a marketing team streamlining your workflow by integrating ClickUp with your social media platform. No more manual data entry – engagement metrics flow seamlessly into ClickUp, saving you time and boosting your ability to track progress. Similarly, imagine a software development team that juggles multiple platforms, using ClickUp for tasks and separate tools for bug tracking and QA collaboration. By integrating ClickUp with their existing environment, they established a unified workflow, keeping track of tasks, bugs, and feedback, all under one roof. These real-life examples showcase the power of integration, fostering efficiency and collaboration across diverse teams and functions.

By integrating ClickUp with your communication tools, the software development team experiences improved efficiency and a faster release of software features.

Having explored the general advantages of integration, let's delve deeper into the realm of communication tools. The next topic unveils how integrating ClickUp with platforms such as Slack, Microsoft Teams, and Zoom can turbocharge your team's collaboration, streamline communication, and eliminate frustrating app switching.

Incorporating ClickUp with communication tools

Integrating ClickUp with communication tools offers several advantages. It enhances collaboration and streamlines communication among team members. Additionally, it reduces the need to switch between applications, resulting in time savings and increased efficiency.

Recommended practices to integrate ClickUp with communication tools

Consider the following practices when integrating ClickUp with your chosen communication tool:

- **Select a communication tool that meets your teams' specific needs (e.g., Slack, Microsoft Teams, or email)**: Prioritize ease of use.

- **Determine which features of both ClickUp and your chosen communication tool need integration**: Identify the functionalities that will benefit your team the most.

   For instance, if you want to stay updated on tasks or send messages seamlessly, you might consider connecting ClickUp with your preferred communication tool. Selecting the right integration platform is crucial. Options include Zapier and Integromat. Make sure to choose a user platform that supports the integrations you require.

- **Set up your integrations**: Once you've chosen your integration platform, proceed to set up the integrations. The process will differ, depending on the platform and tools involved.

- **Test your integrations**: After setting up your integrations, testing them to ensure functionality is essential.

Here is an example of how marketing teams can leverage ClickUp Slack integration for collaboration:

- **This particular team utilizes ClickUp to manage social media campaigns while relying on Slack as a communication channel**: By integrating ClickUp with Slack, they can receive task notifications and effortlessly send messages from within ClickUp

- **This seamless integration enables the team to stay connected and collaborate efficiently**: For instance, if a team member receives a task for a social media campaign, they can easily reach out to the team in Slack to seek assistance or share ideas

A real-life example

Frustrated by scattered conversations and wasted time searching for information, the software development team sought a solution. Juggling ClickUp for tasks, Slack for communication, and various other tools created a fragmented workflow. Enter the power of integration! Connecting ClickUp and Slack transforms the team's collaboration. Now, task notifications and discussions seamlessly flow within Slack, eliminating the need to switch between platforms and dramatically reducing time spent searching for updates. This integration becomes the team's bridge to a centralized conversation hub, boosting collaboration and propelling their productivity to new heights.

Now that we've mastered the art of communication integrations, let's shift gears and empower your productivity. The following section will explore ClickUp's seamless integration with tools such as Google Calendar, Dropbox, and Evernote, transforming your workflow into a well-oiled machine. Let's automate tasks, centralize information, and eliminate app-hopping distractions for productivity.

Leveraging ClickUp's integration capabilities with productivity tools

Integrating ClickUp with productivity tools can significantly boost efficiency and streamline workflows. It also minimizes the need to switch between applications, saving time and improving productivity.

Best practices to integrate ClickUp with productivity tools

Here are some recommended practices when integrating ClickUp with productivity tools:

- **Select the most suitable productivity tools for your team's needs**: There are various options, including Google Drive, Microsoft Office Suite, and project management software. When selecting tools for your team, prioritize the ones that are user-friendly and cater to your team's requirements.

- **Begin by identifying the features you want to integrate**: Determine which aspects of ClickUp and your productivity tools you wish to combine. For instance, connect ClickUp with your productivity tools to automatically save files or create tasks within ClickUp.

- **Choose an integration platform that suits your needs**: Platforms such as Zapier and Integromat are available. Opt for one that's easy to navigate and supports your required integrations.

- **Setting up integrations**: Start setting up your integrations based on the chosen platform and the tools involved.

- **Testing integrations**: Testing the integrations once established is essential to ensure functionality.

Examples and case studies

Here's an example that illustrates how a marketing team utilizes integration with Google Drive, resulting in increased efficiency:

- **The marketing team employs ClickUp as its campaign management tool and Google Drive as its repository for marketing materials.**

- **They have successfully connected ClickUp and Google Drive, enabling file saving and direct access to marketing materials from within the platform**: This integration significantly enhances the team's productivity and efficiency. For instance, when a team member works on a marketing campaign, they can effortlessly retrieve the marketing materials directly from ClickUp.

In a case study, the software development team faced challenges managing its work across applications. They utilized ClickUp for task management, Microsoft Office Suite for documentation creation, and additional tools for bug tracking and collaboration with the QA team. They integrated ClickUp with Microsoft Office Suite and other relevant tools to streamline their software development process. This integration resulted in a workflow where they can now handle tasks, documentation, bug tracking, and QA feedback all in one location.

By integrating ClickUp with their existing tools, the software development team achieved improved efficiency. This expedited the release of software features.

Summary

This chapter explored the possibilities of integrating ClickUp with tools and applications. This integration caters to a range of users, from entrepreneurs to high-level executives. The chapter started by explaining the benefits of integration, such as improved data flow and streamlined workflows across platforms. It provided examples and case studies to showcase how integration has helped teams, such as marketing and software development, become more efficient by reducing tasks.

This chapter was valuable because it discussed the advantages of integration and gave practical insights and real-world applications. By sharing practices and case studies, you understood how to integrate ClickUp with communication and productivity tools, leading to better collaboration and smoother workflows.

Looking ahead, the upcoming chapter will focus on task management with ClickUp. It will guide you in managing your tasks using ClickUp while providing insights and strategies to optimize personal productivity and organize tasks efficiently.

Sign up to download your free workbook and productivity resources for each chapter

ClickUp is constantly evolving. Get help and explore each chapter in depth, receive the latest productivity updates and ClickUp tips, and download your free workbook at `http://bluecreative.com/clickup`. Specializing in ClickUp implementation, configurations, systems development, process implementation, and more.

Unger, E. (2024). Clickup. BLUECREATIVE.

`https://bluecreative.com/clickup`

Part 3:
Understanding ClickUp

In this part, you'll dive into the basics of ClickUp, understanding what it's all about, its benefits, and what it can do. You'll get the hang of navigating the workspace, adjusting the settings to suit your needs, and using features with ClickApps. Whether you're new to ClickUp or a user looking to broaden your knowledge, this information will be helpful. By mastering the concepts and capabilities of ClickUp, you can set up your workspace for maximum workflow efficiency, boost productivity, and effectively handle projects and tasks using the platform. Moreover, with ClickUp AI, you can automate tasks, improve teamwork, and make informed decisions to drive your projects forward.

This part has the following chapters:

- *Chapter 9: Personal Task Management with ClickUp*
- *Chapter 10: Project Planning and Collaborating on Personal Events with Friends and Family*
- *Chapter 11: Managing Household Chores and Home-Life Responsibilities*
- *Chapter 12: Personal Habits, Goal Achievement, and Routines for Success*

Personal Task Management with ClickUp

Welcome to *Chapter 9*, where we delve into the world of task management using ClickUp. Whether you're an everyday person, business owner, or executive taking on the role of project manager, this chapter aims to provide valuable insights into effectively managing your tasks with ClickUp. In this chapter, we will cover the following topics:

- Organizing and prioritizing personal tasks
- Techniques for managing time and boosting productivity
- Setting goals and tracking progress

By the end of this chapter, you can expect to have gained practical knowledge on leveraging ClickUp for personal task management. This comprehensive guide offers tips and strategies for organizing tasks, optimizing time management skills, and aligning goals with measurable progress. Regardless of your background or role, you'll find guidance in these pages.

Organizing and prioritizing personal tasks

When organizing your tasks in ClickUp, the first step is to create a structure that suits your needs. One method is to establish a hierarchy of folders, lists, and tasks.

For instance, you can create folders and lists for different aspects of your life, such as work, school, and home. Another method to organize your task lists is through filtered views, tags, and custom fields. Tags enable you to filter your work. Home, work, and school are good tag starters. Filtered views are customizable by assignee, due date, or custom field. Then, select the ClickUp filter according to how you need to process your work.

Once you have established the structure, you can begin adding tasks. When adding a task, include all the information, such as task name, description, due date, custom fields, and any other pertinent details.

Using the Eisenhower Matrix as a planning tool to set priorities

After adding all your tasks, it becomes crucial to set priorities. This will assist you in concentrating on the tasks while avoiding overwhelm. One effective method for prioritization is utilizing the **Eisenhower Matrix**. The Eisenhower Matrix is a tool that helps prioritize tasks based on their importance and urgency.

To utilize the Eisenhower Matrix, all you need to do is create a grid divided into four quadrants:

- **Quadrant 1**: Tasks that are both important and urgent
- **Quadrant 2**: Tasks that are important but not urgent
- **Quadrant 3**: Tasks that are not important but urgent
- **Quadrant 4**: Tasks that are neither important nor urgent

The following figure shows Eisenhower Matrix four-quadrant method:

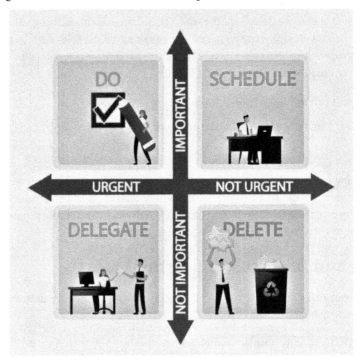

Figure 9.1 – Eisenhower Matrix four-quadrant method (https://www.vectorstock.com/
royalty-free-vector/characters-at-huge-eisenhower-matrix-time-vector-31880364)

Once you have set up the grid, assign your tasks to their quadrants. For instance, if you have a task that's both important and needs attention, such as completing a work presentation, it should go into **Quadrant 1** for the next day.

You can plan your time accordingly after adding all your tasks to the Eisenhower Matrix. Prioritizing the tasks in **Quadrant 1** is crucial since they are essential and urgent.

Next, you can move on to tackling the tasks in **Quadrant 2**. These tasks are important but don't require urgent attention. You can allocate them for later in the day or week.

Tasks falling under **Quadrant 3** are of low importance but still carry some urgency . You have options such as delegating these tasks to others or rescheduling them for a later date.

Lastly, we have neither important nor urgent tasks in **Quadrant 4**. You may discard these tasks or postpone them until a suitable time arises.

How to use the glass jar analogy with ClickUp's priority levels

To effectively prioritize tasks and project backlog work, we can also use the analogy of putting big rocks, small rocks, sand, and water into a glass jar. This method is easier to adopt and is recommended. Just as we must prioritize the big rocks first to fit everything in the jar, we must prioritize our tasks and projects accordingly. Let's compare ClickUp's four priority levels – Urgent, High, Normal, and Low – to big rocks, small rocks, sand, and water for our project and task prioritizations.

Step 1 – Identifying the big rocks (Urgent)

Start by identifying the most critical and time-sensitive tasks or projects. These are your *big rocks*, or the urgent priorities that require immediate attention. Assign them the highest priority level, **Urgent**, in ClickUp.

Step 2 – Addressing the small rocks (High)

Next, focus on the smaller but still important tasks or projects. Your *small rocks* or high-priority items contribute significantly to your goals. Assign them the **High** priority level in ClickUp.

Step 3 – Tackling the sand (Normal)

Now, it's time to address the less critical tasks or projects. These are your *sand* or normal-priority items that may not have immediate deadlines but still need to be completed. Assign them the **Normal** priority level in ClickUp.

Step 4 – Handling the water (Low)

Lastly, deal with the least urgent tasks or projects. These are your *water* or low-priority items that can be postponed if necessary. Assign them the **Low** priority level in ClickUp.

Step 5 – Processing priorities (recommendation for making it work for your schedule)

When processing your backlog for today, save Urgent for today's to-do items. Similarly, do this for projects, initiatives, ideas, and other work areas. High, Normal, and Low then become the next planned priorities. In summary, plan according to High, Normal, and Low and use the Urgent tasks for items to do today/immediately.

Managing urgent tasks efficiently with ClickUp's Personal List

ClickUp's Personal List enables the creation of distinct tasks that are fully autonomous from your project framework. It is ideal for overseeing swift tasks, personal chores, immediate idea processing, or any other items you need to monitor apart from your ClickUp Workspace environment. When you're ready to refine your thoughts, return and transfer them to the appropriate list. This maintains the organization of your ClickUp Workspace and your personal workflow, allowing you to concentrate on your priorities as shown in the following image:

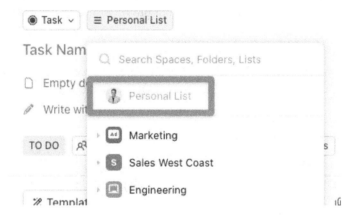

Figure 9.2 – ClickUp's Personal List (https://help.clickup.com/hc/
en-us/articles/18377842006167-Use-Personal-List)

Accessing your personal lists is a breeze. Simply look for the dedicated Personal List button (or find it within the sidebar, depending on your ClickUp view). From there, you can quickly start managing your personal tasks.

Using ClickUp features to stay organized and maintain focus

ClickUp offers features that can keep you organized and focused on your tasks.

One helpful feature is the Everything view if you are an Admin or Member. This will be the Shared with me view if you are a guest:

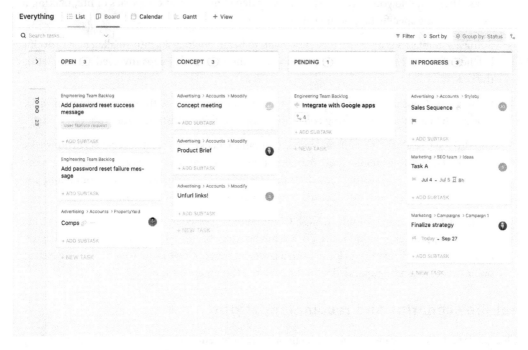

Figure 9.3 – Clickup's Everything view (https://help.clickup.com/hc/
en-us/articles/6310138041367-Add-an-Everything-view)

The ClickUp **Everything** view offers a powerful central location to manage your workload. It displays all tasks within your Workspace, organized by the status assigned in their parent Spaces, Folders, or Lists.

> **Note**
> Personal task lists are not included by default in the Everything view.

ClickUp's robust **List** view provides a summary of all your tasks no matter whether they are stored in Folders, Lists, or Spaces. This feature enables you to do the following:

- Establish deadlines, priorities, and start dates for your tasks
- Visually map out your workload and spot bottlenecks
- Use filters to concentrate on tasks or the work of team members

Additionally, ClickUp provides features that assist in organizing and prioritizing personal tasks:

- **Tags**: These enable you to categorize tasks by departments and categories of life, making it easier to locate specific tags or filter them by category.

- **Subtasks**: Subtasks is a feature that allows you to break down tasks into smaller, more specific batches of work. This can be used as the base outline for all the steps involved in completing the task.

- **Comments**: Comments provide a way for you to communicate with others about your tasks. This can be handy when working collaboratively or seeking assistance from others.

- **Checklists**: Use ClickUp's built-in Slash Command/Checklist to create checklists inside tasks, documents, and comments. These features allow you to break down tasks into smaller, more manageable work. By utilizing these features inside your tasks, documents, and comments, you can quickly organize and stay focused on your personal task management.

- **Toggle list**: Use ClickUp's built-in Slash Commands (accessed by typing `/Toggle List`) to create collapsible lists within tasks, docs, whiteboards, chat views, text block dashboard cards, and notepads. This feature helps organize large amounts of text into visually pleasing bullet-point lists that can be expanded with the touch of the toggle button.

Real-life scenarios and recommendations

We'll explore real-life scenarios and provide actionable recommendations for maximizing productivity using ClickUp:

- **Start the day in ClickUp's Personal List and add your daily tasks. This list can include checking emails, making phone calls, and running errands**. You can then use tags and priority flags to label these tasks based on urgency and category of work. After you capture tasks and ideas in your Personal List, schedule a time to sort them into the correct project lists.

- **To streamline your strategic planning, consider using ClickUp's toggle lists**. These collapsible lists, created with Slash Commands (/), can help organize complex information. By condensing your knowledge base into a clear format, you can bridge the gap between planning and action.

- **Build a project using a task as the project name and subtasks as the project steps**. Document your process steps and meeting notes in the task description using the toggle list function. Also, use the **/checklist** to add a quick checkbox on line items that don't require admin work to create a task. When you've finished planning, kick off the project steps by priority with start and due dates.

- **Use comments to track meeting notes and ideas in the comment section of a task**. Also, comments can be used to document status updates and collaborate with team members, using toggle lists and checklist function Slash Commands for quick access to large amounts of important information in collaboration without getting overwhelmed.

Now that you have built a base for arranging and prioritizing your tasks, let's change our focus and delve into the importance of time management. The following section will explore methods such as allocating time and task batching. We will uncover how ClickUp's features can significantly enhance your productivity and assist you in accomplishing your goals within a specific timeframe.

Techniques for managing time and boosting productivity

Having good time management skills is crucial to productivity. It enables you to get more done in a certain time while minimizing stress levels.

In this section, we will explore various time management techniques that individuals can apply to their task management. We'll delve into time allocation task batching and how leveraging ClickUp's features can enhance productivity.

Effective time allocation

To manage your time effectively, it's essential to start by understanding how you spend your time and where you invest your time. One way to do this is to log your activities for one day. Afterward, begin to watch the clock while you work. When starting a new task, check the clock and recheck it when finished. As you get better at this habit, you can add your time directly to the time-tracking areas of the tasks in ClickUp. Once you have a picture of how you use your time, you can identify areas where improvements can be made.

Creating a schedule is another strategy for time allocation. Include all tasks such as work, school, and personal commitments in your schedule. Remember to allocate time for breaks and relaxation. Enter these as tasks and experiment with time blocking your schedule.

Lastly, when creating your schedule, you must be realistic about how much time you can dedicate to each task. It's also wise to consider events and interruptions that may arise.

Task batching

Task batching is a technique for managing time. This involves grouping tasks and completing them at the same time. For instance, creating a task to check emails throughout the day designates a time each day for email checking. This helps minimize distractions and allows you to focus on tasks.

Another example of task batching is combining all errands into one trip rather than making separate trips. Similarly, it is a best practice to batch your categories of work together to improve efficiency.

Utilizing ClickUp's features to enhance productivity

While ClickUp doesn't currently offer a dedicated **Time Estimate view**, you can still leverage the built-in time estimate functionality. Assign estimated completion times to tasks and utilize ClickUp's filtering and sorting options based on these estimates. This can help you visualize your workload and manage deadlines effectively.

> **Future feature**
> A dedicated Time Estimate view might be available in future ClickUp updates.

ClickUp offers powerful tools for deadline management:

- **Deadline feature**: Assign deadlines directly to tasks' due dates while creating or editing them. This automatically adds them to your **Home** workspace and the **List view**, organized by due date.

- **List view sorting and filtering**: Utilize ClickUp's robust List view options. Sort your tasks by due date to prioritize your workload and ensure you meet upcoming deadlines. You can also filter tasks by specific date ranges to focus on tasks that are due soon.

In addition to these features, ClickUp provides tools that can enhance productivity, including timers for tracking task durations and identifying areas for improvement in efficiency. Recurring tasks can also be automated to save time and maintain organization. Dependencies enable task linking for better workflow management.

By leveraging these features, you'll be able to save time and streamline your work process effectively:

- **Timers**: Timers allow you to track your time on each task. While working, pay attention to your time on tasks, enter your notes directly in the task, and manually add your time or use the timer like a play button. This can help you identify areas for improvement in efficiency.

- **Recurring tasks**: Recurring tasks allow you to automate tasks that you need to do regularly. Automate your bills, exercise routines, and other routines. Add a **Calendar Meeting** status to your standardized statuses and experiment using ClickUp as a calendar replacement that does not require meeting links or locations. This can save you time and help you stay organized.

- **Dependencies**: With dependencies, you can establish links between tasks. If you have a quick series of project steps with an urgent deadline, add **waiting on** or **blocking dependency** to the tasks. This proves beneficial to ensuring that tasks are completed in the desired sequence. For commands, type `/blocking`, `/waiting`, or `/link to`. Press *Enter* on PC or *Return* on Mac. Search or browse for the task.

Here are a couple of ways you can use ClickUp to boost your productivity:

- **Prioritize your schedule by creating a Time Estimate view**: Start by estimating the time needed for each task, and then organize and schedule them accordingly. Use the **Workload view** to see all your tasks by time estimate and drag and drop your tasks like puzzle blocks. View tasks filtered by **Time estimate** to jump back into your work quickly.

- **Use ClickUp's Calendar view to plan out your week**: Begin by reviewing all tasks due for the week and updating their start and due dates to ensure all priority items are in your schedule. Connect your calendar to ClickUp to see all your tasks and meetings for the day.

- **Prioritize for productivity**: Start your day by dedicating 15-30 minutes to plan your tasks. Focus on identifying top priorities and outlining the steps involved. Consider realistic time estimates for each task, avoiding complex dependencies if possible. This helps you stay focused and avoid feeling overwhelmed.

  ClickUp tips for prioritization are as follows:

  - Use ClickUp's priority system (High, Medium, Low) to categorize your tasks. Then, use the Urgent priority only for tasks to do today.

  - Leverage ClickUp's List view to visually organize tasks based on priority.

Now that you have become adept at managing your time and increasing productivity, let's take your understanding to the next level. In the following section, we will delve into the realm of setting goals and monitoring progress. Explore the effectiveness of SMART goals, discover tracking techniques, and uncover the motivating features within ClickUp that will help you stay on course and accomplish your objectives.

Setting goals and tracking progress

Setting goals and tracking progress are aspects of task management. **SMART** goals are **specific, measurable, achievable, relevant, and time-bound**. By setting goals and regularly monitoring your progress, you'll stay motivated and focused on achieving your objectives. In this section, we'll delve into goal-setting, progress-tracking techniques and learn how ClickUp's features can help you maintain motivation while accomplishing goals.

Setting SMART goals

When setting goals for yourself, it is important to make sure they are SMART so that you are more likely to achieve them. Here in this image, we show you how to set these goals:

Figure 9.4 – SMART goals (https://clickup.com/templates/smart-goals-t-222168692)

Here are some tips for setting SMART goals:

- **Be specific**: For a goal, such as "*get healthier*," be clear about what you want to achieve. For example, aim to lose 10 pounds within a three-month period.

- **Make it measurable**: Ensure your goals are measurable so that you can track your progress effectively. Then, aiming for increased productivity, set a target of completing five daily tasks.

- **Seek achievability**: It's important to set challenging yet attainable goals. If they're too easy, they won't motivate you, and if they're too difficult, you might become discouraged and give up.

- **Stay relevant**: Align your goals with your objectives. For instance, if your aim is getting a promotion, focus on improving your skills and enhancing your job performance at work.

- **Set a deadline for yourself to achieve your goals**: Having a time-bound target is important, as it keeps you motivated and focused.

Effectively tracking progress

Once you've established your goals, it's crucial to track your progress so that you can assess it and make any necessary adjustments.

There are ways to monitor your progress. One approach is to maintain a journal where you can jot down your goals, track your advancement, and reflect on both successes and challenges.

With ClickUp, you can manage your goals through its notepad, docs, tasks, subtasks, and milestones while also tracking your progress toward your goals. Experiment with each possible workflow and select what works best for you.

Leveraging ClickUp's features to maintain motivation and accomplish personal objectives

ClickUp provides features that aid in maintaining motivation and accomplishing personal objectives.

ClickUp's **Goals view** provides a central hub to manage and visualize your progress toward achieving your objectives:

Figure 9.5 – ClickUp's Goals view (https://clickup.com/features/goals)

While the visual layout of the platform might differ slightly from marketing materials, the core features remain consistent. Here's what you can expect:

- **Clear progress tracking**: Monitor the progress of your goals with intuitive visualizations and progress bars, keeping you motivated and focused
- **Measurable targets**: Break down your goals into actionable key results (targets) to track your advancement step by step
- **Centralized management**: You can manage all your goals, update progress information, and collaborate with your team within the familiar ClickUp interface

The following figure illustrates the **Dashboard view**, showcasing how ClickUp's customizable and comprehensive dashboards can streamline your workflow and provide real-time insights into your projects and tasks.

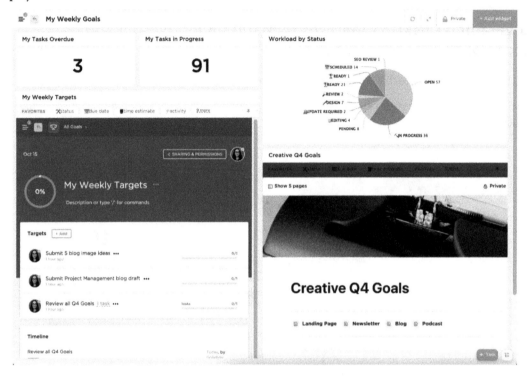

Figure 9.6 – Dashboard view (https://clickup.com/blog/dashboard-examples-in-clickup/)

ClickUp allows you to design customized dashboards that act as your hub for organizing work and tracking progress. While the visual layout within the platform may vary slightly from materials, the core features remain robust. Here's how ClickUp dashboards can be advantageous to you:

- **Personalized command center**: Arrange widgets by dragging and dropping to create a dashboard that showcases your tasks, projects, and objectives, customized to meet your specific requirements

- **Practical insights**: Obtain real-time updates on the progress of tasks, projects, and goals through representations and data

- **Improved concentration and orderliness**: Have a view of your workload and deadlines to ensure you remain focused and on course to achieving success

This can be really helpful when it comes to managing your time and ensuring that you stay on schedule to meet your objectives and deadlines. ClickUp also provides a range of features that can assist you in staying motivated and accomplishing your objectives. These features include the following:

- **Dashboard view**: Use dashboards in your workflow to quickly access your top metrics and key indicators. Add one of the pre-configured dashboards to get started right away. Customize your dashboard as you go or custom program all of your important metrics.

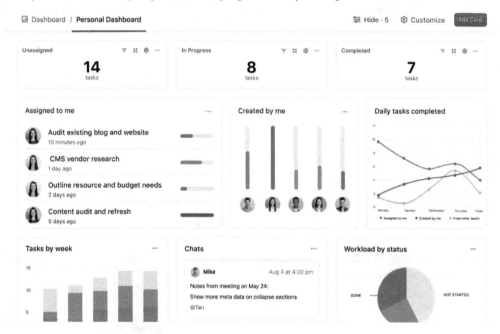

Figure 9.7 – Personalized ClickUp dashboard (https://clickup.com/features/dashboards#productivity)

It serves as a reflection of where your attention lies, guiding you through a satisfying, productive day. Take control of your workday with the ClickUp dashboard. Prioritize tasks, track progress, and get things done.

- **Timeline view**: The ClickUp **Timeline view** lays out your tasks in a visual calendar format, offering a clear view of deadlines and project schedules:

Figure 9.8 – ClickUp's Timeline view (https://help.clickup.com/hc/
en-us/articles/6310399909143-Add-a-Timeline-view)

- **Gantt view**: ClickUp's Gantt view provides a bar-chart-like timeline, ideal for visualizing project dependencies and overall workflow:

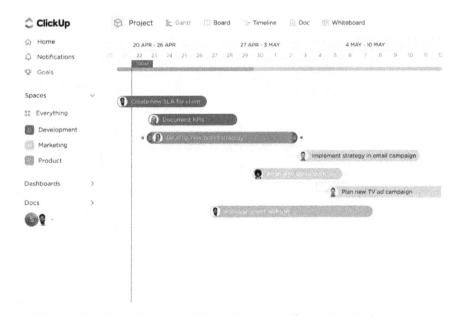

Figure 9.9 – ClickUp's Gantt view (https://clickup.com/features/gantt-chart-view)

- **Reminders:** ClickUp's Reminders feature provides an option for setting task reminders within the platform. Additionally, reminders can be used as an idea management tool. Any time you have an idea or need to be reminded quickly of a task to work on, use your computer or mobile device and add a reminder with the *R* shortcut (make sure to enable hotkeys/shortcuts in your ClickUp settings). Currently, reminders are only visible in your ClickUp **Home** Workspace. You can effortlessly convert them into tasks when you're ready to work on them.

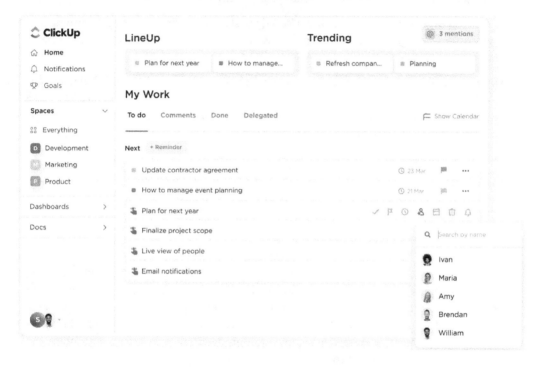

Figure 9.10 – ClickUp's Reminders (https://clickup.com/features/reminders)

Here's a simple guide on how to make the most of them:

- **Quick creation:** Use the /reminder command directly in ClickUp to set reminders for tasks
- **Streamlined organization:** Keep track of all your reminders from your ClickUp **Home** workspace to ensure you meet deadlines effectively
- **Turning reminders into actionable tasks:** When it's time to turn your ideas into actions, use the **Convert Reminder to Task** button and continue working on your priority work with all the features of a task

> **Note**
> Reminders are currently only visible within your ClickUp **Home** Workspace.

Real-life scenarios and recommendations

Here are some ways to leverage ClickUp to maintain motivation and achieve objectives:

- **Start your workflow process with ideas**: Use reminders as ideas throughout the day, and enter them on mobile devices and in the office. When scheduling your workload, convert the reminders to tasks and schedule them into your priority list.

- **Create a central area for goal setting**: Use a dedicated doc or list for strategy planning and goal setting. ClickUp provides lightning-fast ideation-to-action capabilities with tasks to create your planning system.

- **Once you have established your goals, create tasks that will help you accomplish those goals**: In a list, use tasks to outline your plan. Think of it like a table of contents for a book. Then, use tasks to write the contents of the project steps to complete your work, and begin using ClickUp's task features to launch the project.

- **Take advantage of the Timeline view within ClickUp:** See all the project's moving parts.

- **Reference the Gantt view to map out your day effectively:** This ensures you stay aligned with your desired outcomes.

Summary

In this chapter, you explored the intricacies of personal task management using ClickUp, gaining actionable insights applicable to various professional levels. The chapter addressed the needs of solo entrepreneurs and enterprise-level executives involved in project management, offering a strategic guide to effective personal task management. Three main topics were covered: organizing and prioritizing individual tasks, implementing time management and productivity techniques, and setting and tracking progress toward meaningful goals.

The section on organizing and prioritizing personal tasks educated you on structuring tasks in ClickUp and introducing hierarchical lists, labels, and task details. The information proved helpful, emphasizing the significance of adding relevant details to tasks and setting priorities for enhanced focus and efficiency. Practical examples and case studies illustrated the application of ClickUp in creating daily and weekly task lists, showcasing the effectiveness of labels in prioritizing and organizing responsibilities.

Transitioning to time management and productivity techniques, the chapter introduced strategies for effective time allocation, stressing the importance of realistic schedules that include breaks. The proven technique of task batching to streamline activities and increase overall efficiency was explored. ClickUp's features, such as Time Estimate and Due Date views, were highlighted as valuable tools for planning and maintaining productivity. Examples and case studies demonstrated how ClickUp's functionalities enhance personal productivity.

The final topic, goal setting and progress tracking, underscored the significance of setting SMART goals and offered tips for creating meaningful objectives aligned with overall aspirations. The chapter emphasized progress tracking, providing insights into leveraging traditional methods and digital tools such as ClickUp for effective monitoring. ClickUp's features, including Goals view, Timeline view, Progress bars, Reminders, and Comments, were explored as essential components for maintaining motivation and achieving personal objectives.

In the next chapter, you will gain insights into utilizing ClickUp for collaborative project planning involving personal events with friends and family.

Sign up to download your free workbook and productivity resources for each chapter

ClickUp is constantly evolving. Get help and explore each chapter in depth, receive the latest productivity updates and ClickUp tips, and download your free workbook at `http://bluecreative.com/clickup`. Specializing in ClickUp implementation, configurations, systems development, process implementation, and more.

Unger, E. (2024). Clickup. BLUECREATIVE.

`https://bluecreative.com/clickup`

Project Management and Collaborating on Personal Events with Friends and Family

Welcome to *Chapter 10*, where we will explore project management and collaborating on personal events with friends and family. Whether you're organizing a birthday party, a family vacation, or any other private event, this chapter aims to offer valuable insights into effectively planning and collaborating on these special occasions using ClickUp. In this chapter, we're going to cover the following main topics:

- Project management – simplified
- Agile scrum methodology – simplified
- Defining goals and objectives for personal events
- Collaborating and assigning responsibilities
- Managing budgets and resources

By the end of this chapter, you will have gained a holistic understanding of how ClickUp can be harnessed to turn personal event planning into a collaborative project management and organized endeavor. This chapter's insights, tips, and real-world examples provide a valuable resource for individuals looking to create memorable and well-executed events for themselves and their loved ones.

Project management – simplified

"Project management is the process of leading the work of a team to achieve all project goals within the given constraints. This information is usually described in project documentation created at the beginning of the development process. The primary constraints are scope, time, and budget."- Wikipedia

Project management is critical for making personal events successful. Before getting started, clearly define how you'll manage the project. There are two ways to simplify managing and executing your project: essential project management and agile scrum project management.

Essential project management and its terminology

Five phrases come up often when managing projects: project scope, project brief, **statement of work (SOW)**, discovery, and deliverables. Let's take a closer look at this terminology:

- A **project scope** defines the boundaries of a project, outlining what will be done and what will not be done. While project briefs and scopes of work can be interchangeable, depending on their use, they are, in fact, different.

- A **project brief** is a document that outlines the goals and objectives of a project. It is usually created at the beginning of a project and can contain any amount of information. It helps define what the project is and any special requirements and helps us understand the entire project from the client's perspective.

- A **SOW** is a more detailed document that includes the scope of work and other specifics regarding how and when the work will be completed. It describes how the project goals listed in the SOW will be accomplished.

- A **discovery** in project management refers to the initial phase where project stakeholders gather information, identify requirements, and explore potential solutions to define the project's goals and objectives.

- **Deliverables** are the tangible or intangible products, services, or results that are produced by completing a project. The outcomes must be delivered to meet the project objectives and satisfy the stakeholders' requirements.

Agile scrum methodology – simplified

Imagine that you and your team are nearly done with a tough project. You've worked with others in the company to get it done. But suddenly, the client wants changes, messing up your schedule. If this sounds familiar, it might be time to try Agile project management. It helps you quickly adjust while saving resources.

Before agile scrum can be simplified, we must break down the agile methodologies and ceremonies.

Agile ceremonies and methodologies – mindsets and workflows

Agile project management breaks down projects compared to how software companies such as Apple, Google, and Microsoft iterate their software releases by versions. These versions focus on frequent value delivery and getting fast feedback to adapt to emerging changes quickly. It focuses on the following aspects:

- Working on small batches
- Visualizing processes to create transparency
- Working collaboratively with the team/client/customer
- Getting feedback as fast as possible

Understanding how Agile project management operates allows you to promptly adapt to changing requirements and produce higher-quality solutions. Within agile, there are many methodologies and "ceremonies."

Traditional versus Agile project management

In traditional project management, a project manager assigns tasks, which can lead to inefficiencies and information loss. In contrast, Agile projects empower team members to make decisions and actively participate in planning and execution. This shared ownership fosters collaboration and problem-solving, making teams more efficient and motivated.

Continuous improvement

Agile promotes continuous learning throughout the project rather than waiting for a post-project review. This iterative approach allows teams to adapt and improve incrementally.

The following are the four key values of Agile:

- Individuals and interactions over processes and tools
- Working solutions over comprehensive documentation
- Collaboration over contract negotiation
- Responding to change over following a plan

Agile project management methods

Agile project management is an iterative and flexible approach to managing projects, particularly in software development.

Kanban

Kanban focuses on evolutionary change and continuous process improvements through visualizing work, limiting work-in-progress, managing flow, and implementing feedback loops.

Scrum

Scrum is an iterative framework that divides projects into fixed intervals called sprints. It aims to support teams in delivering high-value products creatively. The framework includes three roles: Product Owner, Scrum Master, and Team. The Product Owner manages the product backlog, while the Scrum Master facilitates the team's adherence to Scrum principles. Scrum events include Sprint Planning, Daily Scrum, Sprint Review, and Sprint Retrospective.

Sprint-based Agile project management

Sprints are a unique way to plan, schedule, and execute project work in the Agile framework. They are defined by a timeframe for completing a selected set of tasks from a backlog of prioritized work. Sprints can be recurring or one-time. Backlog meetings such as retrospectives are a mandatory part of the sprint process. The sprint defines the work to be done and who will complete it within a specific period.

A sprint is a defined period during which specific tasks or user stories are completed. It is like a focused sprint toward achieving a set goal within a predetermined timeframe. Sprints empower collaborators to manage a massive amount of work and delegation efficiently, giving them a sense of control over their tasks and time.

It is essential to capture all the tasks or projects that need to be worked on in a backlog. The backlog planning phase involves identifying and defining user stories, which are the results or goals that need to be achieved. These user stories, which are the very essence of the project, become the foundation for planning and executing the work that's most important to you, making the team's work purposeful and impactful.

Once the user stories have been defined, the next step is to manage the execution of these tasks through sprints. A sprint typically has a start date, a due date, and designated timeframes for meetings and check-ins. During a sprint, the team focuses on completing the assigned tasks within the given timeframe.

The backlog replenishment process ensures fresh work is prepared and continuously added to the next backlog. At the same time, ongoing work is replenished based on previous commitments. Keeping an updated backlog of work waiting to be worked on at any moment ensures that the team has a clear view of the tasks and their order of priority.

Sprint-based Agile project management includes various ceremonies or meetings that facilitate effective collaboration and progress tracking. These include backlog meetings, stand-ups, and retrospective meetings. Backlog meetings help review and prioritize the work, stand-ups provide regular check-ins and updates, and retrospective meetings allow for reflection and improvement.

By implementing sprints, collaborators can streamline their workflow, vote on work to be done, and manage a budget that keeps changing within the allocated timeframe. The step-by-step design of sprints allows for flexibility, enabling the team to manage ongoing challenges and changes productively. This flexibility instills a sense of adaptability and capability in the team.

In conclusion, sprint-based Agile project management is a valuable approach that enables teams to break down projects into manageable tasks and execute them efficiently. By utilizing sprints, teams can improve collaboration, track progress, and achieve their project goals effectively.

Defining goals and objectives for personal events

Defining goals and objectives for personal events is essential for planning and executing a successful event. By clearly understanding what you want to achieve with your event, you can make informed decisions about everything, from the budget and venue to the guest list and activities.

Identifying the purpose

The first step in defining goals and objectives is to identify the purpose of your event. What do you hope to achieve by hosting this event? Are you celebrating a special occasion, connecting with friends and family, or raising money for a cause?

Once you know the purpose of your event, you can start to brainstorm specific goals and objectives. For example, if you're hosting a birthday party, your goals might be to celebrate the birthday person uniquely and to create a fun and festive atmosphere. If you're hosting a charity fundraiser, your goals might be to raise a certain amount of money and to increase awareness of the cause.

Once you have set your objectives and targets, ClickUp's Custom Fields enable you to capture details to guarantee a seamless event execution. These personalized fields act as information points that can be included in tasks to help you customize your planning process according to your requirements. For example, if one of your goals is to provide *food and beverages* at a birthday celebration, you could establish a Custom Field named *Dietary Preferences* to monitor any guest allergies or dietary limitations. This way, you can ensure that everyone enjoys a pleasant dining experience.

Desired outcomes

When defining goals and objectives, it's also essential to consider the desired outcomes of your event. What do you want your guests to experience? What do you want them to take away from the event?

Your desired outcomes might be as follows:

- A memorable and enjoyable experience
- A stronger sense of connection with friends and family
- Awareness of a cause
- Support for a charity
- Promotion of your business or brand

Critical elements of successful personal events

No matter the type of personal event, a few critical elements are essential for success:

- **Planning**: Thorough planning is critical to executing a successful personal event. This includes developing a budget, timeline, and guest list. You should also create a contingency plan in case of unexpected events.

- **Organization**: Once you have a plan, it is crucial to stay organized. This includes keeping track of RSVPs, vendor contracts, and other important details.

- **Communication**: Communication is key to ensuring that your event runs smoothly. Communicate with your guests, vendors, and any other people involved in the event planning process.

- **Flexibility**: Things don't always go according to plan, so it is essential to be flexible. Be prepared to adapt to changes as needed.

Examples

Here are some examples of goals and objectives for personal events:

Events	Goals	Objectives
Birthday party	Celebrate the birthday person in a unique and memorable way	• Have a fun and festive atmosphere • Serve delicious food and drinks • Play music that the birthday person enjoys
Wedding	Create a romantic and unforgettable wedding experience for the bride and groom and their guests	• Have a beautiful ceremony and reception venue • Serve delicious food and drinks • Play music that the bride and groom enjoy • Gather friends and family to celebrate

Events	Goals	Objectives
Charity fundraiser	Raise money for a worthy cause	• Attract a large number of guests • Serve delicious food and drinks • Hold a silent auction or other fundraising activities • Raise a certain amount of money for the charity

Table 10.1 – Sample goals and objectives for personal events

Ensuring that the goals and objectives for personal events are clarified is important to help you plan, ensure all the necessary resources are allocated effectively, and execute successful celebrations.

Building out the project in ClickUp

With these examples, we have three projects we can implement in ClickUp and apply tasks with Custom Fields:

- The *Birthday Party Project* is set as a top-layer task and is the project
- The goals are milestones in ClickUp and have a diamond-shaped symbol.
- ClickUp offers progress bars to visualize progress toward completing tasks. These bars are typically represented by a **circle symbol** and can help you stay motivated.

> **Note**
> Progress bars are primarily available for tasks with the **Task** type.

Now, we can begin assigning and scheduling tasks.

ClickUp offers a range of customization options that can enhance your event planning experience:

- **Custom Fields**: You can customize fields to suit your event requirements. For example, you could add fields such as "Gift Suggestions" or "Dietary Preferences" for guests attending a birthday party. Custom Fields can be used to personalize tasks further and help you capture details directly within each task.
- **Task relationships**: You can provide connections between tasks to maintain a sequence. For instance, finalizing the guest list may depend on choosing the venue. ClickUp adjusts task schedules automatically based on these relationships ensuring progress.

- **Gantt view**: You can visualize the timeline of your event using Gantt charts. These charts display task overlaps and potential bottlenecks, allowing you to make decisions. ClickUp's interactive Gantt charts allow you to make modifications to task durations and dependencies.

By utilizing these functionalities, you can elevate your event planning within ClickUp to create a platform for all your needs, leading to a well-coordinated and successful event. While our examples and templates offer a great starting point, some features, such as Custom Fields, may require a ClickUp paid plan for full functionality. Note that users can change anything they see to fit their needs, ensuring a stress-free and successful outcome.

For additional value, ClickUp integrates with various apps to enhance your experience. Here are two key integrations to consider:

- **Google Calendar integration**: ClickUp seamlessly integrates with Google Calendar, allowing you to sync events between the two platforms. This ensures that all your planned tasks and events appear on your Google Calendar, providing a holistic view of your schedule and keeping you organized. Users must create a new Google Calendar specifically for ClickUp integration to avoid privacy concerns.

- **Slack integration**: Integrate ClickUp with Slack to streamline communication and collaboration with your team or family members involved in event planning. You can create and assign tasks directly within Slack channels, receive notifications, and discuss details without switching between different apps.

By leveraging these integrations, you can improve communication, manage your time more effectively, and ensure everyone involved in your event planning is on the same page.

With ClickUp's customizable features, you can tailor your event planning experience to fit your specific needs, ensuring a stress-free and successful outcome:

- **Birthday party**: With ClickUp, you have the option to craft a task template specifically tailored for planning your birthday celebration. This template can encompass all the tasks that must be accomplished, such as sending invitations, arranging for food and beverages, and beautifying the venue. Each task can be assigned to team members, guaranteeing that everyone is clear on their roles:

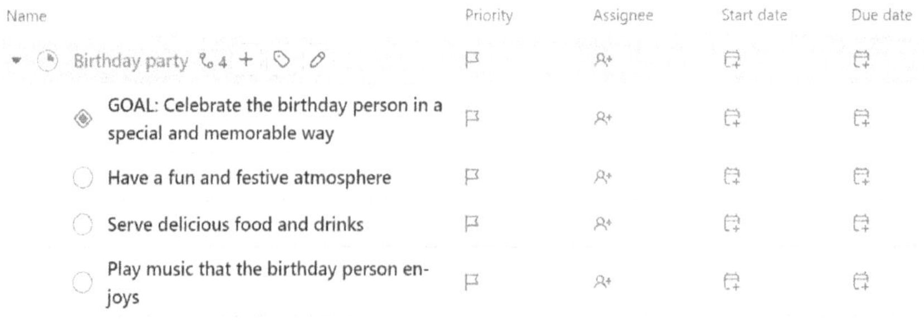

Name	Priority	Assignee	Start date	Due date
Birthday party 4 +				
GOAL: Celebrate the birthday person in a special and memorable way				
Have a fun and festive atmosphere				
Serve delicious food and drinks				
Play music that the birthday person enjoys				

Figure 10.1 – Birthday party event example using ClickUp

Moreover, deadlines can be set for each task to ensure everything stays on schedule. Nothing slips through the cracks. This organized approach not only assists in staying on top of things but also streamlines the planning process, making it more effective and less overwhelming.

- **Wedding**: Planning your wedding with a board streamlines the process, allowing you to oversee every aspect of your day efficiently. You can list tasks for all the elements, such as securing the venue, selecting outfits for the bride and groom, and deciding on the reception menu. Each task can be personalized with descriptions, deadlines, and priority levels for clarity:

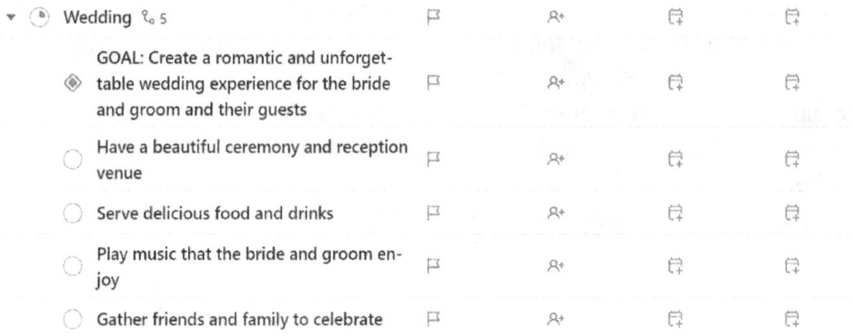

Figure 10.2 – Wedding event example using ClickUp

Moreover, you can assign tasks to your support team – family members, wedding coordinators, or friends – who can assist with duties. By setting timelines for each task, you ensure that everything is completed promptly, easing stress and providing a planning experience. This structured approach enables you to monitor progress, manage expectations, and guarantee no detail goes unnoticed, ultimately resulting in an orchestrated and unforgettable wedding celebration.

- **Charity fundraiser**: Setting up a board for your charity event can help you streamline and organize all the planning details. Begin by listing tasks for activities such as securing sponsors, promoting the event, and arranging the venue. Each task should include descriptions, deadlines, and priority levels to guide everyone involved. You can assign these tasks to team members or volunteers, ensuring accountability in each area:

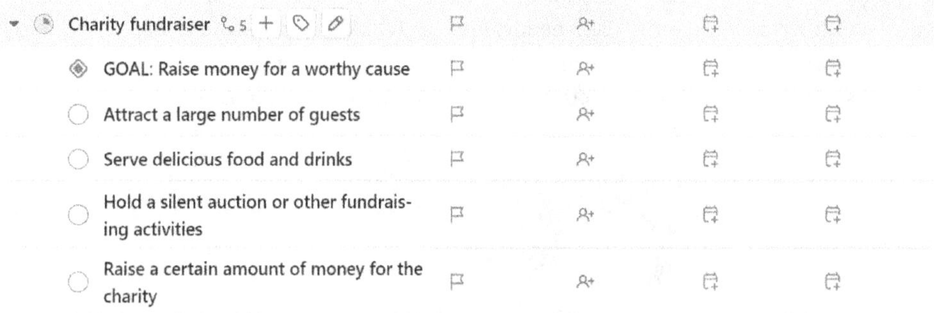

Figure 10.3 – Charity fundraiser event example using ClickUp

By setting deadlines, you'll keep things on track. Ensure that everything is ready on time. This structured approach fosters effective communication, which increases the chances of a charity fundraiser doing well when a well-coordinated effort is made.

Real-life scenarios and case studies

John dreams of a heartwarming family reunion, reconnecting relatives after years apart. To bridge the generational gap and create lasting memories, he prioritizes clear goals and utilizes ClickUp. ClickUp becomes his central hub for planning. Tasks such as activities, meals, decorations, and even a family photoshoot are meticulously planned. John capitalizes on family strengths, assigning tasks such as "Sports Tournament" to his athletic cousin while his culinary-gifted aunt oversees meal planning. A Custom Field named "Dietary Restrictions" ensures everyone enjoys the meals. ClickUp chat fosters excitement by allowing family members to share activity ideas, photos, and memories. Through ClickUp's collaborative features, John transforms reunion planning from a solo mission to a collective effort, guaranteeing a successful weekend filled with laughter, shared stories, and a renewed sense of family connection.

Now that you understand your event's goals and objectives, let's discuss the importance of working and sharing tasks. Here, you will discover how to leverage the support of your friends and family by efficiently delegating responsibilities and how to turn your event planning from an endeavor into a successful collaboration. Let's embrace the power of teamwork and witness your event vision come to fruition effortlessly.

Collaborating and assigning responsibilities

Collaboration and task delegation are essential for planning and executing successful personal events. Working with friends and family can help you share the workload and make the planning process more enjoyable.

Assigning tasks in ClickUp

Thanks to ClickUp's user interface and powerful collaboration tools, assigning tasks is easy. Users can change anything they see to fit their needs, making ClickUp a versatile platform for various workflows. A crucial aspect is inviting people to join ClickUp, which makes it easy to assign tasks to team members (refer to the following section for details on inviting guests):

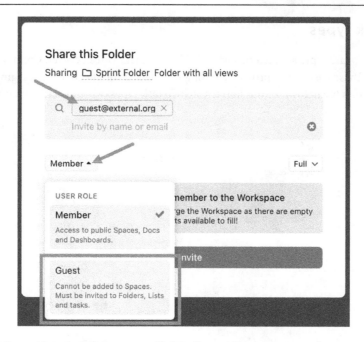

Figure 10.4 – Inviting guests to ClickUp (https://help.clickup.com/hc/en-us/
articles/6310498173079-Invite-people-to-join-your-Workspace)

Here's how you can invite guests to ClickUp:

1. Go to the workspace or project where you want collaborators:

    I.   Click on the **Invite** button and go to **Settings**.

    II.   Enter the email addresses of those you wish to invite.

    III. Customize their permissions based on their roles and set the required access levels.

2. Send the invites. Guests can start collaborating on tasks once they are accepted.

Inviting guests to ClickUp allows you to effectively assign tasks to team members, external partners, or clients for communication and streamlined project management. Everyone on board the same platform ensures collaboration, boosting productivity and project outcomes.

ClickUp task types

The starter ClickUp task types are included with all ClickUp plans (Free Forever, Unlimited, Business, and Enterprise). These basic types provide a strong foundation for effectively managing your tasks and projects. Here's a breakdown of the starter ClickUp task types, which users can customize to fit their needs:

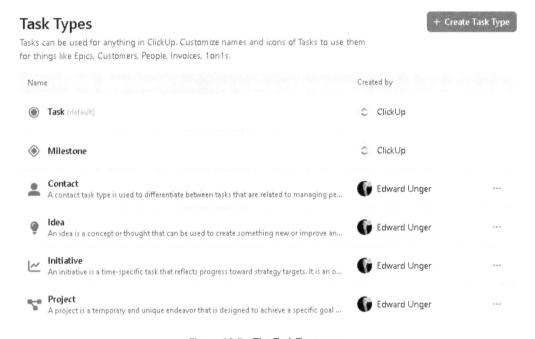

Figure 10.5 – The Task Types page

Let's take a closer look:

- **Task (default)**: A task represents a job that must be completed within a set timeframe or by a deadline to achieve work-related objectives. It acts as a component of a job that distinguishes between parts of a project. Tasks may vary in complexity and can be divided into subtasks and checklists. Within ClickUp, tasks serve as the elements of work that can be tailored to certain needs and segmented into subtasks and checklists.

- **Milestone**: A milestone is a significant event or achievement in a project that marks a specific point in the project timeline. It is a way to measure progress and ensure that the project is on track. Milestones can signify the completion of a significant phase of work, the start or end of a project, or any other important event.

- **Contact**: A contact task type differentiates between tasks related to managing people, vendors, clients, and accounts, a customized ClickUp CRM system, email contact management within ClickUp, and more.

- **Idea**: An idea is a concept or thought that's used to create something new or improve an existing product, service, or process. It is a mental representation of something that does not yet exist but has the potential to be developed into something tangible. Ideas can come from anywhere and anyone, and they are often the starting point for innovation and creativity.

- **Initiative**: An initiative is a time-specific task that reflects progress toward strategy targets. It is an organization's way of prioritizing and achieving a goal or vision. Initiatives can be internal or external campaigns that seek to improve the work environment, company culture, business strategy, services, processes, and more.

- **Project**: Projects are temporary and unique endeavors that are designed to achieve a specific goal or objective. They are a sequence of interrelated tasks that are executed over a fixed period and within certain limitations. Projects can be simple or elaborate, but all projects can be broken down into milestones and tasks that need to be completed to achieve them. Projects can be part of initiatives, small or large, and involve considerable money, personnel, and equipment.

Effective communication

The key to successful collaboration is effective communication. Be sure to communicate clearly with your collaborators about your goals and expectations. It is also essential to be open to feedback and suggestions.

Here are some tips for effective communication:

- **Be clear and concise**: When communicating with your collaborators, be clear and concise in your instructions and requests. Avoid using jargon or technical terms that your collaborators may not understand.

- **Be specific**: When assigning tasks to your collaborators, be as specific as possible. This will help them understand what you need them to do and when you need them to do it.

- **Set deadlines**: When assigning tasks, be sure to set realistic deadlines. This will help to ensure that your collaborators have enough time to complete the tasks without feeling overwhelmed.

- **Be flexible**: Things sometimes go differently than planned, so your communication must be flexible. If something unexpected happens, be prepared to adjust your plans and communicate the changes to your collaborators.

Task delegation

Task delegation is another important aspect of collaboration. When delegating tasks, it is vital to consider your collaborators' skills and experience. You should also make sure that the tasks are appropriate for their level of responsibility.

Here are a couple of ways to delegate or assign tasks in ClickUp:

- Assigning during task creation:

    I.   To start creating a task, click on the + button and select **Task** or select an existing task.

    Look for the **Assignee** field, usually denoted by a person icon.

    II.   Click the icon to select the person to whom you want to delegate the task. You can also search for team members by name and pick them from a list.

- Delegating from existing tasks. There are various methods you can use to delegate tasks you've set up:

    - **List view**:

    I.   Navigate to the **List view** area, which includes the task you wish to assign.

    II.   Open the task by clicking on it.

    III.   Find the **Assignee** field (person icon). To assign someone, follow the steps mentioned for *Assigning during task creation*.

    - **Board view**:

    I.   In the **Board view** area, locate and select the task you want to delegate.

    II.   Click and hold the task to drag it.

    III.   Move the task by dragging it onto another team member's picture or a team name (if you want to assign it to a team).

- Assigning the task by dropping it onto the selected person or team:

    IV.   You can assign individual tasks individually by choosing their names in the **Assignee** section.

    V.   ClickUp provides task delegation methods, such as slash commands, /, or bulk actions. These alternatives may be better suited for users or specific workflows.

Following these guidelines, you can efficiently distribute tasks among your team members in ClickUp, ensuring responsibility and smooth project progression.

Here are some tips for task delegation:

- **Choose the right person for the job**: When delegating a task, consider the skills and experience of your collaborators. Choose someone with the skills and knowledge necessary to complete the task successfully.

- **Provide clear instructions**: When delegating a task, be sure to provide clear and concise instructions. Explain what needs to be done, when it needs to be done, and what resources are available.

- **Set clear expectations**: When delegating a task, be sure to set clear expectations. Let your collaborators know what level of quality and performance you expect.

- **Provide support**: Once you have delegated a task, be sure to support your collaborators. Let them know you are available to answer questions and assist as needed.

Utilizing ClickUp's collaboration features

ClickUp offers several features that can help you to collaborate effectively on personal events.

One of its most valuable features is the ability to create and assign tasks. You can create tasks for individual collaborators or groups of collaborators and assign deadlines and priorities to them.

Another helpful feature is the ability to create comments and discussions on tasks. This allows you to communicate with your collaborators about the task, ask questions, and provide feedback.

ClickUp also offers several other features that can be helpful for collaboration, such as the following:

- **Boards**: Boards allow you to visualize your workflow and see how tasks progress:

Figure 10.6 – Clickup's Board view (https://clickup.com/features/kanban-board)

- **Calendars**: ClickUp's **Calendar** view offers a powerful tool to visualize your tasks and plan your schedule effectively. While the exact layout might differ slightly from marketing materials, the core functionality remains robust:

Figure 10.7 – Clickup's Calendar view (https://clickup.com/features/calendar-view)

Here's what you can expect:

- **Schedule tasks with ease**: Drag and drop tasks directly onto the calendar to visually plan your schedule and manage deadlines
- **Multiple views**: Choose between day, week, or month views to customize your calendar according to your planning needs
- **Quick access and management**: View and manage task details directly from the calendar interface, ensuring smooth workflow management

- **Files**: Files allow you to share and store files with collaborators in a central location:

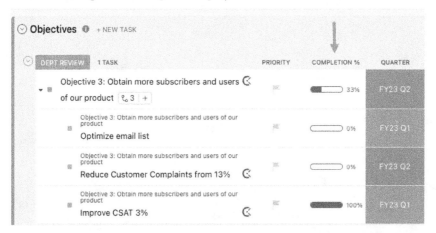

Share this Doc
Sharing all pages of 📄 Doc Doc

| Invite by name or email | Invite |

🌐 Public link ⓘ

🔗 Private link ⓘ   Copy link

⬇ Export Doc ⓘ   Export

◎ Protect Doc ⓘ

SHARE WITH

› 🔵 ACME Marketing and Rocket Fuel [Workspace]

› ▢ **Content team** ⓘ

› 👥 People

ⓘ This Doc is private   🔒 Make Public

Share this Doc   ⌄
Sharing all pages of 📄 Test Doc

| Invite by name or email | Invite |

🌐 Public link ⓘ

🔗 Private link ⓘ   Copy link

⬇ Export Doc ⓘ   Export

◎ Protect Doc ⓘ

SHARE WITH

› 🔵 ACME Marketing and Rocket Fuel

› ▢ Content team ⓘ

PDF PDF

HTML HTML

M↓ Markdown

Figure 10.8 – Clickup – sharing or exporting a file or document (https://help.
clickup.com/hc/en-us/articles/6325333637271-Share-Docs)

- **Progress bars**: ClickUp provides a handy progress bar function that allows you to see how far along you are in accomplishing your tasks and objectives, helping you remain motivated and on track. Progress bars work best when you use a parent task as a project and use the subtasks for all the tasks required to complete the project:

⌄ **Objectives** ⓘ   + NEW TASK

DEPT REVIEW	1 TASK	PRIORITY	COMPLETION %	QUARTER
⌄ ▣ Objective 3: Obtain more subscribers and users ⓒ of our product 👥 3 +			33%	FY23 Q2
▢ Objective 3: Obtain more subscribers and users of our product **Optimize email list**			0%	FY23 Q1
▢ Objective 3: Obtain more subscribers and users of our product **Reduce Customer Complaints from 13%** ⓒ			0%	FY23 Q2
▢ Objective 3: Obtain more subscribers and users of our product **Improve CSAT 3%** ⓒ			100%	FY23 Q1

Figure 10.9 – ClickUp's progress bar (https://help.clickup.com/hc/en-us/
articles/6327987972119-Use-ClickUp-to-track-goals-and-OKRs)

- **Automatic or manual option**: You can decide whether to use a progress bar that adjusts according to subtasks, checklists, and comments or opt for one that reflects your estimated overall completion progress

- **Monitor your progress**: Progress bars visually show how much progress you've made and what tasks or goals still need attention

> **Note**
> Nested subtask progress is not included in the **Progress (Auto)** rollup.

Bonus – ClickUp templates

> **Note**
> These templates aren't compatible with the ClickUp Free Forever plan.

ClickUp's event planning template

ClickUp's event planning template is a tool that was created to make planning and organizing events such as celebrations, weddings, charity events, and more easier. It comes with views such as **List**, **Board**, and **Calendar** to help users manage tasks, schedules, resources, and budgets efficiently:

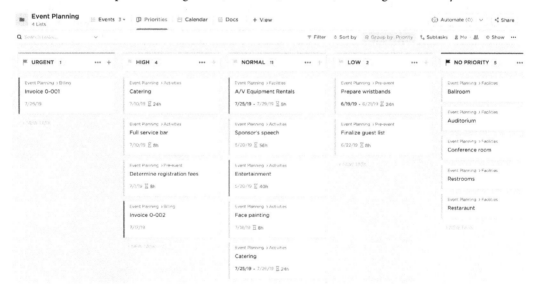

Figure 10.10 – ClickUp's event planning template (https://clickup.
com/templates/event-planning-t-4389476)

Moreover, this template allows customization through features such as Custom Statuses, Custom Fields, and Docs so that users can adjust the planning process to suit their requirements. By enabling task assignments, deadline setting, progress tracking, and team collaboration capabilities, ClickUp's event management template simplifies event planning complexities for execution and successful results.

Clickup's Simple Budget template

ClickUp's user-friendly **Simple Budget** template is a tool that helps users effectively manage their finances. It offers an interface for organizing income, expenses, and savings objectives. Users can personalize categories to distribute funds across their budget and monitor expenditure trends:

#	TASK NAME	JANUARY	FEBRUARY	MARCH	APRIL	MAY	JUNE	JULY	AUGUST	SEPTEMBER	OCTOBER	NOVEMBER	DECEMBER	SUBTOTAL
	Income (6)													
1	Designer	$10,000	$10,000	$10,000	$10,000	$10,000	$10,000	$10,000	$10,000	$10,000	$10,000	$10,000	$10,000	$120,000
2	Virtual Assistance	$15,000	$15,000	$15,000	$15,000	$15,000	$15,000	$15,000	$15,000	$15,000	$15,000	$15,000	$15,000	$180,000
3	Dropshipping	$1,200	$1,200	$1,200	$1,200	$1,200	$1,200	$1,200	$1,200	$1,200	$1,200	$1,200	$1,200	$14,400
4	Stocks	$50	$50	$50	$50	$50	$50	$50	$50	$50	$50	$50	$50	$600
5	Crypto	$50	$50	$50	$50	$50	$50	$50	$50	$50	$50	$50	$50	$600
6	Allowance from Brothers	$500	$500	$500	$500	$500	$500	$500	$500	$500	$500	$500	$500	$6,000
	+ New task													
	Expense (22)													
1	Groceries	-$100	-$100	-$100	-$100	-$100	-$100	-$100	-$100	-$100	-$100	-$100	-$100	-$1,200
2	Food	-$200	-$200	-$200	-$200	-$200	-$200	-$200	-$200	-$200	-$200	-$200	-$200	-$2,400
3	Fuel	-$20	-$20	-$20	-$20	-$20	-$20	-$20	-$20	-$20	-$20	-$20	-$20	-$240
4	Insurance	-$5	-$5	-$5	-$5	-$5	-$5	-$5	-$5	-$5	-$5	-$5	-$5	-$60
5	Car Wash	$0	-$10	$0	-$10	$0	-$10	$0	-$10	$0	-$10	$0	-$10	-$60
6	Cable TV	-$8	-$8	-$8	-$8	-$8	-$8	-$8	-$8	-$8	-$8	-$8	-$8	-$96
7	Netflix Subscription	-$10	-$10	-$10	-$10	-$10	-$10	-$10	-$10	-$10	-$10	-$10	-$10	-$120
8	Spotify	-$3	-$3	-$3	-$3	-$3	-$3	-$3	-$3	-$3	-$3	-$3	-$3	-$36
9	Movies	$0	-$6	$0	$0	-$6	$0	$0	-$6	$0	$0	-$6	$0	-$24
10	Emergency Fund	-$500	-$500	-$500	-$500	-$500	-$500	-$500	-$500	-$500	-$500	-$500	-$500	-$6,000
11	Vitamins	-$10	$0	-$10	$0	-$10	$0	-$10	$0	-$10	$0	-$10	$0	-$60
12	Gym Membership	-$20	-$20	-$20	-$20	-$20	-$20	-$20	-$20	-$20	-$20	-$20	-$20	-$240
13	Credit Card Payments	-$250	-$250	-$250	-$250	-$250	-$250	-$250	-$250	-$250	-$250	-$250	-$250	-$3,000
14	Air Fares	-$2,000	$0	$0	-$2,000	$0	$0	-$2,000	$0	$0	-$2,000	$0	$0	-$8,000
15	Travel Fund	-$5,000	$0	$0	-$5,000	$0	$0	-$5,000	$0	$0	-$5,000	$0	$0	-$20,000
16	Laundry	-$5	-$5	-$5	-$5	-$5	-$5	-$5	-$5	-$5	-$5	-$5	-$5	-$60
17	Accommodations	-$300	$0	$0	-$300	$0	$0	-$300	$0	$0	-$300	$0	$0	-$1,200
18	Clothes	-$100	-$100	-$100	-$100	-$100	-$100	-$100	-$100	-$100	-$100	-$100	-$100	-$1,200
19	Haircut	-$200	$0	-$200	$0	-$200	$0	-$200	$0	-$200	$0	-$200	$0	-$1,200
		$14,415	$21,912	$21,719	$14,649	$21,713	$21,979	$14,429	$21,911	$21,719	$14,618	$21,719	$21,934	$232,604

Figure 10.11 – ClickUp's Simple Budget template (https://clickup.com/templates/simple-budget-t-211273050)

Additionally, the template enables users to establish budget boundaries, track their progress, and generate reports for financial insights. In summary, ClickUp's **Simple Budget** template provides a way for both individuals and businesses to stay on top of their matters and make informed money-related choices.

Clickup's Budget Proposal template

ClickUp's **Budget Proposal** template is a tool that assists users in creating proposals for budget planning. It offers a format to outline goals, expected expenses, projected revenues, and funding needs for different projects. The template includes sections for specifying budget categories, justifying expenses, detailing strategies, and providing supporting data or analysis. Users can customize the proposal with features and formatting choices to meet requirements and preferences:

Figure 10.12 – ClickUp's Budget Proposal template (https://clickup.
com/templates/budget-proposal-kkmvq-6188884)

Furthermore, ClickUp's **Budget Proposal** template promotes teamwork by allowing real-time collaboration through editing, commenting, and sharing options. Overall, this template provides an effective solution for crafting budget proposals that convey financial plans and goals effectively.

Now that we've unlocked the power of collaboration, in the next section, we'll delve into managing budgets and resources. You'll discover how to make every dollar count and how to optimize your resources to ensure your event is financially sound and wildly successful.

Managing budgets and resources

Managing budgets and resources is essential for planning and executing successful personal events. By carefully planning your budget and allocating your resources effectively, you can avoid overspending and ensure your event succeeds.

Setting a budget

The first step to managing your budget is to set a realistic budget for your event. Consider the costs of your event, such as food and drinks, venue rental, decorations, and entertainment. Once you have a good understanding of your costs, you can begin to set a budget.

Here are some tips for setting a budget:

- **Be realistic**: When setting a budget for your event, it is essential to be realistic and consider the cost of things.

- **Prioritize your expenses**: Once you have a good understanding of your costs, prioritize your expenses. This will help you to decide where to allocate your resources.

- **Be flexible**: Things sometimes go differently than planned, so it is important to be flexible with your budget. If something unexpected happens, be prepared to adjust your budget accordingly.

Allocating resources effectively

Once you have set a budget, you need to allocate your resources effectively. This means deciding where to spend your money and how to use your time and energy.

Here are some tips for allocating resources effectively:

- **Prioritize your tasks**: Once you have a list of everything that needs to be done, prioritize your tasks. This will help you to focus on the most critical tasks first.

- **Delegate tasks**: If possible, delegate tasks to friends and family members. This will free up your time to focus on the most important tasks.

- **Use tools and resources**: Several tools and resources are available to help you plan and execute your event. Take advantage of these tools and resources to save time and money.

ClickUp for expense management (workarounds)

While ClickUp doesn't offer a dedicated budgeting feature, you can leverage its functionalities to manage expenses for personal events:

- **Track expenses with Custom Fields**: Create Custom Fields for specific expense categories ("Transportation," "Food," and others) and use them within tasks to categorize expenses.

- **Utilize List Views and reporting**: Create List Views to see all tasks related to your event. Utilize ClickUp's reporting features to analyze spending patterns (available in higher plans).

ClickUp also offers several other features that can help with tracking expenses and managing resources:

- **Reports**: Reports allow you to generate reports on your expenses and resources. This can help you track your spending and identify areas where you can save money.

- **Timelines**: Timelines allow you to see your upcoming tasks and events in a single view. This can help you plan your time and ensure you have enough resources to complete your tasks.

- **Notifications**: You can set up notifications to notify you when your expenses exceed your budget or when you run out of resources. This can help you stay on track with your budget and avoid overspending.

Examples

Here are some examples of how you can use ClickUp to track expenses and manage resources for personal events:

- **Birthday party**: You can create a ClickUp budget for your birthday party and add all your anticipated expenses. You can then track your actual expenses against your budget to see how you spend your money.

- **Wedding**: You can create a ClickUp budget for your wedding and add all your anticipated expenses. You can then track your actual expenses against your budget to see how you spend your money. You can also create ClickUp resources for people, equipment, and other materials. You can then assign resources to tasks and projects to ensure they are used efficiently.

- **Charity fundraiser**: You can create a ClickUp budget for your charity fundraiser and add all of your anticipated expenses. You can then track your actual expenses against your budget to see how you spend your money. You can also create ClickUp resources for people, equipment, and other materials. You can then assign resources to tasks and projects to ensure they are used efficiently.

Bonus – ClickUp templates

The following are some additional ClickUp templates you can use:

> **Note**
>
> These templates aren't compatible with the ClickUp Free Forever plan.

- **Personal Budget**: Creating a budget comes with advantages. It allows people to recognize their spending habits, empowering them to choose and prioritize important long-term objectives such as retirement or college savings. A budget improves your ability to adhere to plans and reach goals efficiently while allowing for flexibility in adjusting expenses when necessary:

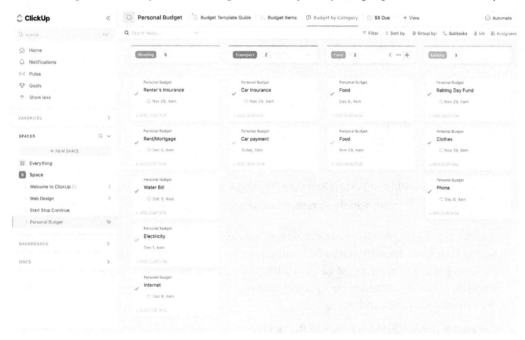

Figure 10.13 – ClickUp's Personal Budget template. (https://clickup. com/templates/personal-budget-t-180546810)

Additionally, it helps individuals prepare for costs, reducing the impact of expenses on their financial situation. Critical components of a personal budget consist of income, savings, essentials, discretionary spending, and debt repayments. While a budget spreadsheet can do the job, free budgeting templates, such as the one provided in ClickUp, offer features and are user-friendly.

- **Resource Planning:** The **Resource Planning** template in ClickUp offers a streamlined approach to allocating resources within a team or department, enhancing project efficiency and organization. This template lets users visualize resource capacity through the built-in **Workload** view, ensuring optimal resource allocation and workload management. With resource planning being a crucial aspect of project success, ClickUp's template helps teams maintain deadlines, budgets, and morale. It facilitates task and resource visualization in one place, optimizing workloads and aligning teams for collective success:

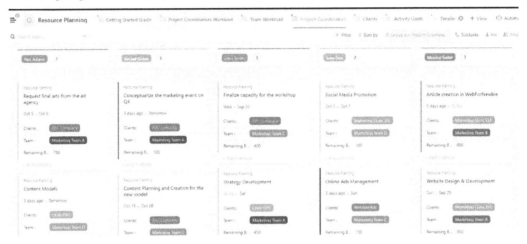

Figure 10.14 – ClickUp's Resource Planning template. (https://clickup. com/templates/resource-planning-t-200533044)

Additionally, the template helps users avoid resource over-allocation, maximize project completion within deadlines, identify potential conflicts, and improve organizational alignment with business goals. Key elements of ClickUp's **Resource Planning** template include customizable statuses, fields, views, and robust project management features such as time tracking, tags, dependency warnings, and more.

- **Expense Report:** ClickUp's **Expense Report** template keeps your business expenses in check and organized. This user-friendly template simplifies the process of recording, categorizing, and predicting expenses, ensuring tracking and efficient resource management. With features such as statuses and fields, you can easily monitor the status of each expense and input important details such as dates, recipients, and amounts:

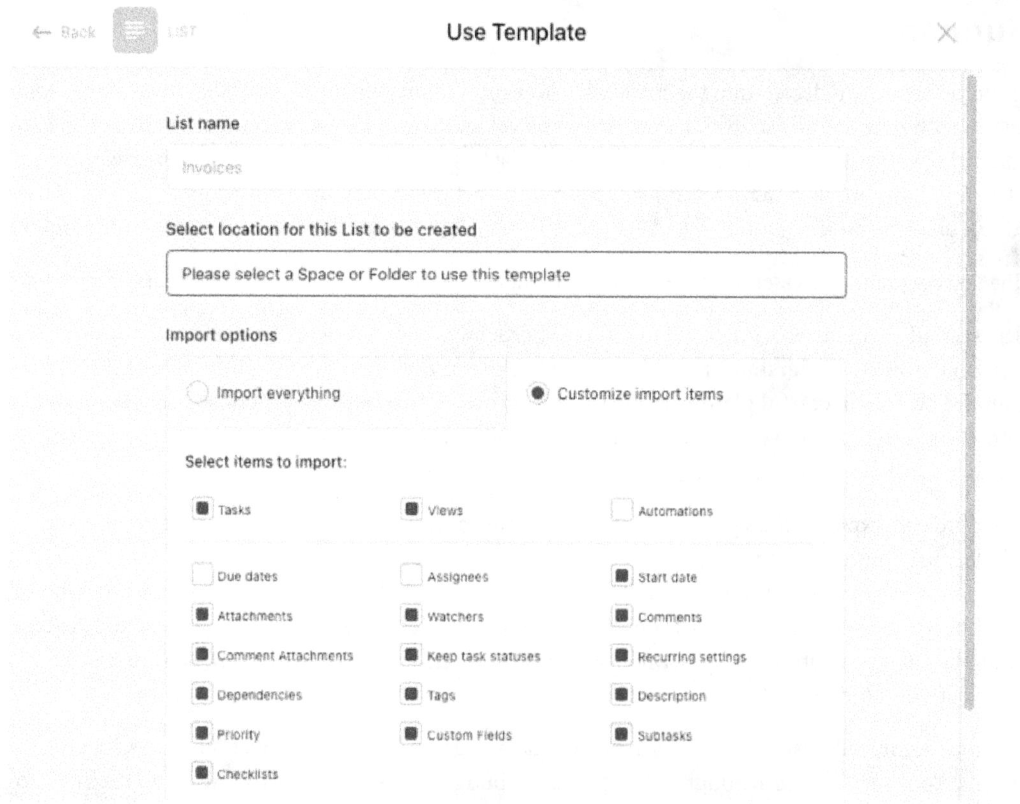

← Back   LIST   Use Template   ✕

List name

Invoices

Select location for this List to be created

Please select a Space or Folder to use this template

Import options

○ Import everything   ● Customize import items

Select items to import:

☑ Tasks	☑ Views	☐ Automations
☐ Due dates	☐ Assignees	☑ Start date
☑ Attachments	☑ Watchers	☑ Comments
☑ Comment Attachments	☑ Keep task statuses	☑ Recurring settings
☑ Dependencies	☑ Tags	☑ Description
☑ Priority	☑ Custom Fields	☑ Subtasks
☑ Checklists		

Figure 10.15 – ClickUp's Expense Report template. (https://clickup.
com/templates/expenses-report-kkmvq-6104128)

ClickUp's interface and project management tools make expense tracking a breeze. They facilitate reimbursement to staff members and enable an insightful analysis of spending habits for potential cost-saving opportunities. Whether you need to print, modify, or tailor the template to suit your business requirements, ClickUp's **Expense Report** template has got you covered with all the tools to keep you organized and make the most of your budget.

Summary

In this chapter, you delved into the intricacies of project management and collaboration for personal events with friends and family. This chapter was a valuable resource for individuals orchestrating and managing various occasions, including birthday parties, family vacations, and other private events. Structured around four main topics, we covered project management, defining goals and objectives for personal events, collaborating and assigning responsibilities, and managing budgets and resources.

The first part reviewed essential project management and Agile scrum project management frameworks.

The second segment provided insights into the crucial process of defining goals and objectives for personal events. Understanding the event's purpose and envisioning desired outcomes laid the foundation for successful planning. Real-life instances illustrated the practical application of this knowledge, emphasizing planning, organization, communication, and flexibility as critical elements for successful personal events.

The third part explored the significance of collaboration and task delegation in effective event planning. You learned how to communicate goals, provide specific instructions, set deadlines, and foster flexibility. Task delegation was portrayed as a collaborative effort, highlighting the importance of choosing the right person for each task. Practical examples demonstrated how ClickUp's collaboration features could be effectively utilized in personal event planning, including task creation, comments, boards, calendars, and file sharing.

The final section addressed the critical aspect of managing budgets and resources for successful personal events. You were guided through setting realistic budgets, prioritizing expenses, and maintaining flexibility. Resource allocation was explored, emphasizing task prioritization, effective delegation, and the use of ClickUp's features for efficient budget management and resource allocation. Real-world examples demonstrated the practical application of ClickUp in scenarios such as tracking expenses for a birthday party or managing resources for a charity fundraiser.

In the next chapter, you will further expand your knowledge of using ClickUp for efficient household chore management and responsibility allocation.

Sign up to download your free workbook and productivity resources for each chapter

ClickUp is constantly evolving. Get help and explore each chapter in depth, receive the latest productivity updates and ClickUp tips, and download your free workbook at `http://bluecreative.com/clickup`. Specializing in ClickUp implementation, configurations, systems development, process implementation, and more.

Unger, E. (2024). Clickup. BLUECREATIVE.

`https://bluecreative.com/clickup`

Managing Household Chores and Home-Life Responsibilities

This chapter delves into ways to handle household chores and innovate new time-saving solutions for your home-life responsibilities. Whether you're managing your home solo, overseeing a business, or taking on an enterprise role while raising a family, this chapter aims to offer valuable insights into optimizing household management through ClickUp. The key topics covered in this chapter include the following:

- Creating a household chore system

- Streamlining communication and collaboration

- Managing supplies and inventories

- Innovating time-saving solutions for your home-life responsibilities

By the end of this chapter, you can expect to gain tips for enhancing household management of your background or role. A chore system outlines how tasks are divided and completed in a home, tailored to suit the needs and dynamics of each household.

Creating a household chore system

A household chore system is a plan for dividing and completing the tasks of running a home. It can be as straightforward or as complex as needed, depending on the size and composition of the household. An organized system for household tasks can bring these benefits:

- Discovering how to create processes for chores and household systems

- Distributing the workload evenly among family members

- Encouraging fairness and equal participation

- Teaching kids the value of responsibility

- Maintaining a clean and orderly living environment

Understanding the principles of forming habits

To kickstart a chore system at home, the first step is to list all the tasks that require regular attention. This includes duties such as dishwashing and bed-making and weekly or monthly chores such as bathroom cleaning and carpet vacuuming.

Once you have a task list, categorize them based on areas or types of chores. For instance, group kitchen-related tasks together or outdoor chores in another category.

Creating a chore timetable

After categorizing the tasks, create a chore timetable. This involves deciding which tasks should be completed daily, weekly, or monthly.

When planning your chore schedule, consider factors such as these:

- Consider the ages and skills of your family members
- Take into account how much time each family member has available
- Determine how often each task needs to be done

Sample chore management

A chore chart template has advantages for running a household. It helps the family stay organized and focused by visually showing daily, weekly, and monthly tasks.

Figure 11.1 – Sample chore board

This ensures that everyone in the house is responsible for their part of the chores and simplifies tracking task completion and distributing responsibilities.

This section delves into establishing a chore system at home by emphasizing the importance of organization and task management through ClickUp's features. Let's now move on to discuss ways to enhance communication and teamwork within the home. Effective communication and collaboration play a role in improving household management, and utilizing ClickUp's tools can help increase productivity while effectively reducing stress levels.

Using ClickUp's tools for better chore management

ClickUp provides features that can simplify the process of managing chores.

One helpful feature is the option to create and assign tasks. Tasks can be assigned to family members or to the household, with deadlines and priorities as needed.

Additionally, ClickUp offers features beneficial for chore management, including the following:

- **Boards**: Visualize your workflow and monitor task progress
- **Calendars**: View all tasks and events in one place
- **Comments**: Communicate with family members regarding tasks and other activities
- **Notifications**: Receive alerts for due dates or completed checklists

Here are a few ways you can utilize ClickUp to simplify chore management:

- **Daily tasks**: Create a board for your chores and list tasks such as making the bed, doing the dishes, and taking out the trash. Assign these tasks to family members and set deadlines.
- **Weekly tasks**: Set up a board for your weekly chores, including vacuuming, bathroom cleaning, and lawn mowing. Assign tasks to family members with deadlines.
- **Monthly tasks**: Use ClickUp to organize chores such as gutter cleaning and window washing. Delegate these tasks to family members and establish deadlines.
- **Seasonal tasks**:
  - **Spring**: For deep cleaning tasks such as oven cleaning, carpet cleaning, and decluttering closets, in early spring, use ClickUp to create checklists and assign tasks with due dates.
  - **Summer**: For exterior cleaning tasks such as power washing the house, cleaning patio furniture, and maintaining gardens, create a ClickUp Board specifically for summer chores and set deadlines before the hot weather arrives.
  - **Fall**: For yard work such as raking leaves, trimming hedges, and preparing gardens for winter, a ClickUp List for fall chores with late summer or early fall deadlines will keep you on track.
  - **Winter**: For decorating for the holidays, organizing holiday storage, and winterizing outdoor plumbing, create a ClickUp Board well in advance to avoid last-minute stress.

- **Yearly tasks**:

  - **Schedule appliance maintenance**: Use ClickUp to set reminders for annual maintenance tasks such as servicing the HVAC system or cleaning the dryer vent.

  - **Deep clean carpets**: In ClickUp, schedule yearly carpet cleanings and assign them to a family member or professional service.

  - **Replace air filters**: Set recurring reminders in ClickUp to replace air filters in your home at recommended intervals.

  - **Inspect and clean gutters**: ClickUp can help you remember to schedule annual gutter cleaning, especially before fall.

Streamlining communication and collaboration

Efficient communication and teamwork are crucial for managing a household. By optimizing how household members communicate and work together, you can streamline household management processes, making them more efficient and less overwhelming.

Enhancing communication

The key to communication is being clear, concise, and direct. When interacting with your household members, ensure you clearly outline tasks, deadlines, and reasons behind them.

Here are some additional suggestions for communication:

- **Be respectful**: Being respectful when communicating with your household members is important even if you are frustrated. Avoid using hurtful words or tones of voice.

- **Be an active listener**: When someone is communicating with you, give them your full attention. Avoid interrupting or multitasking.

- **Be open to feedback**: Be willing to listen to your household members' feedback and make changes as needed.

Task delegation

Assigning tasks to family members is an effective way to improve communication and teamwork. This involves giving responsibilities to each person and ensuring they follow through with them.

When assigning tasks, it's vital to take into account:

- The age and capabilities of each family member
- The time constraints they may have
- The skills and interests they may have

Here are some examples to enhance communication and collaboration within your household using ClickUp:

- **Chore board**: You can create a ClickUp board for your chore chart and add tasks for all of the household chores that need to be done regularly. You can then assign tasks to your household members and set deadlines.
- **Grocery list**: You can create a ClickUp master checklist for your grocery list once. Then, share the checklist with your household members to maintain their eating preferences so everyone can add items to the list. Include a **Re-Order** checkbox to easily have a one-touch view for ordering groceries. If you order online, you'll save even more time.
- **Meal planning**: You can create a ClickUp Board for meal planning. You can then add tasks for each day of the week and assign tasks to your household members. You can also use ClickUp to create shopping lists for your meals.

Now that we have a thought-out communication plan and assigned tasks, it's time to focus on managing household supplies and inventories. Effective communication ensures that everyone is aware of what's needed, and assigning tasks helps share the responsibility of keeping track of these supplies. The link between communication and informed inventory management will streamline your household's operation.

Managing household supplies and inventories

Managing household supplies and inventories can seem overwhelming for households with multiple members. However, by implementing a strategy, you can simplify and optimize the process.

Creating a system for tracking supplies

Establishing a system for monitoring supplies is the first step in managing household supplies and inventories. This system can be tailored to suit your household's simple or intricate requirements.

One method is maintaining a spreadsheet where you document all the supplies that require tracking, including details such as brand, size, quantity on hand, reorder point, and minimum amount.

Figure 11.2 – Sample re-order list

Simply create lists for categories of supplies such as food items, cleaning products, and personal care essentials. When necessary, remember to add items to the lists.

Inventory management with ClickUp Lists

This subsection dives into leveraging ClickUp Lists for efficient household inventory management across various categories.

The following are the benefits of using ClickUp Lists for inventory management:

- **Centralized organization**: All your inventory lists reside in one place, accessible from any device
- **Customization**: You can create separate lists for each category (groceries, cleaning supplies, medications, etc.) and tailor them to your specific needs
- **Real-time updates**: Update quantities and track usage in real time, ensuring you always have an accurate picture of your stock
- **Collaboration**: Share lists with family members for collaborative management and informed purchasing decisions
- **Notifications**: Set up reminders to reorder items before they run out, preventing stockouts and maintaining a smooth household operation

These are the benefits of using ClickUp Lists for different inventory categories :

- **Home product system**: This system keeps your household running smoothly by organizing essential items and automating reminders.

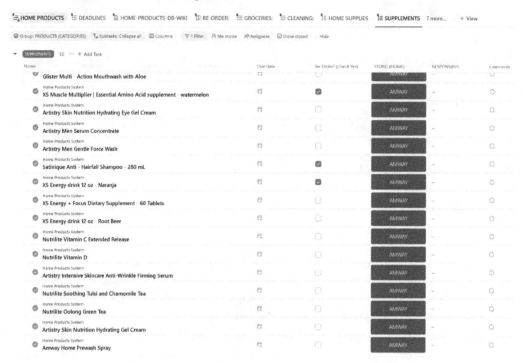

Figure 11.3 – Sample home products system

Here's how it works:

- **Categorized ClickUp Lists**: Create separate ClickUp Lists for different product categories:

   - **Groceries**: Organize items by type (dairy, fruits, vegetables, etc.). Include details for each item:

   i.   **Brand (optional):** Optional, but helpful for price comparisons or identifying preferred brands.

   ii. **Quantity needed**: Indicate how much of each item you typically need (e.g., 1 gallon of milk, 3 apples).

   iii. **Reorder point**: Set a minimum stock level (e.g., enough for 2-3 days) to trigger a grocery list update.

- **Cleaning products**: Track cleaning supplies categorized by usage (bathroom cleaner, floor cleaner, laundry detergent, etc.). Include details for each item:

  i.   **Brand (optional)**: Track preferred brands if desired.

  ii. **Size**: Specify the size (e.g., 32 oz bottle, 100 ct. wipes) to track usage and estimate lifespan.

  iii. **Purchase date**: Track when you bought the product to gauge how long it typically lasts.

  iv. **Estimated lifespan**: Estimate how long the product lasts with regular use. This helps predict replacement needs.

  v.   **Remaining quantity**: Track the amount of product remaining (e.g., half full, almost empty).

  vi. **Reorder point**: Set a minimum stock level (e.g., 25% remaining) to trigger a reorder reminder.

- **Collaborative List building and reminders with ClickUp**: Family chores and errands can feel overwhelming, but ClickUp helps you streamline the process with features that make shopping for essentials a breeze. Here's how:

  - **Smart Lists with ClickUp Brain AI**:

    i.   Forget the constant back-and-forth! Leverage ClickUp Lists to categorize items you need. Need to restock cleaning supplies? Start a list titled *Cleaning Products*. Running low on groceries? Create a list named *Groceries*. ClickUp AI Brain can even suggest items based on your previous purchases and typical consumption.

    ii. **Knowledge base integration**: Wonder how long that bottle of all-purpose cleaner typically lasts? ClickUp's knowledge base integration allows you to store information about product lifespans and reorder points. This eliminates guesswork and prevents overbuying. If you haven't built your knowledge base yet, ClickUp AI Brain can help you create articles with relevant details!

    iii. **Family collaboration**: Gone are the days of forgotten items! ClickUp allows everyone in your family to add items to the appropriate list throughout the week. This ensures a comprehensive shopping list that meets everyone's needs.

  - **Reminders you can't miss**: ClickUp's recurring tasks feature removes the guesswork from restocking. Set reminders based on the estimated lifespan of cleaning products or reorder points for groceries. This ensures you always have essentials and avoids unnecessary trips to the store.

  - **ClickUp AI (your smart shopping assistant)**: Ask ClickUp AI anything: Can't remember how long that laundry detergent usually lasts? No problem! ClickUp AI allows you to ask questions directly about your ClickUp data. Just type `When should I reorder laundry detergent?` and ClickUp AI will search your knowledge base and previous purchases to provide an answer.

- **The AI StandUp card**: For a weekly review of efficiency, use the **AI StandUp** card feature at the beginning of each week to review upcoming shopping needs. ClickUp AI can analyze your lists and knowledge base to identify potential shortages and suggest adding them to your shopping list. This quick review ensures you're prepared for the week ahead.

Managing your shopping list becomes a breeze with ClickUp's collaborative features, ClickUp Brain AI, and automated reminders. It's like having a personal shopping assistant readily available within your ClickUp workspace, keeping your household stocked and functioning smoothly.

- **ClickUp AI upgrade costs**: ClickUp offers a free plan with basic features. Upgrading to a paid plan unlocks additional features and functionalities, including access to ClickUp AI.

    iv. **ClickUp AI for individuals**: Upgrade to a paid plan to leverage ClickUp AI's capabilities and enhance your productivity, streamline tasks, and improve project management.

    v. **ClickUp AI for teams**: Paid team plans provide team-wide access to ClickUp AI, optimizing workflows, automating tasks, and facilitating better collaboration.

    vi. **Enterprise Plan**: Contact ClickUp sales for a custom quote for the Enterprise Plan. This plan offers tailored AI solutions to fit your organization's specific needs, with advanced features and priority support.

- **Business product system**: Keep track of devices, accessories, and warranty information.

Figure 11.4 – Sample business product inventory

- **Other inventory categories**: Adapt the ClickUp List concept to manage various inventory categories, such as the following:

    - **Supplements**: Maintain a list of your essential vitamins and supplements.

    - **Personal care items**: Track toiletries, shavers, travel kits, and other personal supplies.

    - **Office supplies**: Monitor printer ink, paper, and other office essentials.

By leveraging ClickUp Lists for inventory management, you can streamline household organization, ensure informed purchasing decisions, and avoid stockouts of essential items.

Automating inventory management with ClickUp AI

ClickUp AI can further streamline your inventory management by automating tasks and generating summaries and updates. Here's how:

- **ClickUp AI custom fields**: Create a ClickUp AI custom field named `AI Summary`. Simply click the **Generate** button on the **AI Summary** field when viewing an item in your list. ClickUp AI will then analyze your data to provide a summary of the item's current level (e.g., **Low**, **Medium**, or **High**. This quick overview helps you determine when it's time to reorder.

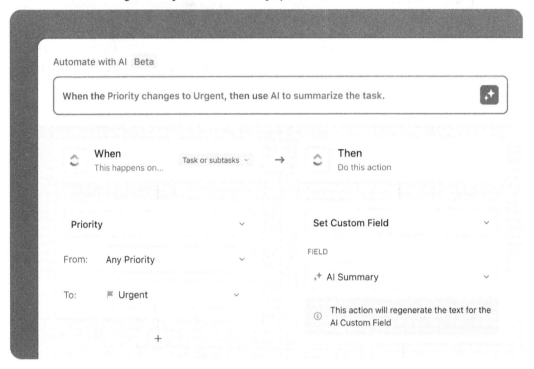

Figure 11.5 – ClickUp AI custom field (https://dev-doc.clickup.com/333/d/ ad-1002505/2024-release-notes/ad-3601017/release-3-20)

- **AI progress updates for inventory usage**: Create a ClickUp AI custom field named `AI Inventory Update`. Choose a timeframe (e.g., **Last Week** or **This Month**) from the drop-down menu next to the field. Click **Generate** for an AI-generated update on how much of the item has been used during the selected period. This helps you track usage trends and anticipate future needs.

- **Automating reminders with AI inventory data**: Combine ClickUp automations with your AI inventory custom fields to set automatic reminders for reordering items. Here's an example:

    I.   Create an automation rule that triggers when the **AI Summary** field changes to **Low**.

    II.   Within the automation rule, set an up an **Add a task** action with the following details:

    - **Task Name**: Reorder [Item Name]

    - **Assignee**: (Assign to yourself or another household member)

    - **Due Date**: (Set a lead time for reordering)

With this automation in place, ClickUp AI will automatically generate summaries and updates for your inventory levels and trigger reminders when it's time to reorder. This will save you time and ensure you always have essential household items.

> **Note**
> ClickUp AI features are available on paid plans only.

Maximizing ClickUp's functions for household inventory management

ClickUp provides features that can streamline the management of household inventories effectively.

Among these features is the option to generate and assign tasks. You can create tasks for every supply you want to monitor and allocate them to yourself or other members of your household.

Another beneficial feature is the capability to develop checklists. Checklists help break down tasks into more manageable steps.

They can also be utilized to monitor the progress of tasks.

ClickUp offers various features for managing household inventory. Boards allow you to visualize your workflow and keep track of task progress. Calendars give you a view of tasks and events. Moreover, notifications can be personalized to remind you about deadlines or checklist completions, ensuring everything gets noticed in your inventory management process.

Examples of using ClickUp for household inventory management include organizing grocery lists, cleaning supplies, and personal care items. For example, you can create a checklist for your grocery list, allowing family members to add items and monitor quantities needed. Similarly, a ClickUp Board can focus on cleaning supplies with tasks assigned for each item and tracking stock levels for restocking. This approach also applies to personal care products, ensuring management and restocking as required.

Innovating time-saving solutions for your home-life responsibilities

This section dives into creative approaches to make chores more engaging and manageable for all family members. Here are three specific examples you can elaborate on.

Gamification system with points and rewards

- **Concept**: Transform chores into a fun competition with a point system and rewards. Assign points to each chore based on difficulty or time commitment. Track points on a visual chart (a physical chart or a ClickUp List) and celebrate achievements with predetermined rewards.

- **Benefits**: Encourages healthy competition, motivates completion, and adds fun to routine tasks.

- **ClickUp integration**: Use ClickUp Boards and Lists to vote and track points for consistency and to promote a great attitude toward accomplishing chores.

Movie night mayhem – gamified movie selection

Following is a sample movie night system:

Figure 11.6 – Sample movie night system

- **Concept**: Turn hang-out night into a collaborative adventure with a point system that influences the chosen media! Assign points to different media selection activities, allowing everyone to contribute and earn points that shape the final viewing experience.

- **How it works**:

  - **Earning points**: Points are awarded for the various ways participants contribute to choosing the media to enjoy together:

    - **Adding media**: Everyone gets points for adding a movie, TV show, audiobook, music, podcast, documentary, or skill-set course

    - **Researching options**: Digging up interesting media details (e.g., movie details, including cast, description, and reviews) earns bonus points when all custom fields are entered

    - **Creating a movie trailer parody**: Extra points are awarded for hilarious homemade trailers promoting the hang-out night or the media selected

    - **Creating themed snacks**: Designing and preparing themed snacks related to the hang-out night or suggested media earns bonus points

  - **Point value ladder**:

    - **1 point**: Add a vote to any media item and assign yourself to that media task

    - **2 points**: Add a new movie, TV show, book/audiobook, podcast, music, documentary, or online course task you would like to enjoy together, and assign yourself to the new task

    - **3 points**: Enter all custom field content about the media and assign yourself to the task

    - **4 points**: Add new media, enter all custom field content, and assign yourself to the media task

    - **5 Points**: Create delicious, movie-inspired themed snacks for hang-out night (or day)

    - **7 points**: Create a funny and engaging parody or movie trailer

    - **10 points**: Create a movie trailer and an event promo video for movie night, including a music soundtrack (incorporate any skills you want to learn together, personally or professionally)

  - **Deciding the winner**: The person with the most accumulated points from suggestions and contributions is the winner! Rewards could be special snacks, thoughtful notes, gifts, adventure time at a particular theme park together, or an outing. Everyone gets to enjoy the fruits of their collaborative effort.

- Benefits:

  - **Shared decision-making**: Encourages everyone to participate in the media selection process

  - **Teamwork and creativity**: Promotes collaboration and creative thinking by suggesting and promoting movies

  - **Engaging build-up**: Adds an exciting build-up and something to always look forward to throughout the week

- **ClickUp integration**: Use ClickUp to create a fun and interactive board dedicated to movie night selection. Here's how:

  - **Movie suggestion list:** Create a list where everyone can submit movie suggestions

  - **Point tracking**: Assign points to each list item based on the contribution type (suggestion, research, etc.)

  - **Discussion board**: Create a separate board for discussions, reviews, and movie trailer parodies

This system transforms media selection into a team effort, building anticipation and excitement for the time spent together!

Chore rotation charts with visual aids (for younger children)

- **Concept:**Create a visually appealing chore chart with pictures or age-appropriate symbols representing each task. Rotate chores weekly or bi-weekly to ensure everyone participates in different tasks and avoid monotony.

- **Benefits**: Provides clear expectations, fosters a sense of responsibility, and makes chores more engaging for younger children.

- **ClickUp integration**: While ClickUp might not be ideal for young children, you can use ClickUp to create a master chore list and rotate tasks within the chart manually.

Integrating chores into family routines (such as music time while cleaning)

- **Concept**: Weave chores into existing family routines to make them feel less like a burden. Play upbeat music while cleaning together, turn folding laundry into a family game, or assign tasks during designated "cleaning sprints" after meals.

- **Benefits**: It creates a sense of teamwork, reduces the feeling of isolation during chores, and makes the tasks more enjoyable.

- **ClickUp integration**: Utilize ClickUp to schedule dedicated "cleaning time" blocks on the family calendar and assign tasks beforehand.

These are just a few examples to get you started. Feel free to adapt and personalize these ideas to fit your family's dynamics and preferences.

Inventory for your business, electronics, and studio

This section explains how to manage your electronics and tech inventory using ClickUp Lists. This category encompasses various devices, accessories, and warranty information.

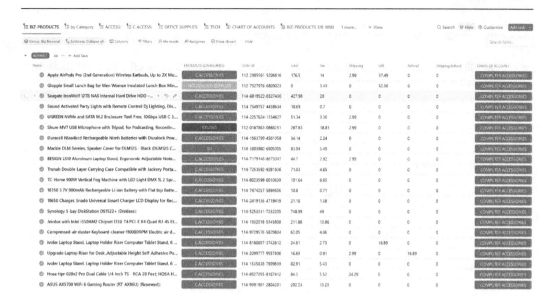

Figure 11.7 – Business inventory

The following image shows a sample studio inventory:

Figure 11.8 – Sample studio inventory

Here are the benefits of tracking the electronics inventory:

- **Organization**: Maintain a centralized location for all your electronic device information, eliminating the need to search for manuals or receipts

- **Warranty tracking**: Set reminders for approaching warranty expirations to ensure you take advantage of valuable coverage windows

- **Loss prevention**: Having a detailed record of your electronics, including serial numbers, can be helpful in case of loss or theft, for insurance or recovery purposes

- **Upgrade planning**: Easily track the age and model of your electronics to determine whether upgrades are necessary

Here's how to organize your electronics inventory with ClickUp Lists:

1. **Setting up a list**: Make a list in ClickUp called `Electronics and Tech Inventory`.

2. **Listing your items**: Add each gadget you have as a task in this list.

3. **Task details**: Make sure to include the following information for each device in the task description or custom fields:

   - Device type (laptop, smartphone, tablet, etc.)

   - Brand (such as Apple, Samsung, or Sony)

   - Model number (specific model designation)

   - Purchase date (date of purchase)

   - Warranty expiry date (if applicable)

   - Serial number (consider using a custom field for secure storage – see the security note that follows)

4. **Accessories**: For each device, you can do the following:

   - List any associated accessories (chargers, headphones, etc.) within the same task description

   - Alternatively, create a sub-list linked to the main device task for a more organized breakdown of accessories

5. **Tracking warranties**: Utilize ClickUp's due date feature to set reminders for approaching warranty expirations. This ensures you're notified before the warranty window closes:

   - **Security considerations**: While ClickUp offers a secure platform, consider storing sensitive information such as serial numbers in a separate password manager or encrypted notes app for an extra layer of security.

- **Physical inventory checks**: Remember that ClickUp provides a digital record. It's recommended that you conduct periodic physical checks of your electronics to ensure that your records are accurate and reflect any changes (lost items, upgrades, etc.).

6. **Inventory pain management system for CBD, medical marijuana, and dispensary use**: Managing your inventory of pain management items, such as CBD, medical marijuana, and other related products, requires a system to protect your information.

> **Note**
>
> Always use HIPAA-compliant related apps and compliance laws. This demo is for personal or company database management only. Referencing the data provides inventory assistance similar to vitamin supplementation or prescription medications, describing their effects and negatives and taking notes on which ones are more effective.

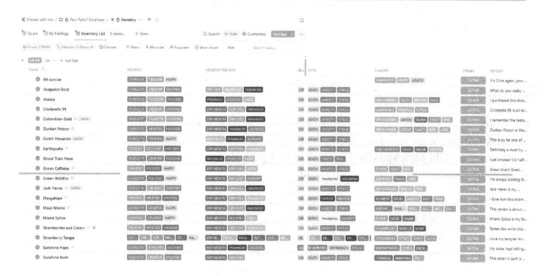

Figure 11.9 – Sample pain management system

Here are the benefits of having such a system:

- **Safeguarding privacy**: Personal details such as medications and treatment strategies are private. They should be kept confidential. A secure system guarantees that this data is shielded from individuals.

- **Adherence to HIPAA regulations**: The **Health Insurance Portability and Accountability Act (HIPAA)** establishes guidelines for protecting health information. Utilizing an app that complies with HIPAA ensures these rules are followed accordingly.

Alternative solutions

There are HIPAA-compliant medication management apps. Explore dedicated apps explicitly designed for medication management. These apps often offer features such as the following:

- Secure storage of medication details, dosages, and schedules

- Medication reminders and tracking tools

- Interaction checks for potential drug conflicts

- Secure messaging with healthcare providers (depending on the app)

Here are some considerations for choosing an app:

- Look for apps certified as HIPAA-compliant

- Research features and functionalities to meet your specific needs

- Ensure there is a user-friendly interface and accessibility

- Read reviews and compare features before choosing an app

Summary

This chapter discussed aspects of managing household chores and responsibilities to cater to a broad audience, from individual business owners to executive-level professionals taking on project manager roles. The three main topics covered in this chapter provided a manual on optimizing household management with ClickUp.

The initial section, *Creating a household chore system* shed light on the importance of having a structured chore system. It delved into aspects of forming habits, guiding you on grouping tasks logically and creating a chore timetable. ClickUp's functionalities, such as task creation, checklists, boards, calendars, and notifications, were highlighted as resources for simplifying chore organization. Real-life scenarios demonstrated how ClickUp can be used for weekly and monthly tasks, to turn household duties into a planned and manageable routine.

Moving forward to *Streamlining communication and collaboration*, the section underscored the role of communication and task distribution in household management. It offered communication advice, emphasizing clarity and respect while exploring ClickUp's tools for task allocation, checklists, boards, calendars, comments, and notifications. Examples showed how ClickUp can aid in creating chore schedules, grocery lists, and meal plans to enhance interaction among household members.

The last section, *Managing household supplies and inventories*, tackled the complexities of managing household resources. It introduced a method for monitoring supplies, setting reminders, and efficiently handling inventories. ClickUp offers a range of tools, such as task management, checklists, boards, calendars, and notifications, that are particularly useful for keeping track of household supplies. Real-life examples showcased how ClickUp can monitor groceries, cleaning items, and personal care essentials to ensure that homes stay well-supplied and organized. The chapter advised enhancing household management by promoting organization, communication, and teamwork.

After establishing household routines and communication methods, the focus shifts to self-development. The next chapter dives into using ClickUp to create habits and accomplish personal goals. It explores ways to maximize ClickUp's functionalities – not for managing household chores but for creating routines and monitoring progress toward individual goals.

Further reading and free resources

Here's a breakdown of which ClickUp features mentioned in this chapter are included in the Free and Paid plans:

ClickUp Feature	Free Plan	Paid Plans
Creating and assigning tasks	Yes	Yes
Boards	Yes	Yes
Calendars	Yes (limited view)	Yes (full view)
Comments	Yes	Yes
Notifications	Yes (limited)	Yes (customizable)
Checklists	Yes	Yes
Recurring tasks	No	Yes
Custom fields	No	Yes
ClickUp AI	No	Yes

Table 11.1 – ClickUp plan details

Here are some additional details about the ClickUp plans:

- **Free plan**: The free plan works well for individuals or small teams seeking task management capabilities.
- **Paid plan**: Each offering has paid subscription options. These plans provide features not included in the free plan, such as recurring tasks, customizable fields, and ClickUp AI integration.

> **Note**
>
> For further details, you can contact the ClickUp sales team:
>
> `https://clickup.com/contact/contact-sales`
>
> Sign up to download a free workbook and productivity resources for each chapter.

Sign up to download your free workbook and productivity resources for each chapter

ClickUp is constantly evolving. Get help and explore each chapter in depth, receive the latest productivity updates and ClickUp tips, and download your free workbook at `http://bluecreative.com/clickup`. Specializing in ClickUp implementation, configurations, systems development, process implementation, and more.

Unger, E. (2024). Clickup. BLUECREATIVE.

`https://bluecreative.com/clickup`

12

Personal Habits, Goal Achievement, and Routines for Success

Welcome to *Chapter 12*, where we will explore how to use ClickUp to create habits that lead to accomplishing personal goals. Whether you are a solo owner, a medium-sized business owner, or an enterprise-level executive taking on the project manager role, this chapter is designed to provide valuable insights into leveraging ClickUp's features to establish and maintain productive habits that drive personal goal achievement. In this chapter, we're going to cover the following main topics:

- Recognizing the impact of habits on goal achievement

- Creating time in your life with habit-stacking routines

- Objectives and key results (OKRs) – simplified

- Progress tracking and managing milestones

- Cultivating effective habits and routines with ClickUp

Upon completing *Chapter 12*, you will learn to utilize ClickUp to cultivate habits that support goal accomplishment. This chapter guides individuals at professional levels by providing a roadmap to turn aspirations into concrete achievements through intentional habits and using ClickUp's versatile features effectively.

Recognizing the impact of habits on goal achievement

Habits play a role in shaping your life. They can propel you toward success or hold you back from realizing your potential. Understanding how habits are formed and utilizing them to your advantage can pave the way for success in every aspect of your life.

The scientific elements of habit formation

The process of creating habits involves repetition and reinforcement. As you consistently engage in a specific habit, your brain develops pathways facilitating its execution. This explains why falling into habits such as procrastination or overeating is easy. However, the silver lining is that you can harness this mechanism to cultivate new habits by practicing desired behaviors, reinforcing the neural pathways associated with them.

The impact of habits on productivity

Habits determine our productivity levels. Establishing habits enables us to accomplish tasks efficiently and effectively. For instance, being accountable to a morning workout routine sets the day's tone. However, succumbing to habits such as scrolling through social media upon waking or delaying essential responsibilities can significantly impede productivity.

ClickUp contains my accomplishment system so I can spend time with family, passion projects, and pursue purpose with my strengths.

Let's use ClickUp as a tool to cultivate habits. Here are a few ways to utilize ClickUp for habit development:

- List your desired habits as recurring tasks in ClickUp to keep them organized and visible

- Assign deadlines to your tasks to maintain accountability and progress toward your goals

- Use reminder notifications within ClickUp to help stay on track with your habits, particularly email notifications when starting out

For instance, you can use ClickUp to establish a routine exercise habit by creating an "exercise" task and a due date reminder for a specific time. Keep track of your progress by journaling notes in the task description and using ClickUp's time to track how much time you exercise daily. Another instance is cultivating a reading habit by creating a task labeled "read" in ClickUp. Assign a due date reminder at a specific time. Monitor your progress by recording the number of pages you read each day in the description. Lastly, if you aim to establish a studying routine, create a task named "study" in ClickUp. Set due date recurring task reminders to prompt you at specific times daily. Track your progress by logging the hours spent studying each day.

Additional tips for developing good habits

Here are a few additional tips for developing good habits:

- **Start small**: Avoid changing habits simultaneously; focus on one or two habits before moving on.

- **Be consistent**: Consistency is critical to developing habits. Aim to perform your desired actions at the time each day and in the setting.

- **Make it easy**: Make it as easy as you can to capture and maintain your habits. For instance, to make morning exercise a habit, lay out your workout clothes the night before. If studying is your priority, create your study plan list the night before so you can wake up inspired and begin immediately.

- **Reward yourself**: When you reach a goal or stick to your routine for a while, invest in yourself with time-blocked rest and reward habits. Schedule time within your week to rest and reward yourself with something that inspires you while celebrating your accomplishments. Be mindful of the different choices between healthy rewards and bad choice rewards that stop your momentum. Choosing rewards that align with your values will keep you motivated and help you maintain the momentum of your habit.

It's okay to make mistakes

Everyone messes up occasionally. Don't be too hard on yourself if you miss a workout or accidentally have a cheat day. Instead, get back on track the next day, catch yourself going off track a little sooner next time, do your best, and forget the rest. Consistency is key.

Initially, we discussed how your productivity is impacted by the goals you set and the efficiency and effectiveness of your habits. The following section will delve into habit-stacking routines and how ClickUp can help keep you accountable for the goals you set. Most importantly, ClickUp can help you be accountable to yourself.

Creating time in your life with habit-stacking routines

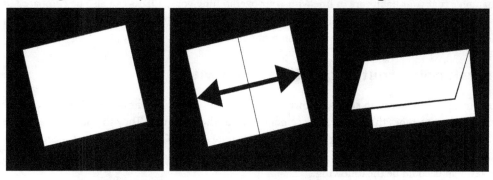

Figure 12.1 – "What is the fastest distance between two points? It is to fold the paper."

Habit-stacking routines for reaching your objectives are like the ingredients in your kitchen to cook a delicious meal. Habit stacking introduces a few new phrases and involves combining habits with other habits that are **batched** together for **multi-purpose** scheduling for **timeboxing**. One of my favorite phrases is, *"What is the fastest distance between two points? It is to fold the paper."* The purpose of habit stacking is to fold the paper in your habits and routines. It is to create time.

Tips for integrating habits with established routines

When merging habits with existing ones, it is important to select habits that complement each other. A fundamental approach is to start small. Avoid attempting to add a new habit that you are not consistent with yet. Introduce one or two habits you are confident about and concentrate on stretching your capacity and maintaining your composure while adding another habit. For example, you can multi-purpose the time you have scheduled to batch the tasks of exercising while listening to an audiobook and taking notes. When you are confident in your regular scheduled habit of learning/journaling/exercising after two weeks, then add another habit such as tracking your heart rate and organizing your calendar for the day while maintaining your habits and composure of exercising, actively listening to your audiobook, and journaling. In another example, you can then batch together all of the phone calls you are required to make for the week, scheduled into a two-hour **timebox** in your calendar.

Linking multiple habits together increases the likelihood of sticking to them since they're associated with an existing one. The purpose of creating these new habit-stacking routines is to fold the paper in those areas and create time back in your life.

OKRs – simplified

We've touched upon the significance of habits in reaching our goals. Knowing there are many ways to brainstorm and set goals is also important. However, I have learned that from preparation to production, the characteristics of a robust goal system require planning, extra speed, agility, and great work habits. It's crucial to introduce a popular goal-setting approach called **OKR**. OKRs aid in establishing objectives and monitoring results. Utilizing ClickUp can serve as a method for incorporating OKRs to guarantee that your habits are in line with your overarching goals. OKRs can also be compared to user stories within the Agile scrum framework. However, where a user story focuses on the work to be done, OKRs focus on the strategy and vision of what to do.

Understanding routines and planning with OKRs

A goal you aim to achieve can also be known as an **objective**. Objectives should be within reach. **Key results** are the outcomes that show advancement towards the Objective. They should be measurable and have a deadline. When planning your routine, integrate your OKRs by scheduling time for habits that directly impact your key results. For example, if your objective is to improve your physical health, your key results could be the following:

- 30-minute workout, five days every week
- Three servings of veggies each day
- Lowered body percentage by 5% within six months

Implementing OKRs in ClickUp – simplified

However, a simplified way of implementing OKRs should also be considered. For instance, if you imagine your goal and then consider the projects and tasks required, it can be beneficial to think 10 more steps forward about how much work and resources will be required. How will the objectives look over time, moving slowly and steadily while simultaneously tracking the progress of the end result and the entire project?

Implementing OKRs can be awkward at first, but I found a simple way to begin adopting them is to define them using a new acronym, **OP: objectives and projects**. It can be confusing to tell someone who has used OKRs for many years, just like OKRs can be confusing to someone who has never heard of them. What is a win-win solution? A best practice for efficient and effective planning and execution combines key results and project management using ClickUp.

By combining OKR strategy and project management within the same list of ClickUp, you can instantly track key results and see roadblocks within the project. This is a great example of folding the paper by batching tasks to multi-purpose your time. Make only one minor tweak in your habits and configurations inside of ClickUp, and now you can see metrics and project health while working on the project together at the same time. To use ClickUp with simplified OKRs, follow these steps:

1. **Create an objective**: Make a new task, change the task type to **Milestone** in ClickUp, and label it with the name of your objective. This will serve as your primary goal.

2. **List key results**: Create subtasks for each key result under this task. These will be the specific outcomes you're aiming for.

3. **Track progress**: While you work on your OKRs, track them. While you work on your habits, update the status of your key results in ClickUp. This will give you a visual representation of your progress.

4. **Review and adjust**: Schedule your goals as recurring tasks to regularly review your OKRs in ClickUp. If you're not making the expected progress, adjust your habits and update your project plan or key results accordingly.

Benefits of OKRs

- **Focus**: OKRs help you concentrate on what's truly important, avoiding distractions
- **Alignment**: By linking habits and project work to OKRs, you ensure daily actions contribute to larger goals
- **Motivation**: Seeing progress in ClickUp can boost your motivation to maintain habits
- **Flexibility**: OKRs can be adjusted as needed, allowing for adaptability

Celebrating OKR achievements

Just like celebrating milestones, when you achieve a key result, mark it as complete in ClickUp and give yourself a healthy reward. This reinforces the positive behavior and encourages you to keep pushing toward your next objective.

Integrating OKRs into your ClickUp workflow gives you a structured approach to turning your personal goals into reality. Review them regularly and celebrate every win, no matter how small. Every day, you have the opportunity to see your tasks differently and innovate an easier approach with ClickUp.

Optimizing productivity through routine development

To develop a routine, begin by pinpointing the habits you wish to integrate. Arrange these habits in an order that works best for you. Consider starting with tasks and ending with pressing ones. Utilize tools such as ClickUp to monitor your progress. Create tasks for each habit in your routine, assign deadlines, and track how much time you dedicate to each habit or how often you complete them.

After exploring ways to blend habits with our routines and make the most of ClickUp's features for effective habit stacks, let's now focus on the significance of progress tracking and milestone celebrations in reaching our goals and how ClickUp can support us in these areas.

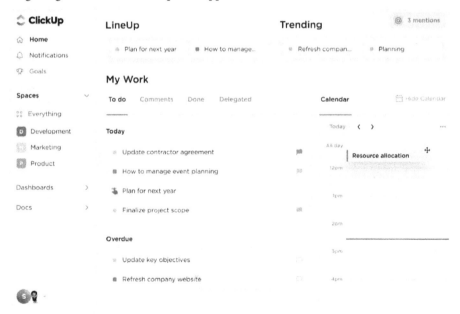

Figure 12.2 – Habit-stacking visual representation (https://clickup.com/teams/personal)

ClickUp, with its 10+ customizable views, empowers you to visualize your daily tasks and routines with ease. Whether you like keeping things organized with a list, planning ahead with a calendar, or getting creative with a mind map, ClickUp gives you the freedom to customize your workflow to match your preferences perfectly.

Progress tracking and managing milestones

Monitoring progress and managing milestones are components of any goal-setting process. Tracking progress can help you gauge your progress and pinpoint areas for enhancement. Managing milestones increases your confidence in keeping consistent habits that lead to successful habits. ClickUp provides features that aid in tracking and managing milestones and progress.

One straightforward approach is to track the frequency of your habits. Another method is to create a task for each habit you wish to track by assigning start and due dates, then mark them as completed upon execution.

Utilizing ClickUp's progress-tracking features

ClickUp's progress-tracking features are pretty handy. ClickUp provides tools to assist you in monitoring your progress toward achieving your objectives. One of the most valuable features is the ability to create and track tasks. You can effectively track your progress by setting deadlines and monitoring the time spent on each task.

Additionally, ClickUp provides an array of tools for monitoring progress. This includes boards, which visually represent workflows and task progression. Calendars consolidate upcoming tasks and events into a unified view for easy management. Progress bars indicate the completion percentage of tasks, providing a quick overview of progress. Moreover, reports enable the generation of comprehensive progress reports, aiding in tracking advancement toward set objectives.

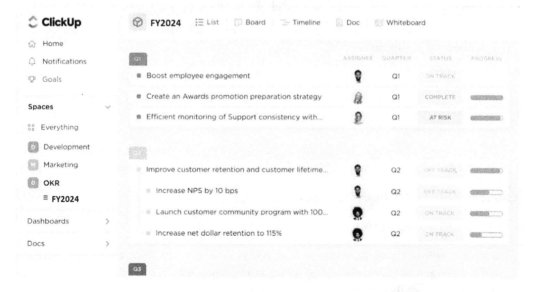

Figure 12.3 – Progress bar visual representation (https://clickup.com/teams/startup)

Here are a few illustrative examples demonstrating how ClickUp can be utilized to monitor progress toward various goals. For instance, in weight loss, individuals can create recurring tasks such as "weigh myself" and set daily deadlines to track their weight over time. Similarly, for those aiming to establish a regular exercise routine, tasks labeled "exercise" with daily deadlines can be created, allowing users to log their workout durations daily for progress tracking. Furthermore, in academic pursuits such as test preparation, users can create tasks for each study topic with respective deadlines to systematically monitor their progress by marking tasks as complete upon mastering each subject.

Cultivating effective habits and routines with ClickUp

ClickUp empowers you to design effective habits and routines that pave the way for achieving your goals. Here's a comprehensive guide that merges the strengths of both sections:

ClickUp functionalities for habit success – a step-by-step guide

Roadmap strategy includes goals in ClickUp for daily, weekly, monthly, and yearly project planning:

1. **Folder and list**: Create a folder with your name and a list named Roadmap Strategy in your new folder.

2. **Goals**: Write four new goals, create four new tasks, name them by the goal name, change their task type to a milestone, name each task BIG ROCK, SMALL ROCK, SAND, or WATER, and prioritize each by ClickUp's priorities – **Urgent**, **High**, **Normal**, and **Low**.

3. **Prioritize**: Create new milestones in the roadmap strategy list of all the projects and accomplishments prioritized by what you would like to achieve within a 2-5 year time period. Organize by the priority analogy that your day is a glass jar; to finish the day effectively, the big rocks, small rocks, sand, and water are prioritized throughout the day.

4. **Think ahead**: Begin by thinking 10 steps forward about what projects and tasks need to be completed to accomplish the goal.

5. **Finish planning**: Then, create subtasks for each project until your backlog of priority tasks is ready for scheduling.

6. **Scheduling**: Next, process all of your work and put it into your calendar. Look at your schedule and find the time you can commit to.

7. **Kanban view with boards**: Use boards to visualize your milestones and track task progress. Arrange tasks to see how your habits fit together within your daily routine.

Creating a Habits and Routines list in ClickUp

The following steps illustrate how to create a habits and routines list:

1. **Capture routines**: Create a new list and call it Habits and Routines, and then brainstorm habits and routines to start doing, stop doing, and update. Create tasks and subtasks to further define the steps of the routine.

2. **Capture habits**: Identify and define specific and achievable habits you want to develop and create them as tasks or milestones accordingly. Write tasks with five W's and one H. WWWWWH/**5WH**. Include who, what, where, when, why, and how to hold yourself accountable.

3. **Schedule recurring tasks**: Create, schedule, and assign new habits and routines as recurring tasks on a specific date and time.

4. **Automation**: Explore automation during your habits and routines. Pay attention to what you do repeatedly, take notes in a ClickUp document, and journal time-saving ideas. Then, implement your ideas by scheduling recurring tasks and learning how to create time. For example, every time you create a task, have it automatically assigned to you, set the priority, and set the start and due dates.

5. **Simplicity with subtasks**: Use subtasks to break down complex habits into smaller, more manageable steps. This simplifies the process, allowing you to track progress on each subtask and maintain motivation.

6. **Custom notifications**: Stay on track by customizing your notifications to receive specific alerts for you that do not slip through the cracks.

7. **Set start and due dates**: Assign deadlines to your habit tasks to ensure consistent completion.

Starting your day whenever it starts – routine

Depending on your priority schedule and responsibilities, you can plug and play working on your goals, routines, habits, and daily work, no matter how difficult your days go, and leave the office on time. Here are some examples of a starting-your-day routine:

- **Learning habit routines**: Throughout the day, expand your capacity for learning, like a bodybuilder expands their capacity for training. Or, like a dog lover who designs their life around their dogs, they will naturally meditate and focus on their passion. It is easier to grow your strengths than to grow your weaknesses. Similarly, find your strengths and create learning routines around them.

- **Using reflective critical thinking to plan**: Listen for inspiring things to do throughout your day, or perhaps you're in a season of battling obstacles head-on for many months and years. In any case or similar, throughout your time, listen for inspiration, thoughts that contain actions that give joy, or exciting ideas that help you move past the current obstacles in your path. This habit will help inspiration, vision, and the required action steps to emerge. It is within moments of deep focus and relaxation the action step ideas will emerge through your thoughts and inspiration. Make sure to type or write them down.

- **Work habit routines**: Imagine your work habit routines are like an ice-cold glass of water. It takes effort and thoughtfulness to keep the water ice cold. Every day, we get a new opportunity to find new ways to keep the water cold with the resources around us. It takes effort to keep up to date with technology. When Henry Ford designed the automobile in a time when horse carriages were the primary source of transportation, what if someone said to him, "Can you make the automobile easier to understand? The horse is so much simpler, and I want a faster horse, not this... what do you call it... automobile? I didn't ask for that." Cars have stood the test of time on that issue, but how will the test of time show up in your life based on your current routines?

Hard work always pays off. However, the greater the effort and the more time spent in your work routine, wherever you discover how you spend or invest your time, that is where your payoff will be. Work habit routines help ensure that what we work on leads us to where we want to go.

- **Soul time**: Reminisce about memories of things you always wanted to do but never had the time to do. Where are your favorite places to go or small things in life that give you joy for absolutely no reason? What action items give your mind and heart rest? These are all ideas of what you can begin to call soul time for yourself. Maintain routines around writing new ideas about where you can take yourself out to a place you want to go, on a date, adventure time, think time, journal time, or rest and relax.

By incorporating these actionable steps and leveraging ClickUp's functionalities, you can transform the concepts of habits and routines into a practical and achievable plan for achieving your goals and creating time back in your life. Remember, consistency is key! Utilize ClickUp to stay organized, motivated, and ultimately triumphant in your journey toward efficiency and personal development.

Summary

In *Chapter 12*, you learned how to use ClickUp to establish and maintain habits that contribute to achieving personal goals. You were introduced to the concept of habit formation and its scientific basis, emphasizing the importance of repetition and reinforcement in creating neural pathways that facilitate consistent behavior. The chapter provided practical advice on using ClickUp for habit development, including listing desired habits as tasks, assigning deadlines for accountability, and utilizing notifications and progress tracking to stay motivated.

The information presented was helpful because it offered a structured approach to goal setting and productivity enhancement by implementing OKRs. You discovered how to define achievable objectives and measure progress with key results using ClickUp's features, such as task creation, checklists, boards, calendars, and reports. The benefits of OKRs, such as focus, alignment, motivation, and flexibility, were highlighted, along with tips for integrating them into daily routines.

Overall, the chapter served as a comprehensive guide for professionals at any level to turn aspirations into concrete achievements by cultivating intentional habits and leveraging ClickUp's versatile features effectively. It underscored the significance of setting clear milestones and consistently working toward them.

In the next chapter, you will learn about creating processes, workflows, and automation in ClickUp to further enhance productivity and goal attainment.

Further reading and free resources

Here's a breakdown of which ClickUp plans by each feature mentioned in this chapter are included in the Free and Paid plans:

ClickUp Feature	Free Plan	Paid Plan
Task creation and assignment	Yes	Yes
Checklists	Yes	Yes
Boards	Yes	Yes
Calendars	Yes	Yes
Recurring tasks	Yes	Yes
Notifications	Yes	Yes
Progress bars	No	Yes
Reports	No	Yes
Mind maps	No	Yes
OKR tracking	No	Yes
Advanced views	No	Yes
Custom fields	No	Yes
Goal folders	No	Yes
Workload view	No	Yes
Time tracking	No	Yes

Table 12.1 – ClickUp plan details

Here are some additional details about the ClickUp plans:

- **Free plan**: The free plan works well for individuals or small teams seeking task management capabilities.
- **Paid plan**: Each offering features and pricing structure has paid subscription options. These plans provide features not included in the free plan, such as recurring tasks, customizable fields, and ClickUps AI integration.

> **Note**
>
> For further details, you may contact the ClickUp sales team:
>
> `https://clickup.com/contact/contact-sales`.

Sign up to download your free workbook and productivity resources for each chapter

ClickUp is constantly evolving. Get help and explore each chapter in depth, receive the latest productivity updates and ClickUp tips, and download your free workbook at `bluecreative.com/clickup`. It specializes in ClickUp implementation, configurations, systems development, process implementation, and more.

Unger, E. (2024). ClickUp. BLUECREATIVE.

`https://bluecreative.com/clickup`

13

Processes, KPIs, and Automation – Simplified

Welcome to *Chapter 13*, where we will explore the power of creating processes, Dashboard KPIs, and automation in ClickUp. Whether you're an entrepreneur, a small business owner, or a high-level executive stepping into the project management realm, this chapter aims to offer insights on maximizing your work efficiency using Clickup's functionalities.

In this chapter, we're going to cover the following main topics:

- Creating repeatable steps to accomplish your goals – processes simplified
- Harnessing the power of ClickUp's automation tools
- Implementing top-notch strategies for processes
- Using Dashboards to track processes with KPIs

By the conclusion of this chapter, you'll possess the know-how and resources required to transform your work procedures, tap into ClickUp's automation capabilities, and integrate effective practices for seamless processes. This chapter acts as a roadmap for individuals to refine their work approaches and make the most out of ClickUp's offerings.

Creating repeatable steps to accomplish your goals – processes simplified

Whether you know it or not, every day, you follow a series of steps in work and home life. Crafting simple and repeatable processes is fundamental for the efficiency and effectiveness of accomplishing your goals. By devising standardized processes in all areas of your life, you can enhance the efficiency, productivity, and overall quality of your life. ClickUp provides features that can aid in creating, maintaining, and managing these elements by yourself and with others.

Creating processes in ClickUp – a step-by-step guide

When it comes to outlining processes in ClickUp, you can make the most of its task functions. Here's a simple how-to:

- **Start with a folder**: To get started, create a folder called PROCESSES and a new list titled General Processes.

- **Break it down**: Start creating tasks, where each task becomes a process, and each sub-task represents a step in the process.

- **Task type**: Create a new process task type to visually distinguish processes from other task types.

- **Due dates**: Assign start and due dates to yourself and others to write and maintain processes.

- **Attachments and comments**: Include original process document attachments, diagram images, and links for context. Utilize comments for team communication or progress updates.

- **Templates**: Create task templates to simplify creating and maintaining processes. Write instructions, and maintain current links and resources.

- **Automation**: When you find yourself spending too much time on low-level admin tasks, capture that info and create a new task to schedule a time to figure out how to refine that process with automation.

- **Metrics with dashboards**: As you continue to be efficient with your tasks, habits, and routines, selecting metrics and statistics to track will become obvious. ClickUp dashboards can usefully manage overdue dates, uncleared notifications, status tracking, and nearly all custom fields. Create a new dashboard and select a template, or create your required metrics, including managing, checking, and refining your KPIs in your habits and routines.

By following this guide, you can write and implement processes in ClickUp. The process maintenance guide works with processes in ClickUp.

Analyzing and mapping out your existing processes

When it comes to creating processes from steps that are already in place, it can be tricky. The first step is to examine and outline your current processes. Gather all of your documents and notes into one area. Use a document in ClickUp, and drag and drop documents, images, and videos for review. This allows you to pinpoint areas that could use some enhancement.

There are methods to analyze and outline your existing processes. One practical approach is utilizing a whiteboard flowchart or diagram, which visually represents the steps in a process and how they are interconnected. Another option is using a process map, which illustrates the inputs, outputs, resources, and activities within a process.

With the use of ClickUp tasks, task types, whiteboards, docs, and mindmap features, you can easily document your repeatable steps and begin process mapping in ClickUp.

Identifying areas for improvement

Once you've reviewed and outlined your existing processes, the next step is pinpointing areas where improvements can be made. There are several questions to ask, such as the following:

- **Bottlenecks**: Are there any stages in the process that are causing delays in progress?

- **Repetitive tasks**: Are there any steps being done multiple times unnecessarily?

- **Unnecessary complexity**: Is the process more complicated than necessary?

- **Lack of clarity**: Do all team members understand their roles and responsibilities in the process?

- **Communication gaps**: Can communication between team members regarding the process be improved?

Top tools in ClickUp to enhance processes

ClickUp comes with a set of tools aimed at simplifying and enhancing your work processes. Let's delve into the features that contribute to boosting efficiency:

- **Task management**:

  - **Creating and assigning tasks**: Divide your process steps into tasks and subtasks, clearly outlining each step of the process. Pre-assign tasks to team members for accountability and clarity on responsibilities.

  - **Deadlines and due dates**: Set deadlines for each task to ensure completion and keep your project on schedule. Monitor progress by comparing task completion with deadlines.

  - **Sub-tasks**: Break down tasks into subtasks, making them easier to grasp and accomplish. Subtasks also are tracked by dashboards, whereas checklists are not currently.

- **Visualization and organization**:

  - **Boards:** These Kanban-style boards provide a representation of your processes, showing tasks at each stage (e.g., To Do, In Progress, and Done). This enables you to track progress and identify bottlenecks.

  - **Calendars**: Merge all your tasks and events into a calendar view. This centralizes your processes by the due date and gives a picture of your schedule, promoting better organization.

- **Structure and automation**:

  - **Dependencies**: Establish relationships between tasks, ensuring a specific order of completion. A task cannot be started until its dependent task is finished, guaranteeing structured process steps.

- **Rules (automation)**: Simplify tasks within process steps. By automating them with rules, you can establish an action based on conditions (e.g., automatically assigning a task when a new project is created) to reduce manual work and enhance efficiency.

- **Additional features**:

  - **Templates**: Save time by utilizing templates for processes within projects. Easily set up tasks and processes with one click.

  - **Statuses and views**: Define your status and select how you want to view them (e.g., a list, board, or document). This flexibility allows you to customize ClickUp according to your requirements.

  - **Collaboration**: Collaborate with features such as chat, file sharing, task comments, and mentions. Chat functions can replace other apps such as Slack, WhatsApp, and texting so that everyone remains on the same page within the same platform. Note that ClickUp's chat feature requires customized notification and implementation steps so that notifications do not slip through the cracks, no matter which device users work from.

  - **Progress tracking**: Keep track of your process progress using tools such as Boards, Calendars, Progress Bars, and Dashboard Reports. Obtain insights to pinpoint areas for enhancement.

By making use of this set of tools, ClickUp enables you to optimize your processes, enhance team productivity, and reach your objectives efficiently.

Examples

Here are instances where ClickUp can enhance process efficiency:

- **Customer onboarding**: Utilize a board view to manage the customer onboarding process. Create tasks such as "send email," "schedule demo," and "create customer account," and assign them to team members, set deadlines, and drag and drop the tasks between statuses as they move toward completion.

- **Order fulfillment**: Organize the order fulfillment process with a list view. Assign tasks such as "pick order," "pack order," and "ship order." You can then assign the tasks to the right team members and establish deadlines for each task.

- **Product development**: Consider setting up a board to manage your processes. Add tasks for stages such as "requirements," "design product," and "develop the product." Ensure that you allocate these tasks to the team members and set deadlines accordingly.

In a case study, a start-up struggled with efficiently onboarding new customers amid high demand for their product. Realizing the urgency of the situation and the risk of losing customers to competitors, the start-up integrated ClickUp to streamline its customer onboarding process. By customizing a ClickUp board for their onboarding processes, they meticulously planned out each step, from sending emails to scheduling demos and creating customer accounts, enhancing accountability and productivity.

Through leveraging ClickUp, the start-up successfully optimized its customer onboarding process, reducing customer onboarding time by half. Consequently, their client satisfaction levels soared, resulting in improved customer retention rates and revenue growth. Furthermore, the refined process enabled the start-up to expand, meeting the increasing demand for their product while maintaining a high service quality. This case study showcases the advantages of using ClickUp to optimize operations and improve customer satisfaction.

After covering the basics of creating processes with ClickUp, as discussed earlier, we will now turn our attention to leveraging ClickUp's automation features in the following section. These automation tools provide capabilities to streamline processes and save time, allowing businesses to enhance efficiency and productivity seamlessly.

Harnessing the power of automation tools in ClickUp

ClickUp provides a suite of automation features that can aid in streamlining processes and saving time. By automating tasks, you can allocate your time efficiently toward critical work.

This section dives into recognizing automatable tasks, building processes, and mastering ClickUp's automation features.

Identifying repetitive tasks

The initial step in automating your processes involves identifying recurring tasks. Some of the tasks you might do regularly include the following:

- Recurring calendar schedules
- Adding tasks for potential leads
- Shifting tasks across different team members as they move through a process
- Updating task statuses
- Assigning task priority levels based on custom fields
- Generating reports

After identifying your repetitive tasks, including recurring ones that update daily, weekly, monthly, or annually, you can set them to explore automation options within ClickUp to streamline your processes.

How to set up automation

To automate processes in ClickUp, you'll have to establish a rule. Rules enable you to automate tasks and processes based on triggers and conditions:

- **Triggers** are events that kick off automation. For instance, a trigger could be the creation of a task, the completion of a task, or a change in a task status.

- **Conditions** are requirements that need to be satisfied for automation to run. For example, a condition could involve a task's priority, assignee, or due date.

- **Actions** represent the activities carried out by automation. For instance, a task could involve sending an email, setting up a task, or changing the status of an existing task.

In ClickUp, automation works based on location, impacting all tasks within the specified level of a hierarchy. For example, when automation is configured at the list level, it affects tasks within a list.

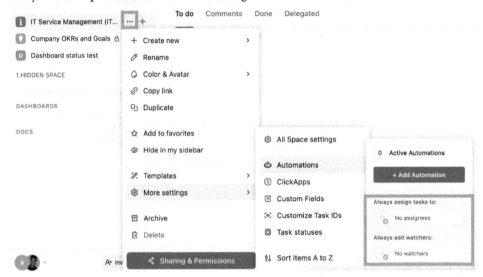

Figure 13.1 – Automation features in ClickUp (`https://help.clickup.com/hc/en-us/articles/6312102752791-Intro-to-Automations`)

Conversely, setting up automation at the folder level extends its reach to all tasks across every list within a folder. While automations themselves are not carried out in a predetermined order, the actions within each automation are executed sequentially to ensure tasks are managed, based on defined criteria.

Maximizing ClickUp's automation features efficiently

Here are some recommendations to make the most of ClickUp's automation capabilities:

- **Start small**: Avoid trying to automate all tasks at once; instead, start with a few. Observe how they progress. Once you have mastered automating a task, you can gradually expand your automated processes.

- **Test your automation thoroughly**: After creating an automation setup, conduct tests to confirm that it functions as intended.

- **Keep track of your automation closely**: After setting up your automated processes, it's important to name them and keep an eye on them to ensure that they function correctly.

Examples

Here are a few instances of how you can utilize ClickUp automation to streamline your work procedures:

- **Sending an email to clients**: Set up a rule that sends a welcome email automatically to new clients once they're added to ClickUp

- **Generating a new task for each new lead**: Establish a rule that automatically generates a new task for every fresh lead generated in your CRM system

- **Shifting tasks between different lists as they move through a process**: Implement a rule that moves tasks automatically between various lists as they progress through different stages of the process, such as moving from the "To Do" list to the "In Progress" list, and then to the "Done" list

- **Updating task statuses**: Create a rule that updates task statuses automatically based on specific criteria, such as a task's due date or when a prerequisite task is completed

- **Assign tasks to team members**: Create a rule that assigns team members from a custom field based on availability and difficulty

In a real-life example, a marketing team dealing with time constraints because of tasks such as sending out weekly email newsletters, creating new landing pages, and managing social media accounts looked for a way to make their work more efficient. They decided to use ClickUp's automation tools and set up rules to help them out. They set up a rule to send the weekly email newsletters to subscribers. They also created rules to make landing pages easily and keep their social media profiles up to date. By using ClickUp's automation features, the marketing team saved time. They could now focus on tasks that could boost productivity.

After exploring ClickUp's automation features that help businesses streamline work processes and save time effectively, we will now turn our attention to implementing strategies for processes in the future.

Implementing top-notch strategies for processes

Streamlining processes with ClickUp's robust tools fosters a culture of efficient collaboration and maximized productivity. This, in turn, translates to improved operations, higher-quality output, and, ultimately, increased customer satisfaction – the key to sustained business success.

ClickUp empowers seamless tools to streamline processes within departments and locations, enabling collaboration between internal teams to elevate productivity and effectiveness. To help you achieve peak efficiency, this section explores practical strategies to organize tasks and leverage ClickUp's functionalities to their full potential.

Task organization

Task organization is an element of process maintenance. Effectively organizing tasks simplifies tracking progress, identifying priorities, and preventing bottlenecks.

Here are some suggestions to organize tasks within ClickUp:

- Establish a consistent naming system to facilitate task management.

- Utilize tags and labels for task categorization to group tasks together and filter them by category.

- Set due dates. Prioritize tasks by focusing on addressing the critical ones first.

- Unpack large projects and continue breaking them down until they are manageable. This approach makes it easier to tackle the tasks and keep track of your progress.

- Utilize checklists to manage the subtasks within an assignment. This method promotes organization and guarantees that all subtasks are executed efficiently.

ClickUp's hierarchy structures your work into manageable levels, from workspaces down to tasks, for seamless project organization.

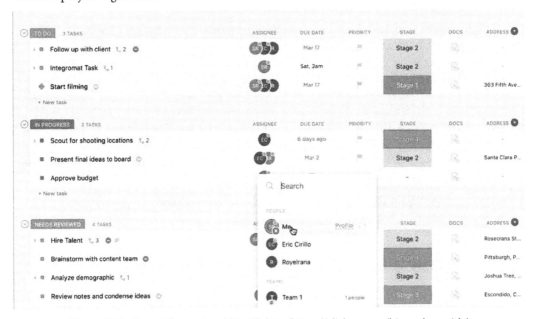

Figure 13.2 – Organizing tasks within ClickUp (https://clickup.com/hierarchy-guide)

Effortlessly navigate complex projects. ClickUp's visual hierarchy lets you see the big picture while staying focused on the details.

Teamwork

Successful teamwork relies heavily on collaboration. It encourages the sharing of ideas, enables the exchange of feedback, and ultimately results in the completion of tasks.

ClickUp supports collaboration by offering a range of features:

- **Assigning tasks to team members**: Ensure clarity on individual responsibilities by assigning tasks with clear descriptions and due dates.

- **Utilizing comments and @mentions**: Streamline communication by using comments to discuss tasks, provide updates, and keep everyone informed with `@mentions`.

- **Establishing task dependencies**: Maintain the logical flow of your project by setting dependencies between tasks, ensuring each step is completed in the right order.

- **Leveraging ClickUp chat**: The built-in chat functionality allows for real-time communication within ClickUp, eliminating the need to switch between different platforms.

- **Boosting collaboration with shared boards**: ClickUp's shared boards allow you to visualize progress and stay aligned throughout the project life cycle.

Using the features of ClickUp to boost your process maintenance efficiency

ClickUp provides tools that can assist you in improving your productivity and efficiency.

Here are some instances:

- **Boards**: These boards enable you to visualize your processes and monitor task progress

- **Calendars**: With calendars, you can view all tasks and events at a glance

- **Gantt charts**: Gantt charts help you see your project timeline and understand task dependencies

- **Time tracking**: By tracking time spent on tasks and projects, you can enhance productivity and estimate task completion times

- **Reporting**: ClickUp offers reports to monitor progress, identify areas for enhancement, and make informed decisions

Process scenarios

Here are a few scenarios that demonstrate how you can leverage ClickUp for processes:

- **Sales process**: Create a board dedicated to your sales process. Add tasks such as "leads," "schedule demos," and "close deals" to streamline operations. Assign tasks to team members. Establish deadlines for each task.

- **Product development process**: Consider creating a board dedicated to your product development process. Break down the steps, such as *gather requirements*, *design product*, and *develop a product*, into tasks, assign them to team members, and set deadlines.

- **Customer support process**: Create a board for your customer support process. Outline tasks such as *log ticket*, *assign a ticket*, and *resolve ticket*, assign them to team members, and set deadlines.

In a real-life scenario, a software company encountered difficulties meeting the demand for their products, facing challenges in project delivery timeline and budget adherence. To solve this, the company opted for ClickUp as their solution. By utilizing ClickUp, they structured their projects into boards on the platform. Each project was carefully divided into tasks, covering every phase of the project life cycle.

By using ClickUp's user layout and task organization tools, the tech company effectively improved its processes, leading to improved project planning, execution, and delivery.

Using Dashboards to track processes with KPIs

Create a visual view to track the important metrics of your work. Dashboards provide a source of truth for accountability and progress within your workspace.

Customizable cards are the building blocks of Dashboards. The customization and flexibility of cards allow Dashboards to be used for various reporting purposes across industries.

Figure 13.3 – Select a template or create Dashboards from scratch,
and use KPIs to track your processes instantly

For example, any sized company can create standardized statuses within their workspace and label specific task statuses as healthy and unhealthy. From there, the company can easily track the health of the organization with statuses and dashboard metrics, increasing personal productivity and team efficiency. For additional productivity, include dashboard KPIs in the process of team meetings, especially when tracking project health.

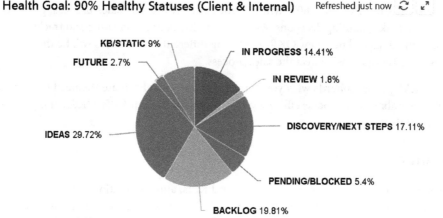

Figure 13.4 – The standardized status KPIs to monitor a project's health

By incorporating dashboards into your processes, you will have all your action steps in one area, reducing unnecessary clicks and clutter while providing a visual view of the important metrics in your work and home life.

Another example is tracking your sales process health in real time. With ClickUp's dashboards allowing real-time reports, your processes inside of ClickUp don't have to be perfect to track them. By using standardized statuses and custom fields and keeping your tasks up to date, the KPI metrics automatically update with automatic refreshes.

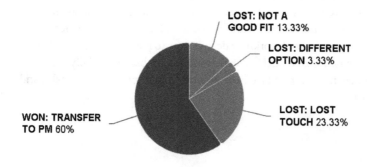

Figure 13.5 – KPIs to monitor the sales process health and opportunities for improvement

In this example, a sales process shows a 60% success win rate. To get a better win rate, we can look at the other KPI statuses to get ideas for improvement. There is a 1-digit percentage at 3.3% for the **LOST: DIFFERENT** option, which is a good target.

The **LOST: NOT A GOOD FIT** and **LOST: DIFFERENT** options could be improved with a new target percentage of 1-5%, which would be another **objective and key result (OKR)** for the next month.

With a new OKR to reach over 60% win rate for the next month's sales process, gives educated information to make planning decisions. As a result of this example, creating and tracking improved follow-up campaigns will be a new OKR. Exploring different lead sources will be the next OKR to track how these two goals will affect the sales process.

By using ClickUp's Dashboards with your processes, you can eliminate the need to print reports and easily streamline your process efficiency, by tracking important KPIs, OKRs, and project status metrics in real time.

Summary

In this chapter, we discussed processes, Dashboard KPIs, and automation in ClickUp to optimize work methodologies and enhance productivity. The chapter covered designing effective processes, provided a dedicated guide to creating processes in ClickUp, leveraging ClickUp's automation features, and implementing best practices for efficient processes. By the end of the chapter, you were equipped with the knowledge and tools needed to revolutionize your work processes, harness the automation potential of ClickUp, and implement best practices for efficient processes, serving as a strategic guide for individuals seeking to optimize their operations.

The information in this chapter is useful because it provides valuable insights into improving efficiency, productivity, and quality through effective processes. Additionally, it introduced you to ClickUp's features to create streamlined processes and automate repetitive tasks, enabling you to save time and focus on more critical work. The chapter's examples and case studies demonstrated the tangible benefits that ClickUp can offer to optimize how you work and live.

In the upcoming chapter, you will delve into a comprehensive exploration of workflows and designing user experience in ClickUp. This chapter is dedicated to providing you with an in-depth understanding of how to create intuitive and efficient workflows that enhance the user experience within ClickUp. You'll learn about the principles of workflow design, how to map out processes that reflect your team's needs, and ways to customize ClickUp's features to streamline your daily tasks. We'll also discuss strategies to minimize friction points, ensure smooth transitions between tasks, and maintain high levels of productivity.

Further reading and free resources

Here's a breakdown of which ClickUp plans, organized by each feature mentioned in this chapter, are included in the Free and Paid plans:

ClickUp feature	Free plan	Paid plan
Task management	Yes	Yes
Checklists	Yes	Yes
Templates	Limited	Yes
Automation	Limited	Yes
Boards	Yes	Yes
Calendars	Yes	Yes
Dependencies	Limited	Yes
Custom fields	Limited	Yes
Real-time chat	No	Yes
Shared boards	Yes	Yes
Gantt charts	No	Yes
Time tracking	No	Yes
Reporting	Limited	Yes

Table 13.1 – ClickUp Plan details

Here are some additional details about the ClickUp plans:

- **Free plan**: The free plan works well for individuals or small teams seeking task management capabilities.

- **Paid plan**: Each offering features and pricing structure has paid subscription options. These plans provide features not included in the Free plan, such as recurring tasks, customizable fields, and ClickUp's AI integration.

> **Note**
>
> For further details, you can contact the ClickUp sales team at `https://clickup.com/contact/contact-sales`.

Sign up to download your free workbook and productivity resources for each chapter

ClickUp is constantly evolving. Get help and explore each chapter in depth, receive the latest productivity updates and ClickUp tips, and download your free workbook at `bluecreative. com/clickup`. It specializes in ClickUp implementation, configurations, systems development, process implementation, and more.

Unger, E. (2024). ClickUp. BLUECREATIVE.

`https://bluecreative.com/clickup`

14

Workflows – Designing User Experience in ClickUp

Chapter 14 is about integrating ClickUp into your own user experience to streamline everything in your life. Whether you're an everyday person, an entrepreneur, or a high-level executive overseeing a project, this chapter aims to offer valuable insights on using ClickUp for both work and home-life-related workflows and tasks. We'll delve into the following main topics:

- Workflows and the user experience in ClickUp: Simplified
- Establishing a workflow in the ClickUp home workspace
- Integrating personal and work tasks
- Making time for home and work-life balance in ClickUp

By the end of *Chapter 14*, you'll have the know-how and tools to make the most out of ClickUp, creating an approach to managing various aspects of your life efficiently. This chapter acts as a guide for individuals looking at ClickUp's potential as an all-inclusive tool for boosting productivity and organizing life effectively.

Workflows and the User Experience in ClickUp: Simplified

It takes much training, configurations, and documentation to confidently understand how to apply goal setting, planning, and execution and to do it well in ClickUp. Your hard work in applying what you have learned up to this point is to design your user experience using workflows.

> **Note**
> If anything needs to be clarified up to this point, now would be a good time to go back and reference previous chapters and follow along with the examples.

A workflow batches together many processes to achieve a goal. They often involve multiple stages and participants. Workflows can be simple, involving a few steps, or complex, encompassing a series of interconnected tasks spanning various departments or organizations. They are designed to ensure that tasks are completed consistently, efficiently, and effectively, minimizing errors and maximizing productivity. In essence, a workflow acts as a blueprint for how work should be carried out, providing a clear path from the initiation of a task to its completion.

The importance of workflows cannot be overstated. First and foremost, they bring structure and clarity to processes, ensuring that you and every team member know their responsibilities and the sequence of actions required. This clarity reduces the likelihood of errors and omissions, which can be costly and time-consuming. Moreover, workflows facilitate better communication and coordination among team members, as everyone knows the steps involved and the status of ongoing tasks. This helps bring relaxed confidence to organizations and complex projects with multiple teams or departments involved.

Another significant benefit of workflows is their ability to enhance efficiency and productivity. By standardizing processes, workflows eliminate unnecessary steps and streamline operations. This not only speeds up task completion but also allows the rescheduling and repurposing of resources for other critical activities. Additionally, well-defined workflows make it easier to identify bottlenecks and areas for improvement. Organizations can analyze their workflows to pinpoint inefficiencies and implement changes that optimize performance. Improving processes and quickly adapting to faster-changing times is a key competitive advantage.

Workflows are essential tools for managing tasks and processes within an organization. They provide a structured approach to task completion, enhance communication and coordination, and drive efficiency and productivity. By implementing effective workflows, organizations can ensure that their operations run smoothly and that they are well-positioned to achieve their goals.

Establishing a workflow in the ClickUp home workspace

ClickUp stands out as a platform for task management and collaboration that can be tailored to suit home and work-related activities.

The Everything view, shared view, folder, and list view allow you to track all your work in any area of ClickUp, allowing the creation of personalized workflows and easy updates for improvement to customize your experience in unlimited ways.

In this part, we'll explore how to set up workflows for a home routine using ClickUp to manage aspects of daily life, such as household tasks, personal objectives, interests, work, and business responsibilities.

Let's look at some examples of home office workflow that can be established in ClickUp:

- **Household chores workflow**: This could encompass tasks such as doing laundry, taking out the garbage, and tidying up the house. You might want to schedule these tasks on a recurring basis so that they are consistently attended to.

- **Personal goals workflow**: This plan involves activities such as working out, eating healthily, and learning. It can be beneficial to keep track of your progress towards your goals and set deadlines for yourself.

- **Hobbies workflow**: This workflow may consist of activities such as playing instruments, sports, exercising, writing, or painting. Monitoring your progress in hobbies and establishing objectives can synergize and create momentum in the other areas of your life.

- **Job workflow**: For those working from the office or from home, organizing a system to handle work-related tasks is crucial. This may involve responsibilities such as checking emails, project work, and attending meetings.

- **Business workflow**: If you run a business, structuring a workflow to oversee all business aspects is essential. From fulfillment to marketing strategies to sales operations and customer service tasks, having a structured process and workflow plan in place is key.

- **Idea management workflow**: Create dedicated lists for personal and work-related ideas. Select the three dots or option, right-click it, and select **Email to List** to find an email address. Add the email address to your email contact list. Create automation rules for how tasks are processed when emailed to the list. Add assignee, priority, start and due dates, and more. Now, you can email home and work ideas to automatically be processed into your schedule and prepared for review, designed, and tweaked to your user experience preferences. Create consistent habits around building and maintaining a backlog of ideas and use statuses to keep track of their development into projects.

- **ClickUp workflow**: When planning your day, begin creating tasks and organizing them by home and work tags. Include start and due dates for reminders, priority, chat, and a dashboard to distinguish your priorities, track progress, and reschedule accordingly.

Utilizing ClickUp functions to optimize your home office workflow

ClickUp provides the views feature that can elevate the efficiency of your home office workflow. Here are some examples:

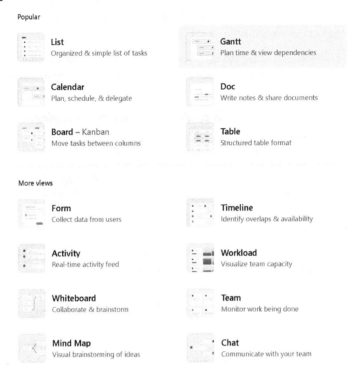

Popular

List
Organized & simple list of tasks

Gantt
Plan time & view dependencies

Calendar
Plan, schedule, & delegate

Doc
Write notes & share documents

Board – Kanban
Move tasks between columns

Table
Structured table format

More views

Form
Collect data from users

Timeline
Identify overlaps & availability

Activity
Real-time activity feed

Workload
Visualize team capacity

Whiteboard
Collaborate & brainstorm

Team
Monitor work being done

Mind Map
Visual brainstorming of ideas

Chat
Communicate with your team

Figure 14.1 – Selecting a view to start creating a workflow in ClickUp

- **Boards**: Visualize your workflow progress and task status effectively using boards

- **Calendars**: The calendar view feature easily keeps track of tasks and events

- **Gantt charts**: Gantt charts represent your project timeline and help you understand the interdependence of tasks

- **Kanban board**: Kanban boards visualize workflow stages using columns, and tasks are represented by cards that move between these columns

- **Time tracking**: Improve time management by tracking time spent on tasks and projects. This will enhance productivity and estimate task durations

- **Reporting**: ClickUp offers reports for progress tracking, identifying areas for enhancement, and facilitating informed decision-making

- **Filters**: You can filter tasks by custom fields, assignees, priority, time tracking, and due dates with many more options on any view, providing unlimited ideas to customize your workflow and free up time

Example of a home workspace workflow in ClickUp

Figure 14.2 – Selecting a home workspace to access cards and reminders

In this example, the demos are starting areas for working internally and with clients to avoid starting from scratch. Build-outs typically involve unpacking how things work and implementing them in multiple spaces to eventually consolidate the workflows into one space, as in *Figure 14.2*.

Look for the **Manage cards** option in the top right of the home workspace screen. When you click on it, you'll have multiple options to select from. Schedule time to explore how each card works within your current workflow:

- **AI StandUp™**: AI generated standup
- **Recents**: Lists all the ClickUp objects and locations you've recently viewed
- **Agenda**: Visualize tasks and events on your different calendars in one place
- **My Work**: A list of all of your assigned tasks and reminders
- **Assigned to me**: Consolidate your tasks across different lists that you have as an assignee

- **Personal List**: Keep track of your personal tasks in a list that is only visible to you

- **Assigned Comments**: Resolve and view any comment that has been assigned to you

- **LineUp:** Prioritize your most important tasks into one concise list

- **Reminders**: Organize and keep on top of all your reminders

Figure 14.3 – Recommended layout to start building your home
workspace cards and use them immediately.

In this example, I am starting the day by reviewing the cards to see the overdue items to reschedule and to organize today's work and the rest of the week's schedule. Once you understand which cards increase your efficiency, you're ready to finalize your home workspace workflow in ClickUp from start to finish.

Creating a home workspace workflow in ClickUp – step-by-step guide

Follow this guide to begin your first workflow for managing your home and work tasks within ClickUp. This workflow requires you to put your project manager hat on. As the project manager of your day, you'll use these features to manage, schedule, and prepare to do your work:

- **Home**: At your home workspace, you can manage reminders, your calendar, and your personal list and view multiple cards to plan, schedule, and do your work.

- **Cards**: Customize your cards and update their settings according to what information is most efficient for you. Add an AI Standup card to get automatic updates of all work, add the agenda card, and select a calendar to have a Google Calendar-like experience. View your personal tasks, comments, LineUp, and Reminders.

- **Capacity**: View cards, including my work card, assigned to me, reminders, and personal list cards to quickly gauge how much work your day will require.

- **Overdue items**: Review all of your tasks within your cards and assess all of the overdue items that require rescheduling in your current calendar. Estimate how long it will take. If it takes more than 15 minutes, create a task and schedule a timeboxed project management session for rescheduling.

- **Everything view and Shared view**: Use views, custom fields and customize ClickUp feature settings to design a custom workflow while you work.

- **Folder and List views**: Update the filters and views to filter the data as you need to see it at the moment, then revert to the default settings when finished.

- **Dashboards**: Create a dashboard for a space, folder, or list while you work and use a template, or start from scratch and track important metrics while planning or working.

- **Start your work**: As you finish managing your tasks and projects, you'll begin to schedule timeboxes to work on the tasks. If your workload is still not prepared, schedule recurring tasks to go through your backlog of work 1-5 times a week, however your schedule permits.

By following this guide, you can use this home workspace workflow to design your user experience for planning, scheduling, tracking, and doing your work in ClickUp.

Feel free to adjust this workflow to suit your individual requirements. For instance, you can include tasks, subtasks, and docs to write process steps and journal your work. You can also modify the deadlines, priority levels, and assignees for tasks.

After delving into the process of establishing a home workspace workflow in ClickUp, which includes creating processes and workflows for managing aspects of personal life such as household chores, personal objectives, hobbies, work-related tasks, and business activities, the attention now turns towards merging personal and work assignments in ClickUp.

Integrating personal and work tasks

Integrating personal and work tasks in ClickUp allows you to obtain a view of your duties while ensuring clarity and balance. When you manage both your work-related tasks in the workspace, it gives you a clearer picture of how you're spending your time. This allows you to make informed decisions on how to prioritize your commitments.

Strategies for integrating personal and work tasks

Here are a few strategies for integrating personal and work tasks in ClickUp:

- Set up areas for your personal and work tasks to keep things organized.
- Use location and tags to categorize your tasks, making them easier to locate and manage regardless of their nature.
- Prioritize tasks using dates, statuses, and ClickUp's priority levels to tackle the crucial ones first.
- Connect tasks using dependencies to maintain the task sequence.
- Leverage ClickUp's dashboards to monitor progress and pinpoint areas for improvement. This enables decision-making regarding time and commitment management.

Utilizing the features of ClickUp to maintain clarity and balance

To maintain clarity and balance while integrating personal and work tasks, ClickUp provides a range of features designed to streamline your workflow. Boards visually represent your tasks, allowing you to track progress and identify potential bottlenecks, ensuring you don't take on too much. Calendars provide a comprehensive view of upcoming tasks and events, aiding in effective planning to manage your time efficiently across both personal and work commitments. With time tracking capabilities, ClickUp enables you to monitor the time allocated to tasks and projects, helping you identify productivity improvements and prevent overworking in both work and home life chores. Additionally, ClickUp's dashboard reporting features offer various reports to track progress, pinpoint areas for enhancement, and make informed decisions. For instance, create a dashboard to analyze time allocation between personal and work-related tasks, facilitating a balanced approach to task management.

Example of a home and work-life balance workflow

Here is an example of an integrated home and work-life balance workflow to create in ClickUp:

- **Goals and Tags**: Begin by brainstorming your goals in a document or task. Brainstorm and capture all the stressors, inspirational ideas, and tasks for home and work. Change task types as necessary and label each task with the tag *Home and Work* or *Home Projects and Work Projects*.

- **Backlog of Work**: You will have a backlog of work after brainstorming. This is a group of tasks to be scheduled and completed, most notably in the Agile scrum framework, where they can be worked on in any order.

- **Tag for Categories of Life**: Further organize your work by creating standardized tags for your categories of life. Use other categories of life to further manage your workload, such as Family, Health, Admin, Chores, Finance, Strategy, Research, AI/Automation, Tech, Shopping, Bills/Expenses, Clients/Projects/Buckets of time. By batching your tasks into these categories and setting start and due dates for the category task instead of individual tasks, you can keep track of all your priorities by as many categories of life as you have.

> **Note**
>
> As a best practice, most users have 5-7 categories of life. Power users can have 7 to 20 categories of life, including defining their home and work-life workload.

- **Board View**: The end of each step of this workflow is to design a user experience that allows you to view all priorities and begin working on the board's top tasks. Use filters and custom board settings to refine your workflow to taste.

Creating a workflow for your home and work-life balance – step-by-step guide

Follow this guide to design your personal user experience for how you would like to manage your home and work responsibilities. As you continue to grow your habits and routines, write processes and build workflows. These assets will be workflows and part of your **personal productivity systems for doing things**:

- **Standard Statuses**: If you haven't already, standardize all spaces, folders, and lists to have the same statuses. Open, In Progress, In Review, Backlog, Recurring, KB/Static, and Mission/Vision are recommended best practices for setting statuses that capture all processes' actions so that nothing slips through the cracks.

- **Custom Fields**: Use custom fields to segment your data, leaving your action status separate from that of processes and workflow. This is critical.

Figure 14.4 – List view workflow

- **List View Workflow:** Filter options for your workflow: Select by status, select by the due date, my mode, view by assignee, and customize settings.

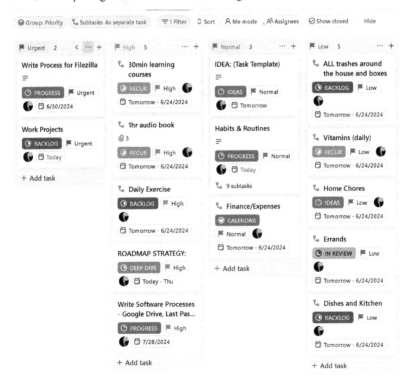

Figure 14.5 – Priority Board view workflow

- **Priority Board View Workflow**: Filter options for your workflow: Select by priority, treat sub-tasks as separate tasks, and drag tasks effortlessly through priority stages.

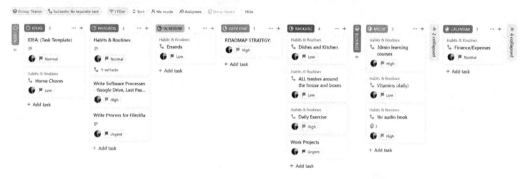

Figure 14.6 – Status Board view workflow

- **Status Board View Workflow**: Filter options for your workflow: Select by status, sub-tasks as separate tasks

Figure 14.7 – Calendar view workflow

- **Calendar View Workflow**: ClickUp's calendar can replace other calendars, such as Google, Apple, and Outlook. Tasks can be used as calendar events. Create a new task type called calendar events.

Figure 14.8 – Workload view workflow

- **Workload View Workflow**: Filter workload by tasks for one week and confirm that you have tasks configured and ready for scheduling and work. Additionally, estimate the hours or number of tasks for each user's capacity.

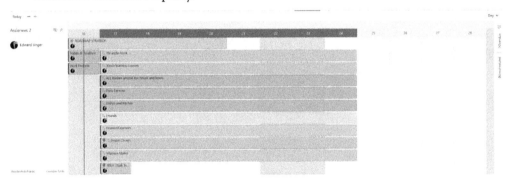

Figure 14.9 – Timeline view workflow

- **Timeline View Workflow**: Filter by an assignee to view scheduling and refine details as needed.

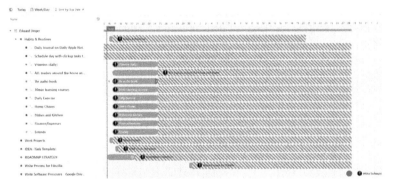

Figure 14.10 – Gantt view workflow

- **Gantt View Workflow:** Filter by Today, Week/Day, and sort by due date.

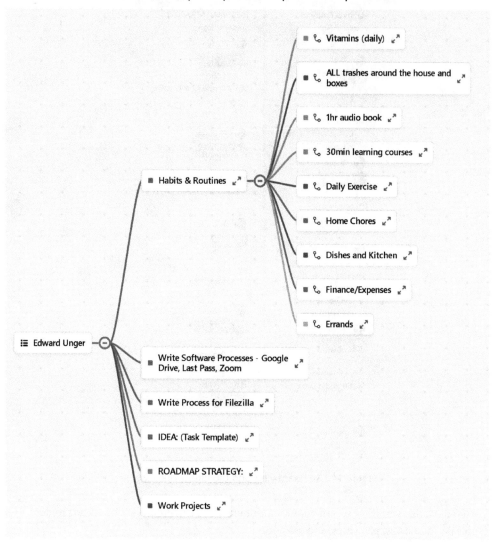

Figure 14.11 – Mind Map view workflow

- **Mind Map View Workflow:** Auto-diagram your processes and workflows and get instant visuals for meetings and internal use.

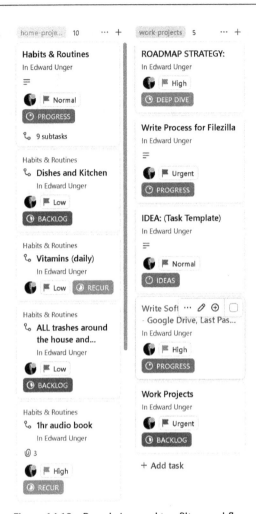

Figure 14.12 – Board view and tag filter workflow

Feel free to adjust this workflow to suit your requirements. You can enhance it by adding folders, lists, tasks, subtasks, due dates, priorities, and assignees.

Having discussed strategies for integrating personal and work tasks in ClickUp, which include creating separate spaces, utilizing labels and tags, setting due dates and priorities, and using ClickUp's features, such as boards, calendars, time tracking, and reporting, the focus now shifts to balancing work and personal life with ClickUp. This transition emphasizes the importance of maintaining clarity and balance in managing work and personal commitments. It introduces the upcoming topic of strategies for time management, setting boundaries, and utilizing ClickUp's features to achieve a healthy work-life balance.

Making time for home and work-life balance in ClickUp

Balancing work and personal life is crucial for sustaining an efficient lifestyle. ClickUp can serve as a tool for achieving this equilibrium. It involves creating new habits and routines and learning new skills every day. In this segment, we will delve into methods for managing time, establishing boundaries, and leveraging ClickUp's functionalities to uphold a work-life balance.

Time management

Time management is key in maintaining a balance between work and personal life. ClickUp aids in enhancing time management through its array of features, including the following:

- **Due dates**: By assigning due dates to tasks and projects, you can stay organized and avoid procrastination.

- **Priorities**: Prioritizing tasks enables you to concentrate on the ones first.

- **Time tracking**: Add ClickUp's time tracking features to workflows to encourage a proactive environment for improvement and not micro-management.

- **Reporting**: ClickUp provides various reports to monitor progress and pinpoint areas needing enhancement. For instance, generating a report can reveal the distribution of time between work-related and personal tasks.

Setting boundaries

Setting boundaries for yourself and others is an unspoken part of balancing work and personal life. Defining distinctions between work hours and personal time is essential to prevent overworking and ensure you have time for yourself.

ClickUp can assist in establishing these boundaries through its features:

- **Working hours**: Customize your working hours on ClickUp to stay focused and avoid working beyond your designated time.

- **Notifications**: Tailor your ClickUp notifications to receive the alerts you need at the times that suit you best, including snoozing alerts. This reduces distractions during your workday by ensuring you only get notified when absolutely necessary.

- **Priorities**: Even though you can turn off alerts, the best practice is to always have them on and check them regularly to ensure everything time-sensitive is noticed and to avoid falling behind due to missed communication, especially during large, high-priority projects. Additionally, I have witnessed team members lose projects and positions they love because they have the right boundaries in the wrong places.

On the other side of this subject, there are times when boundaries and schedules should be thrown out. Scheduling a timebox in the home and work life to extreme focus for many hours without distraction consistently throughout your days is a skillset and a productivity tool to use when extreme innovation or problem-solving is required.

Examples of how to use ClickUp to balance your home and work life

Create a dashboard to monitor progress on work and personal tasks or projects. Include widgets for tasks, projects, due dates, and priorities.

Imagine a dashboard specifically designed for a busy professional to juggle both worlds. Here's what it might look like:

- **Top Priority Tasks and Due Dates**: A prominent Task List card displaying the most critical tasks due today, ensuring nothing gets overlooked.

- **Project Progress Tracker**: Use a bar chart widget visualizing the overall completion percentage of ongoing projects divided between home and work tasks by tags.

- **Team Collaboration**: Create a card showcasing assigned tasks for team members, fostering transparency and accountability.

- **Customize Notifications**: To receive alerts during your working hours and flexible hours, update and refine your notification settings.

- **Workload View**: Use ClickUp's Workload to estimate hours by time or task count. Schedule tasks within your timeboxed working hours to help maintain focus and avoid exceeding designated work hours.

- **Dashboard View**: Create a new dashboard named My Home-Work-Life Dashboard, filtered by home and work tags.

- **Dashboard Card**: Utilize the My Task and Calendar cards to plan your weekly activities, ensuring time is allocated for work-related tasks and personal endeavors.

- **Additional Views to Explore**: Employ Gantt charts to visualize project timelines, pinpoint potential bottlenecks, prevent over-commitment, and stay on target with deadlines.

Case study – How ClickUp restored work-life balance

A ClickUp user found themselves grappling with the challenge of balancing their work and personal life, often working late into the night and sacrificing weekends, leading to stress. Seeking a solution, they turned to ClickUp to manage their tasks and projects. They established a personalized dashboard to monitor progress across both work and personal endeavors, implementing working hours and tailored notifications to maintain boundaries and ensure uninterrupted focus during designated times.

Embracing the My Tasks view, they meticulously scheduled time for work and personal commitments, leveraging Gantt charts to visualize project timelines and pinpoint potential obstacles, thus regaining control over their work-life balance.

Through the utilization of ClickUp, the individual successfully attained a work-life routine, which enabled them to decrease their workload.

By following these suggestions, you can leverage ClickUp to enhance your work-life equilibrium and learn how to continue your growth and work habits to design life how you want to live. You will be amazed at what you can accomplish.

Summary

This chapter has been a guide on how to incorporate ClickUp into your home setup, providing valuable tips on maximizing ClickUp's capabilities for managing various aspects of life outside of work tasks. This chapter focuses on establishing a workflow for your home workspace in ClickUp, integrating personal and work tasks, and finding a healthy balance between work and personal life with ClickUp.

The first part discusses setting up a workflow for your home workspace, highlighting how adaptable ClickUp is for organizing household chores, personal objectives, hobbies, work responsibilities, and business matters. It offers advice on creating processes and workflows for each area of your life by utilizing features such as boards, calendars, Gantt charts, time-tracking tools, and reporting features to improve efficiency and organization.

The second part delves into combining work tasks within ClickUp by suggesting methods such as creating spaces using labels and tags, effectively setting due dates and priorities, utilizing checklists efficiently, and using ClickUp's dashboards for an overall perspective. It includes a sample integrated workflow that can be personalized to meet needs.

The last section addresses the topic of maintaining a balance between work commitments and personal life through the use of ClickUp.

The importance of managing your time and setting boundaries is highlighted, as well as using tools such as dates, priorities, time tracking, and reporting to help maintain a healthy balance between work and personal life. An example is shared to demonstrate how a ClickUp user successfully achieved a work-life balance through these methods.

After completing this chapter, you'll now have an understanding of how ClickUp can be a tool for managing work responsibilities and organizing your life in a balanced and orderly manner. This chapter serves as a guide for those looking to maximize ClickUp's features to boost productivity and handle aspects of their daily routines efficiently.

In the next chapter, we'll cover various topics to enhance your ClickUp experience. You'll discover best practices for task organization and workflow optimization alongside troubleshooting advice for common platform issues. We'll answer frequently asked questions to clarify ClickUp's features and integrations and delve into how AI-powered tools within ClickUp can automate tasks, provide analytics, and support decision-making to boost your project management efficiency.

Further reading and free resources

Here's a breakdown of which ClickUp plans by each feature mentioned in this chapter are included in the Free and Paid plans:

ClickUp Feature	Free Plan	Paid Plan
Boards	Yes	Yes
Calendars	Yes	Yes
Gantt Charts	No	Yes
Kanban Board	Yes	Yes
Time Tracking	No	Yes
Reporting	Limited	Yes

Table 14.1 – ClickUp Plan details

Here are some additional details about the ClickUp plans:

- **Free Plan**: The free plan works well for individuals or small teams seeking task management capabilities.

- **Paid Plan**: Each offering features and pricing structure has paid subscription options. These plans provide features not included in the free plan, such as recurring tasks, customizable fields, and ClickUps AI integration.

> **Note**
> For further details, you may contact the ClickUp Sales Team:
> `https://clickup.com/contact/contact-sales`

Sign up to download your free workbook and productivity resources for each chapter

ClickUp is constantly evolving. Get help and explore each chapter in depth, receive the latest productivity updates and ClickUp tips, and download your free workbook at `bluecreative.com/clickup`. Specializing in ClickUp implementation, configurations, systems development, process implementation, and more.

Unger, E. (2024). ClickUp. BLUECREATIVE.

`https://bluecreative.com/clickup`

Recommendations, Troubleshooting, FAQs, and AI-Powered Productivity

This comprehensive chapter equips ClickUp users of all levels, from solopreneurs to enterprise executives, with the knowledge and tools to navigate the platform seamlessly and unlock its full potential. We'll cover essential topics such as maximizing ClickUp's capabilities, overcoming common challenges, addressing **frequently asked questions (FAQs)**, and leveraging ClickUp's innovative AI features to boost productivity. In this chapter, we're going to cover the following main topics:

- Maximizing ClickUp's potential
- FAQs and additional support
- Troubleshooting common issues and challenges
- Introducing ClickUp AI – your intelligent assistant
- ClickUp AI and the future

Maximizing ClickUp's potential

ClickUp is a powerful task management and collaboration tool for work-life balance that can help you achieve your goals and streamline your workflow. However, its vast array of features and options can be overwhelming at first. This is normal, and rest assured, you will only feel that way for a while. Here's a roadmap to help get you started:

- **Establish a clear structure**: Organize your work using Spaces, Folders, Lists, and Tasks. Assign clear and descriptive names and tags for easy searchability.

- **Best practices**: Implement best practices such as breaking down complex tasks, assigning ownership and deadlines, leveraging comments and attachments for clear communication, and utilizing checklists for managing subtasks.

- **Advanced features**: Explore ClickUp's advanced features to elevate your productivity. Utilize custom fields for additional task information, automate repetitive tasks with automation, visualize progress with dashboards, and share data securely with clients or stakeholders using Portals.

- **Optimize ClickUp**: Enhance your ClickUp experience by utilizing the mobile app for on-the-go access, integrating ClickUp with other tools you use, and taking advantage of ClickUp's training resources, including tutorials, webinars, and documentation.

Case study – how ClickUp boosted a marketing team's productivity

Before ClickUp, the marketing team was drowning in chaos. Disorganized tasks scattered across various platforms made it difficult to track progress, leading to missed deadlines and frustrated team members. Their workflow lacked structure, and communication was a constant struggle. However, ClickUp's structured workspace became their saving grace. The ability to break down complex marketing campaigns into manageable steps within Workspaces, Lists, and Tasks brought much-needed clarity. ClickUp wasn't just about organization, though. Custom fields allowed them to track campaign-specific metrics in real time, providing valuable insights into performance. Automated notifications eliminated the need for manual updates, freeing up time for strategic initiatives. Finally, customizable dashboards became their central hub, offering real-time visibility into progress and allowing for quick adjustments based on data. With ClickUp streamlining their workflow, the team experienced a remarkable 20% boost in productivity. They completed projects faster, achieved better results, and, most importantly, rediscovered the joy of working together efficiently. ClickUp transformed them from a team battling chaos into a marketing machine.

Having explored the strategies for maximizing ClickUp's potential and witnessing its transformative impact on a marketing team's productivity, the focus now shifts to troubleshooting common issues and challenges that users may encounter while navigating the platform.

FAQs and additional support

ClickUp offers a comprehensive platform for managing tasks, projects, and collaboration. Here are some commonly asked questions and resources to help you get the most out of ClickUp.

General FAQs

- **What is ClickUp?** ClickUp is project management software available on desktop, laptop, and mobile for everyday users and medium to enterprise-sized organizations to increase personal productivity and operational efficiency.

- **What are the benefits of using ClickUp?** ClickUp offers a variety of features to improve productivity, including the following:

  - Increased organization and clarity

  - Enhanced collaboration with team members

  - Improved communication and transparency

  - Streamlined workflows and task management

  - Boosted efficiency and time management

- **How do I get started with ClickUp?** Sign up for a free account on the ClickUp website. ClickUp offers a user-friendly interface and provides onboarding resources such as tutorials and templates to get you started quickly.

Additional support resources

- **ClickUp Help Center**: This is a comprehensive resource for all things ClickUp. It includes articles, tutorials, and videos covering basic topics to advanced features (`https://help.clickup.com/hc/en-us`).

- **ClickUp Community Forum**: The ClickUp Community Forum is a platform where you can connect with other ClickUp users, ask questions, share best practices, and find solutions to common challenges (`https://clickup.com/community`).

- **ClickUp support tickets**: If you have a specific issue that you can't resolve using the Help Center or Community Forum, you can submit a support ticket directly to ClickUp. This allows you to get personalized assistance from their support team (`https://help.clickup.com/hc/en-us`).

- **ClickUp Academy**: ClickUp Academy offers online courses and training resources to help you master ClickUp and unlock its full potential (`https://university.clickup.com/`).

- **ClickUp services**: For more advanced needs, sign up for the free workbook resources and learn more about our ClickUp implementation, optimization, migration services, customized curriculums, training, and support (`https://bluecreative.com/clickup`).

> **Note**
> ClickUp is constantly evolving and adding new features. It's a good idea to stay updated on the latest developments by checking the ClickUp blog or following them on social media.

Troubleshooting common issues and challenges

ClickUp is a powerful platform, but occasional issues can arise. Here's a guide to overcoming common hurdles:

1. **Login problems**: ClickUp login problems refer to difficulties users encounter when attempting to access their ClickUp account:

    *   **Double-check credentials**: Make sure you're entering the correct username or email address and password.

    *   **Reset password**: If you've forgotten your password, click the **Forgot Password** link on the login page and follow the instructions to reset it.

    *   **Contact ClickUp support**: If you're still having trouble logging in after trying the preceding steps, reach out to ClickUp support for further assistance.

2. **Notification issues**: ClickUp notification issues describe problems users experience with receiving or managing alerts and updates within the ClickUp platform:

    *   **Enable notifications**: Ensure notifications are enabled in your ClickUp settings. You can usually find this option in your profile settings.

    *   **Clear cache and cookies**: Cluttered browser caches or cookies can sometimes interfere with notifications. Try clearing your cache and cookies and logging back in to ClickUp.

    *   **Log out and and log back in**: Sometimes, a simple logout and log back in can resolve notification issues.

    *   **Contact ClickUp support**: If notifications still don't work after trying these solutions, contact ClickUp support for further troubleshooting.

3. **Data import challenges**: ClickUp data import challenges refer to users' difficulties when transferring information from other platforms into ClickUp:

    *   **Verify data format**: ClickUp supports data import in specific formats, such as CSV, XLSX, and JSON. Ensure your data is formatted correctly before attempting an import.

    *   **Break down large datasets**: Importing large datasets can sometimes cause issues. Try breaking down your data into smaller chunks and importing them one at a time.

    *   **Contact ClickUp support**: If none of these solutions work, contact ClickUp support and get help diagnosing the problem and suggesting solutions.

4. **Performance issues**: ClickUp performance issues encompass slow loading times, lagging functionality, or unexpected crashes that hinder smooth work within the platform:

    - **Close unused programs**: Multiple programs running in the background can consume resources and slow down ClickUp. Close any unused programs before using ClickUp.

    - **Ensure sufficient memory**: ClickUp may run slowly if your computer lacks free memory. Close unnecessary programs and free up RAM.

    - **Clear cache and cookies**: As with notifications, a cluttered browser cache can impact performance. Clear your cache and cookies and try again.

    - **Try a different browser**: If you're using a web browser, try accessing ClickUp with a different browser to see whether the issue persists.

    - **Update the ClickUp desktop app (if applicable)**: An outdated ClickUp desktop app might cause performance issues. If you're using it, update it to the latest version.

    - **Contact ClickUp support**: If none of these solutions work, contact ClickUp directly for troubleshooting and solution-seeking.

5. **Specific feature problems**: ClickUp-specific feature problems refer to malfunctions or glitches users encounter with particular functionalities within the ClickUp platform:

    - **ClickUp Help Center**: The ClickUp Help Center is a valuable resource for troubleshooting issues with specific features. Search for the feature you're having trouble with and see whether there are any relevant articles or tutorials.

    - **ClickUp Community Forum**: The ClickUp Community Forum is a platform where you can connect with other users and ask questions about specific features.

    - **Contact ClickUp support**: If you can't find a solution in the Help Center or Community Forum, contact ClickUp support directly. They have a team of specialists who can assist you with specific feature-related problems.

> **Note**
> When contacting ClickUp support, the more information you provide about the issue you're facing, the easier diagnosing and resolving the problem will be.

Case study – ClickUp support resolves a slow performance issue

A ClickUp customer faced slow performance that hindered their workflow. Even after trying troubleshooting steps on their own, the issue remained unresolved. They reached out to ClickUp support. The support team quickly identified the problem and implemented a solution, resulting in a significant boost in ClickUp's performance for the customer.

Having provided a comprehensive guide to troubleshooting common issues and challenges encountered in ClickUp, including login problems, notification issues, data import challenges, performance issues, and specific feature problems, the focus now shifts to introducing ClickUp AI, your intelligent assistant designed to automate tasks and enhance productivity through its innovative use of **Artificial Intelligence (AI)**.

Introducing ClickUp AI – your intelligent assistant

ClickUp takes project management to the next level. This bonus section explores ClickUp AI, your intelligent assistant that learns from your actions and data to automate tasks.

Leveraging ClickUp AI for enhanced productivity

ClickUp AI empowers you to work smarter, not harder, by automating routine tasks and surfacing valuable insights from your data. Here's a deep dive into ClickUp AI's functionalities and how to leverage them to boost your productivity:

- **Automatic Task Summarization**: ClickUp Automatic Task Summarization is an AI-powered feature that automatically generates concise summaries of your tasks, saving you time and effort:

  - **Effortless overviews**: ClickUp AI can automatically generate summaries of your tasks, including descriptions, comments, and attachments

  - **Actionable insights**: Identify key details and next steps quickly, allowing you to prioritize effectively and stay focused on what matters most

  Let's see how to use it:

  i.   Open a task.

  ii. In the top-right corner, click the **AI** icon.

  iii. Select **Summary** from the drop-down menu.

  iv. ClickUp AI will generate a concise summary of the task.

  v.   You can copy the summary, create a new task or document based on it, or generate a new summary from a different perspective.

ClickUp AI summarizes everything – details, attachments, and comments:

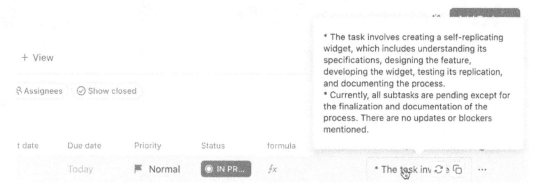

Figure 15.1 – Generating a summary or update in ClickUp (https://help.clickup.com/hc/en-us/
articles/18450100382871-generate-task-summaries-and-updates-with-ai-custom-fields)

Save precious time and stay focused. ClickUp AI condenses task information into clear summaries, keeping crucial details at your fingertips.

- **Smart Comment Thread Summarization**: ClickUp Smart Comment Thread Summarization uses AI to extract key points from lengthy discussions, simplifying complex conversations:

  - **Simplifies complex discussions**: Extract key points from lengthy comment threads to quickly grasp the conversation's essence

  - **Improved communication**: Focus on the most critical points and avoid misunderstandings by referencing the AI-generated summary

Let's see how to use it:

  i.   Open the comment thread you want to summarize.

  ii. Click the **Summarize thread** button in the top-right corner.

  iii. ClickUp AI will generate a summary of the conversation.

  iv. You can copy the summary or generate a new one from a different viewpoint.

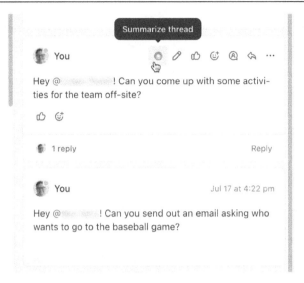

Figure 15.2 – Summarizing task comment threads in ClickUp
(https://help.clickup.com/hc/en-us/articles/18262094491159-
generate-task-summaries-and-updates-with-clickup-ai)

- **AI-Powered Custom Fields**: ClickUp AI-Powered Custom Fields automatically update or summarize data based on your entries, eliminating manual work and providing real-time insights:

  - **Automated updates**: Automatically generates summaries or updates based on custom field data, eliminating manual data entry and providing real-time progress visibility.

  - **Real-time visibility**: Gain instant insights into task progress without manually reviewing every detail. This allows for proactive decision-making and course correction when needed.

  Let's see how to use them:

  i.   Create a custom field for your desired data type (text, number, date, etc.).

  ii. Enable the **Generate summary or update** option in the **Custom Field** settings.

  iii. Click the **Generate** button in the **Custom Field** column to get an AI-powered summary or update for the task.

Figure 15.3 – Adding AI Custom Fields to a workspace (https://help.clickup.com/hc/en-us/articles/18450100382871-generate-task-summaries-and-updates-with-ai-custom-fields)

- **Prioritization Assistant**: ClickUp Prioritization Assistant (currently in development) is an AI-powered feature that analyzes tasks to suggest a prioritized list, helping you focus on the most critical ones first:

  - **Intelligent workload management**: ClickUp AI analyzes your tasks, considering deadlines and dependencies, and assigns team members to suggest a prioritized list. This helps you focus without feeling overwhelmed.

  Let's see how to use it:

  While this feature is not currently available, ClickUp's roadmap suggests it's in development.

Having explored ClickUp AI's functionalities, the focus now shifts to its future. The following section delves into upcoming possibilities such as automated workflows, predictive analytics, and smarter collaboration, highlighting how ClickUp AI continues to evolve to revolutionize project management and team collaboration.

ClickUp Brain – enhancing work-life balance

In the quest for a harmonious work-life balance, ClickUp Brain emerges as a pivotal feature that transforms how we manage our daily tasks and long-term goals. ClickUp Brain is an advanced AI-driven system integrated within ClickUp, designed to streamline workflows, enhance productivity, and simplify complex project management tasks. This feature leverages AI to automate routine processes, provide intelligent recommendations, and ensure that all aspects of your work and personal life are seamlessly integrated.

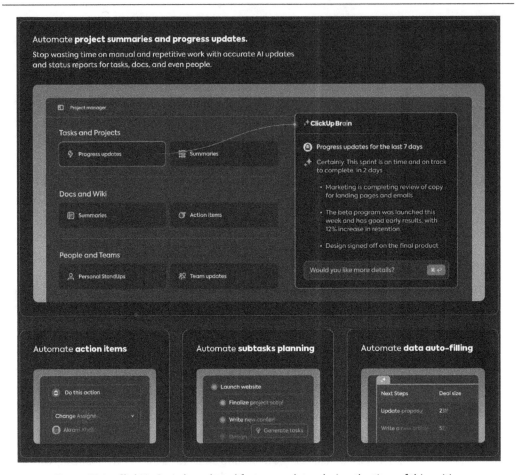

Figure 15.4 – ClickUp Brain launch and feature updates during the time of this writing

One of the most significant advantages of ClickUp Brain is its ability to consolidate various tasks and projects into a single, manageable interface. This integration is invaluable for individuals juggling multiple responsibilities at home and work. By centralizing tasks from different domains, ClickUp Brain helps those losing focus by task switching, thereby saving time and reducing cognitive load. This allows users to believe in the system, processes, and priorities faster. When you can stay on track to create time back in your day, whether personal or professional, and when nothing slips through the cracks any longer, you are well on your way to designing how you live.

Moreover, ClickUp Brain excels at prioritizing tasks based on urgency and importance, allowing users to focus on what truly matters. The AI analyzes your task list, deadlines, and personal preferences to suggest an optimal schedule. This intelligent prioritization helps balance work commitments with personal time, ensuring that you can meet professional deadlines without compromising on family activities or personal hobbies. By fostering a balanced approach to task management, ClickUp Brain helps users achieve their goals more effectively while maintaining a healthy work-life equilibrium.

Additionally, ClickUp Brain's automation capabilities play a crucial role in enhancing productivity. Routine tasks such as setting reminders, updating project statuses, and generating reports can be automated, freeing up valuable time for more meaningful activities. This automation saves time and reduces stress as users can rely on ClickUp Brain to handle repetitive tasks efficiently. The result is a more relaxed and focused approach to both work and personal life, contributing to overall well-being.

In summary, ClickUp Brain is a game-changer for anyone seeking to balance their professional and personal lives. Its AI-driven features simplify task management, prioritize effectively, and automate routine processes, making achieving a harmonious work-life balance more manageable. By leveraging the power of ClickUp Brain, users can enhance their productivity, reduce stress, and ensure ample time for work and personal pursuits.

ClickUp AI and the future

ClickUp AI is constantly evolving, with new features and functionalities released consistently. ClickUp's software development team has incredible habits and routines regarding consistent releases and documentation. Here are some exciting AI features to keep an eye on.

- **Automated workflows**: ClickUp AI could automate entire workflows based on predefined triggers and actions, further streamlining your processes. At the time of this writing, AI automations have been released.

- **Predictive analytics**: AI could analyze historical data to predict potential roadblocks and suggest proactive solutions, ensuring you stay ahead of the curve.

- **Smarter collaboration**: Imagine AI facilitating seamless communication and task delegation within your team, optimizing collaboration and project outcomes.

By embracing ClickUp AI's capabilities, you can unlock a new level of efficiency and productivity in your work. As ClickUp AI continues to develop, it has the potential to revolutionize the way you manage projects and collaborate with your team.

Advanced features (in development)

Unfortunately, as of this writing, there isn't a clear publicly available list of ClickUp's upcoming features or features currently under development.

However, there are a few ways to stay updated on potential ClickUp advancements:

- **ClickUp roadmap**: While an official *ClickUp Advanced Features* list might not be available, they do have a public roadmap (`https://dev-doc.clickup.com/p/ad-3021/click-up-roadmap`) that showcases features currently being worked on. This roadmap is updated periodically and provides insights into upcoming functionalities such as the following:

  - Pages in the sidebar for easier document access

- Private comments for confidential team communication

- Forms improvements for streamlined data capture

- Variables in automation for more dynamic workflows

- **ClickUp blog**: The ClickUp blog (`https://clickup.com/blog/topics/`) regularly posts articles on its website covering topics such as features, updates, and tips for users. They often use blog posts to share features.

- **ClickUp social media**: To stay updated on news and potential feature releases, you can also follow ClickUp on their media platforms with the most current links to LinkedIn, Facebook, Instagram, and X/Twitter at `https://clickup.com/`.

Summary

In this chapter of the book, you learned various strategies and techniques to master ClickUp, a versatile task management and collaboration platform. The chapter covered essential topics such as maximizing ClickUp's potential, troubleshooting common issues, addressing FAQs, and introducing ClickUp's AI-powered productivity features.

You gained insights into maximizing ClickUp's potential by establishing clear structures, implementing best practices, and exploring advanced features such as custom fields, automation, dashboards, and portals. A case study illustrated how a marketing team boosted productivity by 20% through the effective utilization of ClickUp's features.

The chapter also provided guidance on troubleshooting common issues such as login problems, notification issues, data import challenges, and performance issues. Practical solutions and case studies demonstrated how users can effectively overcome these hurdles.

Furthermore, you were introduced to ClickUp's AI capabilities, including automatic task summarization, smart comment thread summarization, AI-powered custom fields, and the prioritization assistant (currently in development). The potential future developments of ClickUp AI, such as automated workflows, predictive analytics, and smarter collaboration, were also highlighted.

The information in this chapter was useful to you as it equipped you with the knowledge and tools necessary to navigate ClickUp effectively, resolve common issues, and leverage AI-powered features for enhanced productivity.

In the next chapter, we'll focus on leveraging ClickUp's advanced features to foster your personal and professional development. You'll learn how to refine productivity habits, manage complex projects, and customize workflows while integrating ClickUp with other tools to create a comprehensive management ecosystem.

Further reading and free resources

Here's a breakdown of which ClickUp plans by each feature mentioned in this chapter are included in the free and paid plans:

ClickUp Feature	Free Plan	Paid Plan
Spaces, Folders, Lists, and Tasks	Yes	Yes
Comments and Attachments	Yes	Yes
Checklists for Subtasks	Yes	Yes
Custom Fields	Limited	Yes
Automation	Limited	Yes
Dashboards	Limited	Yes
Portals	No	Yes
Mobile App Access	Yes	Yes
Integrations	Limited	Yes
Training Resources (Tutorials, Webinars)	Yes	Yes
AI Task Summarization	No	Yes (in development)
AI Comment Thread Summarization	No	Yes (in development)
AI-Powered Custom Fields	No	Yes (in development)

Table 15.1 – ClickUp Plan details

Here are some additional details about the ClickUp plans:

- **Free plan**: The free plan works well for individuals or small teams seeking task management capabilities.

- **Paid plan**: Each offering's features and pricing structure has paid subscription options. These plans provide features not included in the free plan, such as recurring tasks, customizable fields, and ClickUp's AI integration.

> **Note**
>
> For further details, you may contact the ClickUp sales team:
>
> `https://clickup.com/contact/contact-sales`

Sign up to download your free workbook and productivity resources for each chapter

ClickUp is constantly evolving. Get help and explore each chapter in depth, receive the latest productivity updates and ClickUp tips, and download your free workbook at `bluecreative.com/clickup`, specializing in ClickUp implementation, configurations, systems development, process implementation, and more.

Unger, E. (2024). ClickUp. BLUECREATIVE.

16

Next Steps – Personal and Professional Growth with ClickUp

Welcome to *Chapter 16*, where we will explore how to continue innovating in ClickUp and create new systems and processes in your personal and professional life. Whether you're a proprietor, a business owner of a sized company, or an executive overseeing projects at an enterprise level, this chapter aims to offer valuable insights into expanding the possibilities with ClickUp and enhancing your personal and professional frameworks. The main topics we will explore in this chapter include the following:

- Embracing a growth mindset for development

- Utilizing ClickUp's features to foster innovation

- Implementing effective strategies for sustainable progress

- Learning to recognize accomplishments

This chapter acts as a guide for optimizing your utilization of ClickUp while also fostering a culture of continuous improvement in your personal and professional spheres. By embracing the growth mindset, using features, and adhering to best practices, you can unlock ClickUp's full potential as a driver of innovation and advancement.

Embracing a growth mindset for development

Embracing a growth mindset for development involves believing that intelligence and skills can be cultivated through dedication and effort. People with a growth mindset tend to welcome challenges, learn from their errors, and persist in situations. Having a growth mindset is crucial for progress. We are more inclined to invest the effort when we believe we can enhance our abilities. Additionally, being open to experimentation and taking risks can lead to outcomes.

Here are some ways to adopt a growth mindset for improvement:

- Challenge your ingrained beliefs by recognizing any notions that limit your perception of your intelligence or capabilities. Then, question these beliefs. Evaluate whether there is any evidence supporting them.

- When undertaking new tasks or projects, concentrate on the process rather than fixating on the end result. Focus on acquiring knowledge and honing your skills without being overly concerned about the outcome.

- Embrace mistakes as learning opportunities. Errors provide insights for growth. Take time to analyze what went awry when you made a mistake and consider how you can approach situations differently in the future.

- Solicit feedback from others regarding your work to pinpoint areas where you can excel further.

- Welcome challenges as opportunities for growth and development. Don't shy away from challenges. Stepping out of your comfort zone is an opportunity to learn and grow

Here are instances that demonstrate how adopting a growth mindset can result in progress:

- When a student embraces a growth mindset, they are more inclined to work hard to enhance their grades, especially if they're facing difficulties in a specific subject. Moreover, they are more likely to reach out for assistance from their teacher or peers.

- An employee with a growth mindset is more inclined to take on projects and tasks at work. They also show enthusiasm for participating in training sessions and developmental opportunities.

- An athlete who embodies a growth mindset tends to dedicate more hours toward training and honing their skills. Additionally, they actively seek feedback from their coach and teammates.

Illustrative example

Google fosters a growth mindset. Its unwavering commitment to continuous enhancement fuels ground-breaking products and services.

One method by which Google nurtures this mindset is by encouraging employees to experiment and take risks. Google employees are urged to explore avenues, even if they face the possibility of failure. This culture of trying things has resulted in the creation of groundbreaking products and services, such as Gmail, Google Maps, and Google Search.

Google also promotes a growth mindset by allowing employees to learn and develop through training programs and shadowing experiences.

This focus on growth has made Google one of the global companies that is always striving to enhance its offerings.

Having discussed the importance of embracing a growth mindset for continuous improvement and how it can lead to innovation, the focus now shifts to leveraging ClickUp's advanced features for further innovation and creating new systems and processes.

Utilizing ClickUp's features to foster innovation

ClickUp offers more than task organization. It provides a platform that inspires creativity. Through its set of capabilities, you can simplify workflows, discover fresh avenues for teamwork, and address challenges.

Custom fields

Custom fields enable you to include details in your tasks, projects, and other elements within ClickUp.

This feature can come in handy for keeping tabs on data that caters to your requirements. For instance, you could set up a field to monitor the status of a lead, the importance level of a customer service ticket, or the financial plan for a project.

Personalized fields also serve the purpose of streamlining workflows. To illustrate, you could establish a field to monitor the progress of a task. Subsequently, you could set up an automation guideline to automatically allocate the task to the individual in line when its status changes to "In Progress."

Automation

The automation functionality in ClickUp enables you to devise regulations that automate recurring duties. This can help save time and allow you to concentrate on matters.

Here are some instances of how automation can be applied in ClickUp:

- Automatically generate tasks upon generating a lead
- Allocate tasks to the team member based on task type or priority
- Shift tasks across lists or projects as they move through the workflow
- Dispatch notifications to team members regarding impending or overdue tasks
- Create lists and tasks to provide real-time reports on your advancement and performance

Dashboards

ClickUp's dashboards represent your data and enable you to monitor your progress. You can design dashboards in ClickUp to manage your tasks, projects, objectives, and more.

Dashboards can aid in spotting areas for enhancement and making choices. For instance, you could craft a dashboard to monitor your project statuses and pinpoint any projects that might be at risk of falling behind schedule.

Illustrative instances and success stories

The following are instances and success stories demonstrating how ClickUp's advanced features can drive innovation:

- A software company employs custom fields in ClickUp to monitor bug statuses and feature requests. They also utilize automation for task creation and assignment based on bug or feature request categories.

- A marketing team utilizes ClickUp's dashboards to monitor the effectiveness of their marketing campaigns. They also employ automation to produce reports on their progress and pinpoint areas for enhancement.

- The sales team leverages ClickUp's portals to exchange leads and opportunities with their partners, enabling them to collaborate on closing deals.

- Furthermore, a product development team uses webhooks to integrate ClickUp with their **customer relationship management** (**CRM**) system. This integration automates task creation in ClickUp whenever a new lead is generated in the CRM system.

After exploring how advanced features such as custom fields, automation, and dashboards in ClickUp can drive innovation and open up possibilities, the focus now shifts toward implementing practices for sustainable innovation. This shift underlines the significance of utilizing ClickUp's capabilities to nurture innovation in both professional pursuits.

Implementing effective strategies for sustainable progress

Implementing practices for innovation involves developing new products, services, or processes that meet current needs without compromising the ability of future generations to meet their own needs. It's crucial to incorporate innovation into your professional life to help build a more sustainable future for everyone.

Fostering a culture of innovation

The initial step in integrating innovation involves cultivating an environment that promotes creativity. This entails encouraging individuals to think and generate ideas, as well as providing them with the necessary resources and support to bring those ideas to fruition.

Here are a few tips for fostering a culture of innovation:

- **Encourage thinking outside the box**. Embrace challenging the existing norms and inspire individuals to devise solutions.

- **Offer learning and growth opportunities**. Allow individuals to explore technologies, stay informed about trends, and enhance their skills.

- **Recognize achievements**. When someone introduces an idea, make sure to acknowledge their success. This recognition can inspire others to embrace innovation

Managing change effectively

Sustainable innovation often demands change, which can be daunting for some individuals. Therefore, it's vital to handle transitions.

Here are a few pointers on managing change:

- **Communicate effectively**. Foster clear communication and real-time collaboration through ClickUp chat and comments to effectively explain necessary changes and their benefits using ClickUp chat and task discussions.
- **Get buy-in from stakeholders**. Seek approval from stakeholders by involving them and ensuring their support for the proposed changes.
- **Provide support and training**. Offer assistance and training to individuals to help them adapt to the changes.
- **Monitor the change and make adjustments as needed**. Keep an eye on the changes. Make necessary adjustments along the way to guarantee success.

Ensuring long-term success

To ensure long-term success in your sustainable innovation endeavors, it is important to focus on the following:

- Ensuring that your sustainable innovation endeavors align with your overarching goals and objectives
- Engaging in collaboration with others to exchange ideas and pool resources
- Striving for enhancement of your sustainable innovation efforts over time

Implementing leading practices for innovation within ClickUp

ClickUp serves as a platform for implementing top-notch methods for sustainable innovation in various ways. For instance, you can utilize ClickUp to do the following:

- Establish a hub for all your innovation concepts and ventures. This will aid in tracking progress and pinpointing areas where enhancements can be made.
- Utilize customized fields to monitor the advancement of your innovation projects. This way, you can keep track of your progress and pinpoint any roadblocks.

- Develop dashboards to represent your advancements and pinpoint areas that need enhancement. This will enable you to make informed decisions regarding your innovation projects.

- Implement automation to streamline the workflows of your innovation endeavors. By doing so, you'll have time on hand to focus on tasks of greater significance.

- Engage in collaborative efforts with others on your sustainable innovation projects. ClickUp offers seamless collaboration opportunities for tasks, projects, and documents.

Illustrative instances

Here are three scenarios showcasing how ClickUp can be utilized for implementing innovation:

- **A company leverages ClickUp to monitor its progress toward reducing its carbon footprint**. It utilizes customized fields to monitor energy usage, water consumption, and waste generation. Dashboards visualize progress and identify areas for enhancement.

- **A city utilizes ClickUp to oversee its transportation initiatives**. Through ClickUp, it monitors the advancement of initiatives such as expanding bike lanes, enhancing public transportation systems, and alleviating traffic congestion. Additionally, it collaborates with residents and businesses using ClickUp for their transportation endeavors.

- **A non-profit organization utilizes ClickUp to oversee its agriculture projects**. ClickUp helps them monitor the advancement of their efforts to promote farming methods and cut down on food wastage. Additionally, they employ ClickUp to work with farmers and other entities involved in their agriculture endeavors.

Learning to recognize accomplishments

As an efficiency consultant with over 20 years of experience, I have dedicated my career to learning how things work to enhance business systems efficiency and process implementation. My journey has led me to work with diverse teams, both small and large, optimizing their operations through strategic project management and automation. The impact of my work has boosted the efficiency and productivity of these teams, delivering tangible results.

One of my accomplishments is creating business operating systems from scratch. This involved creating robust processes that serve as the backbone for organizations, enabling them to function seamlessly and scale effectively. My expertise in ClickUp has been instrumental in this, allowing me to implement comprehensive project management solutions, CRM systems, and business frameworks that drive productivity.

I am grateful for the opportunity to share my insights on ClickUp and project management. This work encapsulates my extensive knowledge and hands-on experience combined with a simplified version of agile project management principles and various other frameworks, which I've applied to deliver projects successfully while maintaining flexibility and fostering collaboration in both work and home life.

My role as a consultant has also involved providing valuable insights through resume and case study examples, demonstrating the tangible impact of optimized workflows and streamlined processes. I have adapted my schedule to meet project needs and collaborated asynchronously to ensure that deliverables are met within realistic timelines and budgets.

I thrive in dynamic environments, tackling both long-term strategic initiatives and fast-paced short-term projects with equal enthusiasm. I always strive for arrangements that allow me to refine processes and achieve goals efficiently. My approach starts with a comprehensive discovery process, where I gain a deep understanding of team workflows and pain points. I then iterate on solutions until we reach successful project completion, demonstrating my problem-solving skills and commitment to efficient goal achievement.

Regarding compensation expectations, I have managed enterprise projects with a broad scope, varying from $12k to $1.1m+. My goal is always to provide sustainable ongoing refinement until all project priorities are completed and approved by stakeholders.

Beyond my professional accomplishments, I have contributed to various industries by managing projects and building websites, online school systems, music production schools, and support systems. My top strengths—Achiever, Strategic, Futuristic, Learner, and Ideation—have guided my endeavors, including helping organizations achieve ISO certifications and AWS Partner accreditation. Moreover, I have built "business operating systems" for entities ranging from start-ups to large-scale enterprises, encompassing CRMs, processes, systems, workflows, communication tools, and integrations with their business ecosystems.

To recharge, I enjoy spending time with loved ones, the competitive spirit of ice hockey, and the energy of DJing and making music. My passion for leadership development is reflected in my admiration for John Maxwell and the creation of many online courses. My book, *Mastering Project Management With ClickUp For Work And Home Life Balance*, is a testament to my commitment to empowering others with the knowledge to succeed.

With numerous years of project experience and 34+ technical training certificates under my belt, I continue to grow and share my expertise in project management, agile methodologies, AI, productivity, and beyond. My mission is to accomplish many goals in life, and this system has allowed me to design life more of how I would like to live, innovating and maintaining company and personal objectives. Through relentless learning and innovation, I stay adaptable to new challenges while consistently maintaining my expertise to deliver effective solutions as a leader and team.

Innovation and accomplishments

Here is a diverse range of systems I have developed:

- **Project management and time management systems**: Streamlining tasks to enhance productivity
- **Music production systems**: From recording to release, every step is systematized

- **Sound library database**: A comprehensive catalog of sounds and genres for music production
- **Video production and podcasting systems**: Simplifying the creation and distribution process
- **Online music production school system**: Educating the next generation of music producers
- **Book writing and social media systems**: Facilitating content creation across platforms
- **Photoshoot systems**: Tailored for both large and small agencies
- **Marketing agency systems**: Including web development, maintenance, and hosting
- **Budgeting and accounting systems**: Keeping finances in check
- **Medication inventory**: Assisting with pharmaceutical scheduling and pain management solutions
- **Moving system**: Incorporating box scanner barcodes for efficient content tracking
- **Traveling and value system for chores**: Making travel and household tasks easier to manage
- **Home and business product inventories**: Organizing essentials from meal planning to business supplies
- **Hard drive and data inventory**: Ensuring that data is safe and regularly backed up
- **Tech backup and maintenance planning**: For servers, virtual desktops, and workstations
- **Help desk systems**: Providing support when needed

The following are some of my notable achievements:

- **Recording studio**: Successfully ran a studio in Atlanta, Georgia
- **Vintage music sound design company**: Co-founded a company specializing in hardware and software samplers
- **Authorship and mentoring**: Wrote a book on music production, leading to an online course and mentoring program
- **AI music courses**: Custom-tailored AI music courses focusing on workflow
- **Certifications and business operating systems**: Assisted companies with ISO certifications and AWS Partner accreditation and helped build robust business operating systems

As a project manager, I have helped set up systems for digital marketing firms and other entities to improve their daily functions, planning, and project coordination.

Skills, software, and framework experience

Ed is proficient in a wide array of software and frameworks:

- **Project management tools**: ClickUp, Zoho, Notion, Jira, Asana, Monday, Teamwork, Accelo, and many more

- **Communication platforms**: Zoom, Pipedrive, Vonage, and RingCentral

- **Marketing and sales tools**: Better Proposals, PandaDoc, SharpSpring, and Unbounce

- **Cloud services**: AWS, Zoho CRM, and Zoho Desk

- **Financial software**: Xero, Intuit, Freshbooks, and `bill.com`

- **Development and SEO**: WordPress, Magento 2, Onpage SEO, Joomla, and Zendesk

- **Networking and administration**: Windows Server, VMware, and network administration

Ed's expertise extends to designing and developing social networking sites and providing comprehensive training and support for clients:

- **BLUECREATIVE:** Founded by Edward Unger, BLUECREATIVE leverages over two decades of experience to transform businesses through efficient project management and collaboration. Emerging from the success of Blue Sound Studios, this agency specializes in training and implementing systems and processes. BLUECREATIVE is your strategic partner in business innovation, crafting tailored solutions for modern enterprises and driving efficiency with smart, innovative systems.

- **Ed Unger Music:** Ed Unger is also an accomplished DJ and producer based in Miami, FL. His work has been featured on Mix 93 FM and in his podcast, The Cup of Inspiration. He founded an online music production school, ran a recording studio and music-related e-commerce businesses. Ed's music has won dance remix contests and has been praised by mainstream media, showcasing his versatility across genres like progressive house, deep house, and tech house.

Learning to celebrate your choices

Acknowledging your choices that lead to achievements, regardless of their size, is crucial. Doing so boosts motivation and propels you forward. It first starts with thinking about what you're thinking about, what you're feeling, and what you're seeing. When I first started in business, you could not have told me this would be my future self. Success habits do not care about your excuses, and I learned the hard way, over and over and over. Failure after failure. It is embarrassing to think back on who I was, and even today, there are always embarrassments of not knowing what I don't know. Thankfully, curiosity, agility, and great learning and work habits have allowed me to continue to find good choices and make good choices that result in good results in work-life balance.

By focusing on and celebrating your choices, you will be amazed at what you can accomplish; anything I have done is nothing in comparison to what you're capable of according to your goals, objectives, and purpose.

Focusing on daily choices and learning from mistakes will consistently bring joy and inspiration beyond any celebration or party you may have experienced—at least, that did it for me.

When winning in life and family becomes more important than feeling good, things change drastically in your home/work life in an amazing way.

Summary

In this chapter, you learned how to innovate and create new systems and processes in both your personal and professional life using ClickUp. You were taught the value of a growth mindset for development, which involves the belief that abilities can be developed through effort and learning from mistakes. The chapter emphasized utilizing ClickUp's features such as custom fields, automation, and dashboards to foster innovation and manage change effectively.

The information was useful because it provided strategies for sustainable progress, such as fostering a culture of innovation, managing change, and ensuring long-term success. By leveraging ClickUp's advanced features, you can drive innovation and open up possibilities for continuous improvement in your work.

Overall, the chapter served as a guide for professionals to optimize their use of ClickUp, encouraging them to think creatively, embrace challenges, and implement effective strategies for sustained innovation and progress.

As we come to the end of this journey with project management and ClickUp, I trust you will feel empowered and ready to make the most of this tool. Throughout our time, you've picked up techniques to streamline your tasks, save time, and reach your objectives efficiently and clearly. Remember, the path to productivity is ongoing, and with ClickUp at your disposal, you're prepared for any obstacle that may arise. Embrace the wisdom shared in this guidebook, keep discovering functionalities, and continue striving for greatness in all your pursuits. Here's to a future brimming with productivity, achievement, and boundless opportunities!

Further reading and free resources

Here's a breakdown of which ClickUp plans by each feature mentioned in this chapter are included in the free and paid plans:

ClickUp Feature	Free Plan	Paid Plan
Custom Fields	Limited	Yes
Automation	Limited	Yes
Dashboards	No	Yes
Portals	No	Yes
Webhooks	No	Yes
Chat	Yes	Yes
Task Discussions	Yes	Yes

Table 16.1 – ClickUp Plan details

Here are some additional details about the ClickUp plans:

- **Free plan**: The free plan works well for individuals or small teams seeking task management capabilities.
- **Paid plan**: Each offering's features and pricing structure has paid subscription options. These plans provide features not included in the free plan, such as recurring tasks, customizable fields, and ClickUp's AI integration.

> **Note**
>
> For further details, you may contact the ClickUp sales team:
>
> `https://clickup.com/contact/contact-sales`

Sign up to download your free workbook and productivity resources for each chapter

ClickUp is constantly evolving. Get help and explore each chapter in depth, receive the latest productivity updates and ClickUp tips, and download your free workbook at `bluecreative.com/clickup`, specializing in ClickUp implementation, configurations, systems development, process implementation, and more.

Unger, E. (2024). ClickUp. BLUECREATIVE.

Index

packtpub.com

Subscribe to our online digital library for full access to over 7,000 books and videos, as well as industry leading tools to help you plan your personal development and advance your career. For more information, please visit our website.

Why subscribe?

- Spend less time learning and more time coding with practical eBooks and Videos from over 4,000 industry professionals

- Improve your learning with Skill Plans built especially for you

- Get a free eBook or video every month

- Fully searchable for easy access to vital information

- Copy and paste, print, and bookmark content

Did you know that Packt offers eBook versions of every book published, with PDF and ePub files available? You can upgrade to the eBook version at packtpub.com and as a print book customer, you are entitled to a discount on the eBook copy. Get in touch with us at customercare@packtpub.com for more details.

At www.packtpub.com, you can also read a collection of free technical articles, sign up for a range of free newsletters, and receive exclusive discounts and offers on Packt books and eBooks.

Other Books You May Enjoy

If you enjoyed this book, you may be interested in these other books by Packt:

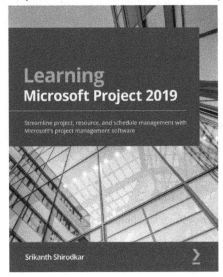

Learning Microsoft Project 2019

Srikanth Shirodkar

ISBN: 978-1-83898-872-2

- Create efficient project plans using Microsoft Project 2019
- Get to grips with resolving complex issues related to time, budget, and resource allocation
- Understand how to create automated dynamic reports
- Identify and protect the critical path in your project and mitigate project risks
- Become well-versed with executing Agile projects using MS Project
- Understand how to create custom reports and make them available for future projects

Enhancing Productivity with Notion

Danny Hatcher

ISBN: 978-1-80323-208-9

- Understand how to set up and build on any device
- Navigate, share and alter the appearance of your workspace
- Import and export data to and from Notion
- Understand how to use all the database views, filters, sorts, and properties
- Create task, wiki, and project management systems
- Connect Notion to third-party applications with the API

Packt is searching for authors like you

If you're interested in becoming an author for Packt, please visit authors.packtpub.com and apply today. We have worked with thousands of developers and tech professionals, just like you, to help them share their insight with the global tech community. You can make a general application, apply for a specific hot topic that we are recruiting an author for, or submit your own idea.

Share Your Thoughts

Now you've finished *Mastering Project Management with ClickUp for Work and Home Life Balance*, we'd love to hear your thoughts! Scan the QR code below to go straight to the Amazon review page for this book and share your feedback or leave a review on the site that you purchased it from.

https://packt.link/r/183546873X

Your review is important to us and the tech community and will help us make sure we're delivering excellent quality content.

Download a free PDF copy of this book

Thanks for purchasing this book!

Do you like to read on the go but are unable to carry your print books everywhere?

Is your eBook purchase not compatible with the device of your choice?

Don't worry, now with every Packt book you get a DRM-free PDF version of that book at no cost.

Read anywhere, any place, on any device. Search, copy, and paste code from your favorite technical books directly into your application.

The perks don't stop there, you can get exclusive access to discounts, newsletters, and great free content in your inbox daily

Follow these simple steps to get the benefits:

1. Scan the QR code or visit the link below

https://packt.link/free-ebook/9781835468739

2. Submit your proof of purchase
3. That's it! We'll send your free PDF and other benefits to your email directly

www.ingramcontent.com/pod-product-compliance
Lightning Source LLC
Chambersburg PA
CBHW080626060326
40690CB00021B/4833